WORKERS AT PLAY

A SOCIAL AND ECONOMIC HISTORY OF LEISURE 1918-1939

STEPHEN G. JONES

Routledge & Kegan Paul
London

For Kathryn, Sam and Ben

First published in 1986
by Routledge & Kegan Paul plc
11 New Fetter Lane, London EC4P 4EE

Set in Times Roman
by Input Typesetting Ltd, London
and printed in Great Britain
by St Edmundsbury Press
Bury St Edmunds, Suffolk

British Library Cataloguing in Publication Data

Jones, Stephen G.
Workers at play: a social and economic
history of leisure, 1918–1939.
1. Leisure—Social aspects—Great
Britain
I. Title.
306'.48'0941   GV75

ISBN 0–7102–0635–6

Contents

Tables

Plates

1 The demand for leisure: *Urban transport systems such as trams and motor traffic stimulated a range of amusements.*

2 The leisure industry: *Leisure was highly commercialized, involving much capital investment and the application of technology. Blackpool Pleasure Beach is a case in point.*

3 Urban pleasures: *The cinema was one of many working-class leisure interests. The Paramount cinema in the centre of Manchester can be seen flanked by ballroom, table tennis rooms, billiard halls, and Cook's Tourist Office.*

4 Association football: *The FA Cup Final was the climax of the English football season. The 1934 Final was between Manchester City and Portsmouth (and was refereed by Stanley Rous).*

5 Picture palaces: *Arguably the cinema was the main leisure institution of the 1930s.*

6 Dances and socials: *The dance craze spread during the 1920s. Dances and socials were held throughout the country.*

7 Theatres: *Despite the growth of alternative entertainments, the theatre survived as a centre of pleasure.*

8 Holidays: *The working-class holiday spread during the period, albeit unevenly. Many resorts benefited from the influx of working-class visitors, in this case the East coast town of Clevelys.*

9 Boxing: *The amateur and professional fight game was especially popular in many working-class districts.*

10 Rambling: *Of all outdoor recreations in the inter-war years, rambling was perhaps the biggest growth area.*

11 Cycling: *Cycling was enjoyed by men and women of all social classes. Here we have two members of the Clarion Cycling Club.*

12 Education: *Independent working-class education was regarded as a rational recreation by certain political activists. The Marxist Summer School held in Skegness from 31 July to 14 August 1937 had (according to the* Daily Worker*) a 'Good holiday programme. Bathing, Boating, Rambling, Socials, etc. Popular lectures and discussion.'*

13 Street entertainment: *The working class created entertainment in the informal arena of the street. Many British streets, such as this one at Salford, celebrated George V's Jubilee in 1935.*

14 Parks: *Public parks were provided by the municipal authorities, giving the opportunity for a variety of recreations.*

15 Open spaces: *A number of pressure groups stressed the need for open spaces, like Belle Vue Gardens (including speedway).*

16 Excursions: *The working-class outing was one alternative to a holiday away from home. The Nelson Labour Women's section organized such an outing in 1934.*

17 Leisure and politics: *The working class campaigned for access to the countryside. There were a number of protest rallies, such as this one in Derbyshire.*

18 Sport and Politics: *The organized working class in London sought facilities for sport. The* Worker Sportsman *was the journal of the Communist-inspired British Workers' Sports Federation.*

Acknowledgments

I would like to thank the following for permission to use material: Cambridge University Press for A. L. Chapman and R. Knight, *Wages and Salaries in the United Kingdom 1920–1938*; B. T. Batsford Ltd for D. H. Aldcroft, *The Inter-War Economy: Britain 1919–1939*; the Controller of Her Majesty's Stationery Office for *British Labour Statistics: Historical Abstract 1886–1968*. Permission was also granted by Frank Cass & Co. Ltd to use material which first appeared in *The Service Industries Journal*, vol. 5, no. 1, 1985.

Acknowledgment is also due to those who allowed me to use illustrations: Mr R. Henshall: no. 2; Mrs C. J. Hughes: no. 3; Manchester Studies Unit: no. 4; Mr Glover: no. 8; Mrs M. Bobker: no. 12. I have tried to trace the copyright owners of the remaining illustrations, but without success.

Many librarians and archivists have helped me during the course of researching this book. In particular, the staffs of the Manchester University Library and the Manchester Central Reference Library have been of great assistance. A number of people have answered my questions and discussed different aspects of the subject, and I should like to mention Ruth and Eddy Frow in this respect. I am also indebted to Audrey Linkman of Manchester Studies Unit for help with photographs. Many colleagues have been willing to provide help and advice. My warmest thanks are to Professor A. E. Musson and Dr Mike Rose of the University of Manchester who welcomed my initial research proposals and encouraged me throughout. Dr Tony Mason and Dr Jim Riordan were also kind enough to offer advice. My greatest debt is to my wife, Kathryn, and I thank her for her typing assistance, suggestions and friendship.

Introduction

The economic and social history of leisure has recently commanded the attention of a number of scholars. It is clear from an overview of the historiography that most of the research has been concerned with the changes and modifications in spare time and ways of using that spare time during nineteenth-century industrialization and urbanization. More specifically, historians have examined the ways in which recreation was affected by the transformation of Britain from a traditional, rural society to an industrial, urban society. It is not the place here to rehearse the claims made about the recreational and cultural implications of industrial change. But in very broad terms, the emergence of industrial Capitalism imposed a number of new constraints on leisure, in particular regular and longer working hours, as well as new codes of organized and regulated recreation. Obviously recreation had to fit in with the needs and demands of an expanding economy. Some pre-industrial recreations, customs and traditions were dynamic enough to survive external economic change, but by and large, popular cultural practices were assimilated into the new society. There has also been some debate as to whether leisure was a form of bourgeois social control or class expression and cultural identity. The economic and social history of leisure, obviously related to wider themes of modernization, has therefore given rise to a fair degree of argument and polemical debate. This is not to argue that work on the new industrial leisure has been exhaustive; there are still many unexplored areas and a pressing need for synthesis. As two of the leading practitioners, John Walton and James Walvin, have astutely observed:

general surveys of themes in the social history of leisure have
sought to take account of regional differences, but their main
task has been to generate introductory hypotheses. These now
need to be tested at the local level in various kinds of setting,
and new themes need to be investigated, before a more
informed and contextually-aware synthesis can be
attempted.[1]

However, despite the need for further research and writing, the
growing consensus demonstrates that by the 1880s a world of
leisure had emerged which would be recognizable a century later.
In the view of Hugh Cunningham: 'there is nothing in the leisure
of today which was not visible in 1880'.[2] Likewise, Stephen Yeo
has concluded that, 'For consumers of leisure, and for producers
and organisers, critical developments took place within this
period, shaping much of modern British culture'; John Lowerson
and John Myerscough agree that, 'Most of today's leisure habits
and expectations remain staunchly Victorian'; and James Walvin
states that leisure 'was already clearly defined in the last quarter
of the nineteenth century'.[3] Given the radical economic and social
changes of the nineteenth century and the fact that Britain
emerged as the first industrial nation, these are not unreasonable
assertions. By the latter part of the century many of the pieces of
a mature industrial nation were in place; not only the economic
and social infrastructure, but also the political institutions and the
class relations, symptomatic of Capitalist society. In the case of
leisure, modern patterns were similarly established. The view of
Chas Critcher is worth quoting at some length:

in a remarkably short period of three-quarters of a century,
the nature of leisure had changed dramatically. Where
previously there had been custom now there was commerce;
where work and leisure had been intermingled now they were
sharply differentiated; where the rhythm of life had been set
by the agricultural cycle now it was by the unvarying routine
of the industrial week; where previously activities had been
chaotic now they were disciplined; where once had been
anarchy now were codes of conduct. Leisure looked very much
as it would be defined and recognised today: something which
went on outside working hours; at regular times; in specially

provided places (where frequently one person's pleasure was another's profit) unequally distributed between classes and sexes.[4]

Certainly, no one would disagree with the notion that in the century or so after 1780 the position of leisure in society was fundamentally changed. Most significantly, commerce entered the leisure domain and a prototype leisure industry was founded.

There are, however, problems with such a view. In the first place, as we have already seen, there are many unexplored areas of nineteenth-century leisure, not to mention the virtually barren areas of the twentieth. If there is need for further research, judgments can only hope to be tentative and partial. Indeed, common sense tells us that significant developments in the leisure sphere had to wait until the twentieth century. Most of all, the process of commercialization was unfinished in the 1890s and many important innovations had to wait until after the Great War. Not wanting to pre-empt the discussion in chapter two, it may be noted that some historians have claimed that it was not until the inter-war period that leisure 'matured' and took on a modern form. As Derek Aldcroft has suggested:

> perhaps the most dramatic developments were in the field of leisure and recreational pursuits. Compared with Victorian and Edwardian England, the working man, no less than his wealthier middle class counterpart, was literally bombarded with opportunities for filling in his increased spare time following the reductions in hours of work.[5]

It is indeed suggestive that, according to the social survey of London in the 1930s, the emergence of mass leisure had brought more fundamental transformations than any other aspects of the people's life since Booth's study of the late nineteenth century.[6] Also, the York survey of the 1930s had as its longest chapter 'Leisure Time Activities', whereas the earlier York study, published in 1901, had no such chapter.[7]

It is therefore the intention of this book to explore the world of inter-war leisure activities in Britain, and to show that the period was crucial in the evolution of modern forms of leisure. As far as the historiography of inter-war leisure is concerned there is only a very small collection of serious work.[8] For the most part, there are a number of dubious, sometimes antiquarian, books which focus on all manner of subjects. As Alun Howkins and John Lowerson have expressed it: 'Leisure studies, especially in relation to the inter-war period, have suffered very badly from a spate of "pop" or "semi-pop" books, designed by publishers with an eye to quick sales, rather than to any lasting or seriously considered research.'[9] Thus it is essential at the outset to stress the somewhat limited objectives of this study. In short, the study will provide an overview of the main trends in inter-war leisure, with particular reference to the manual working class. In a volume of this kind there will inevitably be a number of gaps. For instance, some may protest that not enough attention is paid to the regional dimension or the urban/rural divide, others may point out that gender differences or sectional divisions within the working class are not given due emphasis. Nevertheless, it is hoped that a study of inter-war leisure as offered here will encourage further research into specific recreational and cultural forms at both the national and local level, and stimulate new questions and areas of debate about the nature of and developments in working-class leisure.

There are four main themes which run throughout the book. First, it is tacitly assumed that leisure cannot be studied in isolation as it is related to the main economic and social developments of the period. Here, it is appropriate to provide a very brief, and somewhat simplistic, summary of the salient features of the inter-war economy.

The 1920s and 1930s were once considered to have been plagued by industrial stagnation, mass unemployment, and general gloom and pessimism. In recent years this view has been modified, and the orthodox impression is now one of paradox; that is, economic and social historians have indicated that there were regional disparities in economic development, the contrast being between the prosperous South and Midlands and the depressed regions of South Wales, the North East, and central Scotland. Southern England and the Midlands are said to have been marked by growth industries such as motor-car manufacture and electrical engineering, while the depressed areas were characterized by the declining staple industries of shipbuilding, coal, and iron and steel. Similarly, mass unemployment and social decay were more evident in the industrial North and in South Wales, with rising prosperity in the southern half of the country. In aggregate terms the inter-war years was a growth period, though at the same time a period of painful structural adaptation. Data suggest that over the period 1920–37 industrial growth rates averaged 3.1 per cent each year. Further, conventional quantitative indices show that the standard of living rose.[10]

At this stage it is important to appreciate that these developments in the economy, whether unemployment or rising real wages, affected the demand for and participation in different kinds of leisure activities. It is a basic premise of this study that recreational trends were related to socio-economic change. Although a number of recreations grew in popularity in spite of, and perhaps because of, the slump, there is some evidence to suggest that the success of spectator sport depended to some extent on local economic circumstances – the level of trade, employment and wages. Hence, the relative decline of Cardiff City, Blackburn Rovers and Newcastle United in the 1930s, and the rise to fame of several London football clubs, can be connected to local industrial conditions, namely depression and prosperity.[11] Equally, rugby union in South Wales was adversely affected by the recession in the Welsh economy during the 1920s and early 1930s.[12] In a slightly different way, the growth of a marginal critique of the work ethic had a lot to do with both unemployment and rationalization in industry, while at the same time the Labour Movement's approach to leisure was influenced by the commercial trends of the period. Also, the growth of public provision and State interference in the leisure sphere cannot be divorced from the more general collectivist developments. Working-class leisure, in short, needs to be situated within the political economy, and the determining economic and social context.

Second and more briefly, it is claimed that there was an expansion in leisure provision. This expansion was experienced in different ways by different social groups, but compared to earlier periods there were certainly more opportunities for amusement. During the 1920s and 1930s there were significant developments in the area of leisure, affecting not only business organization, but also the quality of life in all its forms – collective, institutional, familial and personal. From the various 'pop' histories of leisure, these developments are well known, ranging from the growth of the local cinema and dance hall to the proliferation of organizations catering for outdoor recreation. More specifically, leisure goods and services provided by commercial enterprises, the State – at both central and local level – and voluntary organizations all expanded. In addition, earlier associational forms of group-created leisure survived and adapted to the new economic and social context. Undoubtedly, there was a growth in and modification of a number of leisure forms.

The third theme is a rejection of crude notions of social control whereby leisure is viewed as imposed on the working class by their so-called social 'betters'. It is true that the church, employers and the State intervened in workers' leisure. There were attempts by the church to inculcate elevated modes of social and moral behaviour, pressure by employers to shape a more disciplined and healthier workforce, and propaganda, even censorship, by governments to maintain the *status quo*. However, it is debatable whether such aims were successful. It is clearly wrong to depict the working class as impotent consumers, having little or no say in the form and content of the leisure product. In fact, working people had the capacity to resist and contest attempts at social control. There was, in short, a great deal of ingenuity in workers' leisure.

Moreover, leisure did not act as an Althusserian Ideological State Apparatus. According to Louis Althusser, the French Marxist and philosopher, culture – literature, the arts and sport – along with religion, education, the family and so on, are part of an Ideological State Apparatus designed for 'the reproduction of the relations of production, i.e. of Capitalist relations of exploitation'.[13] Within such a theory, sport and other cultural practices are said to carry the ruling ideology of individual competitiveness, chauvinism, nationalism and sexism. Apparently, films and even the football stadium teach the masses the contrasting virtues of 'modesty, resignation, submissiveness on the one hand, cynicism, contempt, arrogance, confidence, self-importance, even smooth talk and cunning on the other'.[14] Despite the fact that the Ideological State Apparatus is viewed as relatively autonomous – 'what the Marxist tradition calls conjointly the relative autonomy of the superstructure and the reciprocal action of the superstructure on the base' – this analysis gives very little room for working-class creativity and resistance to the ideology of the ruling *élite*. The evidence suggests that leisure failed as a superstructural adjunct of capital. There was no question of the working class being programmed or conditioned in their leisure time. Indeed, miners' institutes, the working men's club movement and Labour organizations of all kinds were a sure sign of working-class autonomy in the cultural sphere. Human agency has undoubtedly played an important role in cultural and recreational developments. Cultural production in Capitalist society is not, therefore, a matter of ideological incorporation into the dominant social order. Moreover, working-class attitudes and approaches are an important element in the making (and remaking) of the dominant ideology. As Stewart Macintyre has pointed out, in the 1920s 'the prevailing ideology was genuinely popular among workers', and far from being imposed by some kind of Capitalist conspiracy, popular forms were 'often generated spontaneously in workers' daily activities'.[15] Cultural and recreational forms were not simply a mode of Capitalist expression; true, they were partly a reflection of the dominant culture, but a dominant culture which included 'alternative' and 'oppositional' proletarian values and meanings.[16]

Finally, throughout this volume it is apparent that working-class leisure was, and is, a political thing. In the first place, as most of the chapters in this volume demonstrate, the leisure question was often debated at the heart of the formal British political system, the House of Commons. In addition to this it was an important concern of the various levels of the State, including ministries in the civil service. But perhaps more important, leisure was a central part of everyday life and necessarily gave rise to discussion, dispute, even conflict, which in essence were political. In the informal political arena of the local community, people struggled over the meanings of and rights to particular leisure forms. At another level, representative organs of the working class campaigned for improvements in recreational provision, both in the form of more leisure hours and more amenities. Indeed, it can be argued that the working class, aligned with other progressive groups, were able to extract many benefits out of the system and improve the standards of leisure. Such benefits included paid holidays, Sunday entertainment, sports facilities, and public money for recreation. Certainly the inter-war period witnessed a range of leisure reforms.

Many aspects of this volume will be introductory and suggestive. There is simply not enough space to give full treatment to all the facets of inter-war leisure. Moreover, many research projects need to be undertaken before all the facts are known. It may well be the case that when the groundwork has been carried out, a further study would provide a more considered integration of theory and the historical critique. In brief, this study cannot hope to do justice to all aspects of working-class leisure in inter-war Britain, but at least it provides some kind of starting point.

1
The demand for leisure

During the inter-war years leisure in Britain was provided in three main forms. First, there were commercial providers of recreational products, facilities and services, who regarded leisure as a source of profit. In very broad terms, business enterprises penetrated many leisure activities, including sport, entertainment and the arts, and holidays. Second, recreation was provided in the voluntary sector by a variety of associations and societies. Voluntary recreation and leisure groups banded together in most towns and consisted of youth organizations, outdoor activity groups, sports clubs, cultural organizations and so on. It is correct to say that there were very few leisure pursuits which were not catered for in the voluntary sector. Lastly, there was leisure provision in the public sector, both at national and local level. The central and municipal authorities provided a wide array of recreational amenities such as urban parks, playing fields, swimming baths, concert halls, libraries and museums. As will be claimed in subsequent chapters, there was an expansion of all forms of leisure in the 1920s and 1930s. One of the reasons for this is that the demand for leisure goods and services was buoyant.

This chapter will consider the nature of the demand for leisure; more specifically, the demand for leisure time and the financial means to enjoy that leisure time. The demand for leisure is determined by a number of economic and social variables. For instance, it is clear that real wages, hours of work, the price of recreation, the level of transport systems, and the general commitment of communities and governments to recreational provision will all have an impact on total leisure demand. Here, it is assumed that

9

the demand for leisure is determined by two main factors: first, purchasing power in terms of wages and the cost of living; and second, the amount of spare time available in terms of the number of hours worked and holidays taken. The rationale behind this is that purchasing power provides the consumer with greater command over leisure goods and services, particularly in the commercial sector, while reduced working time simply provides the consumer with more leisure. Having said this, the chapter will examine where appropriate those other factors which directly impinged on demand. Finally, something will be said about the campaign of the trade unions for greater leisure time in the form of the shorter working week and paid holidays. Because of the differences in working-class experience created by the disparities of region, occupation, skill and gender (the average worker is something of a statistical illusion), and also the lack of certain key data, the following analysis is not meant to be conclusive, merely suggestive.

Purchasing power

It is important to examine purchasing power, for without money individuals could not have participated in the commercialized leisure sector. In addition, income was also required in the voluntary sector for membership fees, equipment, club premises and so on. Equally, money was exchanged for municipal services as in the use of swimming pools and park amenities, as well as in the hiring of playing fields and town buildings for organized recreation.

For the account of wages and the cost of living a number of sources have been consulted ranging from the statistical to the impressionistic, though quantitative estimates will be stressed. Various indices have been constructed for the movement of basic weekly rates of wages. Although there are many problems connected with the construction of such an index, the general trend is fairly clear. There was a strong rise in money wages immediately after the end of the first world war. In 1920, however, came a dramatic collapse which lasted until 1923, by which time wages had fallen to approximately twice their 1913 levels. For the rest of the decade they stayed fairly stable, but in 1930 there was a further decline which, though only moderate, lasted until 1934. Thereafter, wages rose slightly, so that by 1938 they were about double the pre-war level.[1] Thus, whereas the average weekly wage in 1913 was £1.60, by 1938 it was about £3.50.[2] A wage index is, however, only an average, so to be more precise about the true movement in money wages it is necessary to investigate further.

It is quite clear from the statistics that there were wide differences in wage rates, determined by occupation and skill.[3] Although these examples follow the overall national trends, they also illustrate the differentials according to industry and grade. It can be seen that not only did wages differ between the skilled and the unskilled, they also differed within these two distinguishable groups. Obviously differences in weekly wage rates had an effect on the workers' ability to consume leisure; a bricklayer on 65s 6d or a hand compositor on 73s 10d in 1934 was likely to consume more units of leisure in the market place (*ceteris paribus*) than was a goods porter on 43s or a building labourer on 49s 4d. Hence one study of income and expenditure patterns made in 1936 found that spending on recreation increased with average weekly income: for a family on £2 11s 4d, expenditure on recreation amounted to 1s 3d, whereas for a family on £3 17s 6d, recreation spending was 5s 0½d.[4] The figures for wage differentials are given in Table 1.1. In addition to this, there were also regional variations in wage rates. In London, for example, the weekly wage in 1928 for wiremen was 84s, for carpenters and joiners 77s, and for engineers' labourers 45s 3½d, compared to the national averages of 74s 5d, 72s 5d, and 41s 11d respectively.[5] If the further complexities of unemployment, short-time working, basis of payment, bonus systems and so on are taken into consideration, the difficulties of using this data would be increased. Nevertheless, enough has been said about the movement in money wages to suggest that those workers in full employment in 1938 were in a better position to purchase leisure than they had been in 1914. The analysis will now continue by considering the cost of living factor.

As with weekly rates of wage, a number of cost of living indices have been compiled.[6] The one used here has 1930 as the base year (see Table 1.2). The movement of prices follows a similar path to that of money wages. There was price inflation in the immediate post-war period followed by a rapid deflation in the

Table 1.1 *Weekly wage rates in certain occupations and industries*

	July 1914		31 Dec 1924		31 Dec 1930		31 Dec 1938	
	s.	d.	s.	d.	s.	d.	s.	d.
Cabinet makers	39	5	74	4	72	5	73	7
Hand compositors	35	8	73	9	73	10	73	10
Bricklayers	40	7	73	5	70	7	73	1
Building labourers	27	0	55	6	52	7	55	1
Fitters and turners	38	11	56	6	59	1	67	2
Shipwrights	41	7	55	10½	60	1½	68	0
Shipbuilding labourers	23	0	38	6	41	2	49	0
Permanent way gangers	27	0	54	0	52	0	52	0
One-horse carters	25	7	53	7	52	6	53	4
Local authority labourers	26	9	53	0	52	5	55	8

Source: Department of Employment and Productivity, *British Labour Statistics: Historical Abstract 1886–1968*, London, HMSO, 1971, pp. 40–1.

two years after 1920. For the ten years after 1923 there followed a much more moderate decline in prices, and from the trough of 1933–4 prices increased slowly to the outbreak of the second world war, so that the cost of living index lost 37.4 points between 1919 and 1938.

Using the movement in money wages and the cost of living as a basis for calculations, what can be said about the overall change in the level of real purchasing power? Both money wages and prices fell in the period after 1920, but prices fell at a faster rate than wages, thus bringing an increase in purchasing power or, to put it another way, an increase in real income per head.[7] Table 1.2 provides figures showing the movements in money wages, the cost of living and real wages. Moreover, the working population also benefited from a change in the distribution of income in favour of wages, a fall in family size, and a fall in the price of foodstuffs – a major component of the working-class budget.[8] Certainly, the conclusion to be drawn from a study of the statistics of money wages, the cost of living and real wages points to an increase in working-class material standards of living, though once

Table 1.2   *Wage and cost of living indices (1930 = 100)*

	Average wage	Cost of living	Average real wages
1913	52.4	63.3	82.8
1919	–	136.1	–
1920	143.7	157.6	91.2
1921	134.6	143.0	94.1
1922	107.9	115.8	93.2
1923	100.0	110.1	90.8
1924	101.5	110.8	91.6
1925	102.2	111.4	91.7
1926	99.3	108.9	91.2
1927	101.5	106.0	95.8
1928	100.1	105.1	95.2
1929	100.4	103.8	96.7
1930	100.0	100.0	100.0
1931	98.2	93.4	105.1
1932	96.3	91.1	105.7
1933	95.3	88.6	107.6
1934	96.4	89.2	108.1
1935	98.0	90.5	108.3
1936	100.2	93.0	107.7
1937	102.8	97.5	105.4
1938	106.3	98.7	107.7

Source: D. H. Aldcroft, *The Inter-War Economy: Britain, 1919–1939*,
B. T. Batsford, London, 1973, pp. 352, 364.

again the significant differentials in wage rates should be stressed. How, then, was leisure provision affected by this increase in purchasing power?

It would seem that with the rise in real wages more money would be spent on leisure. Increased purchasing power led to an increase in total consumer expenditure on commercial leisure forms. Hence, according to John Hilton in *Rich Man, Poor Man* (1944), a significant proportion of the extra income had 'gone, along with what was already going in such directions, on pools, perms, and pints, on cigarettes, cinemas and singles-and-splashes; on turnstiles, totalizators, and twiddlems: and on all manner of two pennyworths of this and that.'[9] Two further trends are worthy of note. First, many staple items in the family budget, such as food, shared in the deflationary trends which meant that a greater proportion of income was available to spend on leisure goods and services. As the Hull Survey thus suggested: 'Significance must be attached to the increased percentage of the family budget which is devoted to leisure time activities.'[10] Second, there was a fall in the average price of entertainment and recreation in the period – the average price index being 336.4 in 1920, falling to 262.5 in 1938.[11] Indeed, the actual cost of many leisure activities was well within the reach of working-class consumption patterns: cinema, theatre and music hall seats for 6d and lower, a pint of beer between 3d and 6d, dance hall admission 3d or 6d during the week, 6d or 1s on Saturday, newspapers ½d and 1d, paperbacks 2d, six inch 'singles' for 6d at Woolworths, a game of bowls for 2d an hour, Sunday evening excursions (in 1937) from York to Harrogate 1s 3d, pool betting between 6d and 2s 6d a time, admission to football matches 6d to 2s, and for craft workers a brand new Raleigh bicycle for under £5 (in 1932) or 9s 7d a month on hire purchase.[12] Clearly, for an important section of the working class who found themselves in regular employment the economic trends of the period favoured the purchase of leisure-type goods and services.

Hours and holidays

Up to this point, the demand for leisure has been examined in relation to purchasing power; in order to take the analysis one step further it is necessary to look at demand in relation to the number of hours available as leisure time. Obviously, the demand for leisure does not depend solely upon purchasing power. It is also affected by the length of the working day and holiday entitlements, and the amount of time within that day which is set aside for leisure. Annual leisure time is increased by reducing weekly hours of work and taking more holidays. Since economists would expect the demand for leisure activities to increase if total working hours were shortened (that is, if wages were maintained at the same level), it would be fruitful to examine the course of working time between the wars.

Most of the economics' literature dealing with the determination of leisure time has been concerned with the influence of the wage rate. It is assumed that the working population has an income-leisure choice by which at a fixed wage rate the employee can sacrifice income to gain more hours of leisure or sacrifice hours of leisure to obtain more income. Another way of expressing this is to say that an employee can choose between taking a rise (fall) in the wage rate in the form of more (less) income or more (less) leisure. Moreover, an increase in the wage rate may in fact mean that an employee will actually take less leisure as it is now financially worthwhile to work longer hours. This means that the effect of a change in wages on hours of work is largely indeterminate: alterations in wages can stimulate either an increase or a decrease in the demand for leisure time. Nevertheless, in view of the fact that both wages and leisure have risen in the last century, it would appear that increases in the wage rate have led to more leisure being taken.[13] In the case of South Wales coal-mining in the period 1874–1914, it has been found that miners chose 'to consume a part of their greater potential income in the form of increased leisure and reduced work intensity'.[14] Likewise, if this interpretation is applied to the inter-war years, then some interesting observations can be made. The demand for shorter hours or longer holidays was never really seriously considered if it involved a subsequent fall in wages. Nevertheless, some trade unions argued that increased income as the predominant workplace concern was misplaced. Hence the foundry workers agreed that a large share of leisure was more important than the attainment of wealth, the post office workers that 'a share-out of leisure and a betterment of life are more vital than money', the printers that greater leisure was more important than increased earnings, and the painters that 'the shorter working week, holidays with pay, and the raising of the age of entry into industry are even more important than wage increases'.[15] Indeed, as some economic historians have suggested, in the immediate post-war period some workers preferred to take a proportion of the gains in employment conditions in the form of more leisure rather than increased income.[16] Although it is difficult to substantiate this idea of a leisure preference, it is possible that workers were as concerned about hours as they were about wages in this period.

The main reductions in hours of work occurred in the years just after the war as a result of the eight hours movement. In 1919, 6½ million workers and a further half a million the following year, obtained reductions averaging 6½ hours a week. As a consequence, the average working week came down to about forty-eight hours, compared with fifty-four hours before the war. By contrast, the period after 1921 was rather barren with a slight decrease in the number of hours worked, so that in October 1938 the average weekly hours of manual men and women were 47.7 and 43.5 respectively.[17] Legislation also had an effect with the Shops Act of 1934 and the Factories Act of 1937 both limiting maximum legal hours to forty-eight or less for certain categories of workers, mainly women and youths. The working class had thus benefited from a substantial reduction of hours in the period 1918–39, with most of the gain being secured in the immediate post-war period.

Once again, however, the differences from industry to industry must be taken into consideration. In 1935, when the average hours worked each week by all workpeople was 47.8, those engaged in mining and quarrying (except coal) worked 45.7, those in metal and engineering 48.2, and those in building 46.9. Figures for average weekly hours are given in Table 1.3. Moreover, a major caveat is required in the case of overtime. Although there is little hard data, overtime certainly continued to be a feature of British working practices in the 1920s and 1930s. During periods of buoyant trade it was common for very long hours, even double shifts, to be worked. In the non-textile firms it was possible for juveniles and female employees to work up to sixty hours a week, at least up to 1937. Furthermore, even during the depression in May 1933 the Ministry of Labour found that an average eight hours of overtime was being worked each week in the woollen industry, brick manufacture and in boot and shoe manufacture, though very little in the carpet and pottery industries.[18] Overtime was also prevalent in the major industries. For example, in May 1919 the National Union of Railwaymen negotiated an agreement with the Government of the day, the terms of which gave the railway workers regular overtime on Sundays, while in 1922 the engineering industry introduced a new Overtime and Nightshift Agreement which gave the employers the right to decide when overtime was necessary. Despite the fact that some unions tried to restrict overtime, as W. Fagan of the Edinburgh Trades Council commented: 'There were a number of people who did not want a shorter working week but merely a chance of getting overtime quicker.'[19] The point to stress is that overtime may well have increased basic weekly hours and so reduced available leisure time.

Table 1.3   *Average weekly hours of manual workers in certain industries*

Industry	1924	1935	1938
Brick, pottery, glass, chemical etc.	47.5	48.0	46.0
Metal, engineering etc.	46.2	48.2	46.1
Textiles	45.3	47.7	46.1
Clothing	43.6	45.4	43.0
Food, drink and tobacco	45.8	48.5	47.6
Building and allied industries	45.1	46.9	46.3
Public utility services	47.7	48.0	40.9
Government industrial establishments	46.5	49.7	47.2

Source: Calculated from, Department of Employment and
Productivity, *British Labour Statistics: Historical Abstract
1886–1968*, London, HMSO, 1971, pp. 96–7, 104–5.

Obviously, further qualifications would have to be made for gender, underemployment and region. Thus, whereas a journeyman in furniture manufacture in 1938 worked forty-seven hours a week in London, he worked 46.5 in Manchester and forty-four in Liverpool.[20] Yet, in spite of these occupational, regional and other differences, it can be said that for the vast majority of working people there was more leisure time in the late 1930s than there had been before the first world war. *The Listener* got it about right in 1937, commenting that 'the major social gain of our day is the increase which has taken place in the individual's leisure time'.[21]

The ending of hostilities in 1918 also marked a period in the extension of holidays with pay. The question of paid holidays was discussed within the Ministry of Reconstruction, and was dealt with and conceded by the newly formed Joint Industrial Councils in the flourmilling industry, tramways, the soap and candle manufacturing trade, and in paint and varnish manufacture.[22] By the beginning of the 1920s, general and district agreements between employers and employees covered an estimated 1 million manual workers.[23] It is true to say that paid holidays covered only a small proportion of workers, but they did represent a significant improvement in conditions of employment, and an additional element in the demand for leisure.

The post-war boom broke in the spring of 1920, and by the following year Britain was experiencing an economic depression. In these circumstances employers resisted holidays with pay on the grounds that they would increase labour costs. Some agreements which had been established prior to the slump were discontinued. In 1922, a holiday provision for paper mill workers, granted in 1920, was dropped on the pretext that luxuries like this could not be sustained: 'The union representative fought hard to reinstate the clause, but the employers would make no further concession.'[24] In those industries under Joint Industrial Council supervision, the application of holidays with pay proved difficult and, in certain cases, they were suspended or postponed. Yet, in spite of these unfavourable conditions, the momentum of the 1919–20 period continued, so that by 1922 a number of agreements covered about 1½ million manual workers. This figure did not increase dramatically until the late 1930s; certain agreements lasted, others lapsed and some were replaced. Nevertheless, this should not hide a number of significant developments which kept the issue of paid holidays in the public eye: many private agreements were introduced by individual firms; statutory recognition was contained in the Shops (Hours of Closing) Act, 1928; and there were a number of formal initiatives taken by the International Labour Organisation and the British Parliament, as well as the continued pressure of organized Labour. Indeed, after the trough of the depression was reached in August 1932 and the economy began to recover, the industrial and political environment was more receptive to the need for social reform. Holidays with pay were again a realistic demand, culminating in 1937 in the establishment of a tripartite departmental committee of inquiry into the question.

The Holidays with Pay Committee was appointed in late March, with Lord Amulree as its chairman and a number of representatives from the trade union and business world. Having taken a great deal of evidence from many interest groups, it reported in April 1938 in favour of the paid holiday principle:

It cannot, in our view, be denied that an annual holiday contributes in a considerable measure to workpeople's happiness, health and efficiency and we feel that the extension of the taking of consecutive days of holiday annually by work-people would be of benefit to the community.

They unanimously recommended that annual holidays with pay 'should be established, without undue delay, as part of the terms of the contract of employment'.[25] In order to give the parties time for negotiation, there should be an interim or probationary period before legislation was to be introduced – the Committee envisaged that legislation should be passed during the Parliamentary session of 1940–1. In the meantime, it was considered that statutory wage regulating bodies should come under immediate legislation to provide them with the means of awarding holiday pay.

Consequently, the National Government's Minister of Labour, Ernest Brown, announced his intentions at the beginning of June. He proposed to introduce a Holidays With Pay Bill and to set up a special 'Holiday' branch in the Ministry of Labour. The main object of the Bill was to enable trade boards, agricultural wages committees and road haulage central wages boards to provide paid holidays when fixing rates of wages. The proposals were not far reaching and could only apply to a potential workforce of two million. Even Brown was moved to say that 'the scope of the Bill is limited'.[26] Nevertheless, it was read a second time and went to a Committee of the Whole House for further consideration, where with Government support it emerged relatively unscathed. The Holidays with Pay Act of 1938 was not a strong piece of legislation. Although it sought to help agricultural workers in certain areas, it retarded existing agreements. The Act proposed that no more than three days' consecutive holiday be given, meaning that some workers were worse off. In Norfolk, for instance, agricultural labourers already enjoyed seven days' holiday remuneration.

It was in the form of voluntary collective agreement that the majority of people came to receive a paid holiday. When the Holidays with Pay Committee was first appointed between 1.5 million and 1.75 million people were under some kind of agreement, yet by the time the report was made the number of people covered by agreements had increased to about three million.[27] This meant that 7.75 million manual and non-manual workers out of a total occupied population of 18.5 million were in receipt of holiday pay. By the beginning of 1939 the number of manual workers who were getting paid for their annual holiday had again increased, this time to four million.[28] Paid holiday figures are given in Table 1.4. Collective agreements had been made in many of the major industries and of these there were at least 175 individual agreements on the files of the transport union, even by April 1937.[29] This was not the end of the story, however, as further gains were made during the course of the second world war. In 1940 and 1942, for example, important agreements were finalized in the textile and building industries, so that by 1945 it was calculated that about ten million manual workers were in receipt of holiday pay.[30] In addition, paid holiday schemes not recorded in the above were introduced by individual firms as part of an enlightened managerial strategy. It is apparent that the content of agreements varied from firm to firm and especially from industry to industry. The lack of uniformity was particularly noticeable as regards the criterion used for entitlement, the length of and payment for holidays, and a plethora of other provisions. Even so, the gains made between 1918 and 1939 had been considerable and, perhaps more important, the principle of holidays with pay had been accepted by the majority of the British people.

Table 1.4 *Approximate number of manual workers provided with paid holidays*

	Number (Millions)	Collective agreements covering paid holidays	
		General	District
1920	1	20	39
1922	1.5	20	94
1925	1.5	27	103
1929	1.5	23	111
1932	1.5	23	111
1934	1.5	24	124
1936	1.5	28	128
1938 (March)	3	39	209
1938 (Sept)	4	57	284

Source: Calculated from *Ministry of Labour Gazette, passim.*

It can be further postulated that the demand for leisure was increased by the greater mobility provided by the transport system. During the inter-war years there was a considerable expansion of new forms of motor transport. The estimated number of passenger miles travelled by final consumers on buses and coaches in the UK increased from approximately 3.5 million in 1920 to 19 million in 1938.[31] Although the motor-car remained a middle-class luxury, the working-class increasingly had access to motor-cycles, trams, motor-buses and, of course, bicycles. As Sir Arthur Balfour claimed: 'The bicycle in this country has ceased to be an upper middle-class thing at all. It is now a working class necessity . . .'[32] Yet, it was motor transport which underwent revolutionary change and provided even the poorer classes with new opportunities for leisure. In urban areas motor-buses were increasingly used to transport workers to cinemas, pubs and other places of leisure. At the same time the rural motor-bus brought villagers into the towns, and presumably some of their time and money would have been spent on entertainment. Equally important was the charabanc (an open motor-coach) which was used for day trips and excursions to the seaside and other places of interest.[33] According to C. Delisle Burns, it was because of these developments that 'a greater number than ever before have the daily experience of . . . entertainment at a distance from their homes'.[34] In fact, the increase in road transport led to traffic congestion and an increasing number of accidents. However, the railways were still an important alternative mode of transport for entertainment purposes. In London, for example, the railways granted special facilities for football supporters.[35] In brief, highly organized transport systems providing cheap travel made it much easier for consumers to reach the centres of entertainment.[36]

Having said all this, transport developments (coupled with suburban growth) may well be an indication that people were travelling longer distances to and from work which could have reduced the number of hours set aside for leisure. One study made in the late 1930s thus showed that many workers spent some considerable time getting to their place of employment. For example, 60 per cent of workers at Standard Telephones in Southgate took between half and one hour travelling to work, while 83 per cent of the labour force at Carreras in London spent over half-an-hour on the work journey. This meant that though working hours were shorter, some of the gain in 'leisure time has been eaten up by the lengthening of the daily journey'.[37]

Notwithstanding this, on balance transport improvements are likely to have brought more people into contact with amusements.

In sum, the demand for leisure was growing during the inter-war years. Given the fact that purchasing power and paid holidays were increasing, the working week falling, and the transport network expanding, it is not unreasonable to suggest that leisure provision was stimulated. To express it simply, there was more money in working-class hands to be spent on recreation, and more time available in which to enjoy recreational activities.

The campaign for shorter hours and paid holidays

The demand for leisure was not simply a sign of economic and social progress, it was in fact organized and articulated by the Labour Movement. The trade unions in particular campaigned for higher wages and reduced working time. Obviously, normative concessions at the place of work such as an increase in wages or a reduction in hours would give the worker more resources and more time for leisure. Similarly, the claim for a paid holiday, if successful, had a direct effect on the pattern and style of life by giving a certain amount of financial security during the annual break from work. Thus the demands and struggles for better conditons of employment necessarily had implications for recreational provision. Of special interest is the union fight for the shorter working week and holidays with pay, both of which were salient features of Labour programmes in the 1920s and 1930s.

As has already been pointed out, the main advances on the hours front were achieved in the immediate post-war period. There was a proliferation of working time demands and agree-ments, a point stressed by a memorandum presented to the war cabinet:

> The result has been that in practically all the important industries claims for reductions in hours of labour have been put forward either alone or accompanied by . . . claims for annual holidays of a week or two weeks, without loss of pay.[38]

There were a number of factors in the unions' claim for shorter hours. First, and possibly the most important, was the fear of unemployment which the unions were anxious to prevent. Even before the first world war had been concluded the TUC envisaged that because of technological change, demobilization and labour dislocation, unemployment would result. Congress therefore declared that this could be averted or, at the very least, cushioned by the universal reduction in the hours of labour.[39] Second, during the war many wage earners had worked very long hours and this undoubtedly produced a degree of illness and fatigue, which, so it was claimed, could be relieved by the shorter working week. Lastly, the war, having forced great sacrifices from all concerned, brought forth new ideas and approaches; against the background of Lloyd George's promise of a 'land fit for heroes', organized Labour demanded more leisure:

> The war has changed the worker's ideas of values. No longer will he be content to be a wage slave, existing to produce only that others may enjoy. The war was won by the wage-earning classes. . . . The worker in this country therefore claims that he is entitled to conditions of life that will enable him to live as a citizen of a wealthy, victorious nation. Good wages is not sufficient. Leisure is required to enable the worker to live up to the obligation that citizenship imposes.[40]

The arrival of the shorter working day in industry was first achieved by the engineering and shipbuilding workers, who were soon followed by the majority of the industrial labour force.

After the initial gains of 1919–20 the shorter working week was primarily regarded as a demand for leisure and a solution to unemployment; it was recognized as 'a means of increasing the amount of leisure and of reducing the volume of unemployment'.[41] As W. Sherwood of the National Union of General and Municipal Workers said: 'It was foolish that two men should be working long hours and that a third man should be idle, when the three men working shorter hours and enjoying more leisure could maintain the output.'[42]

It was first and foremost an employment measure, a means of sharing work evenly throughout the labour force; that is, a policy which purports that if working time was to be reduced for those in the existing labour force, the unworked hours could provide employment opportunities for the out-of-work.[43] Throughout the inter-war years the TUC, supported by Labour groupings as diverse as the moderate General Federation of Trade Unions and the Communist-inspired National Minority Movement (NMM), claimed that the policy would stimulate employment. Yet, the policy also had a strongly flavoured social content which assumed the need to improve the cultural side of life. Hence, Richard Wallhead, the MP for Merthyr Tydfil, remarked that it was essential in order 'to raise the whole standard of living, not only on the physical side, but on every other side, so far as intellectual development, artistic development and appreciation of the good things in life are concerned'.[44] In short, reduced hours of work was said to have a social value which gave the 'opportunity of a richer and fuller life'.[45] It was further argued that this would enable workers 'to have facilities for self-improvement and more healthy recreation and it would also enable them to devote their leisure time to extracting some joy out of life'.[46] The hours option was thus regarded as an integral measure of employment stimulus and social advance.

Closely related to the question of unemployment and hours was the question of new technology. This was so for two reasons. Labour argued that modern machinery and new methods of production had caused technological unemployment, and that the workers had a right to share in the benefits of productive ingenuity in the form of more leisure. It was concluded that if technology was going to provide the opportunity for leisure and not lead to unemployment, shorter hours of work were necessary.

With the use of modern technological methods, trade unions judged that the working class would benefit from guaranteed work, in the guise of work-sharing and increased leisure. The phrases used by the working-class movement to express contemporary trends were optimistic in tone, especially when referring to the work process: new technology would 'Lighten the load of labour', reduce the 'bondage of incessant toil', 'liberate our folk from toil and moil', decrease the 'expenditure of human effort' and help men to 'escape from the drudgery of toil'.[47] According to this view, the machine had the potential to free people from constant and unremitting labour – a view far removed from that of the machine-breaker. Union officials, such as J. A. Gibson, the General Secretary of the National Society of Painters, and M. J. Bell Richards of the Union of Boot and Shoe Operatives, claimed that improved methods of production should bring the workers leisure and recreation and not further unemployment.[48] In brief, for labour-saving devices to 'fulfil the promise of their name', they must act 'as a measure of spreading employment instead of concentrating employment in few hands and leaving a large mass constantly unemployed'.[49]

Notwithstanding this, the belief that more productive machinery and efficient managerial strategies would reduce hours, free the workforce into more leisure and so provide occupational opportunities for the out-of-work was unproven. As some commentators tartly observed, the reality of new technology sometimes departed from the expectation – instead of spreading the work load, rationalization schemes were creating further instability in the labour market. The engineering workers were one of many unions who pointed out that the benefits of productivity increases were being destroyed: 'Instead of more leisure we had more unemployment.'[50] Then again, in the printing industry, with the advent of composing machines and the advances in the linotype and monotype, the workers also pointed to technological unemployment.[51] The fact that science was not benefiting the working class led critics, like the Tailors and Garment Workers' trade unionist Anne Loughlin, to pose the following important question. Was labour-saving machinery, she asked, 'to bring to the majority of the people more and more of the good things of life and more leisure, or are they to be allowed through maladjustment to bring poverty, distress and misery to our people?'[52] Miss Loughlin hoped that they would result in improved living standards for all, but there was the doubt in her mind that, under the prevailing economic and social system, the consequences would be detrimental to the interests of the workers. Trade unionists clearly believed that there was more to machinery than nuts and bolts and increased production targets. What also mattered were the social ramifications of the new innovations. Did they intensify work schedules and accentuate monotony, increase unemployment or provide more leisure? These were the important questions being asked.

It would therefore have been understandable had trade unions taken the short-term point of view by opposing technical and organizational innovation, and introducing restrictive practices. In certain cases this did happen but, despite the immediate adverse effects of new technology, the Labour Movement still continued to favour invention. Indeed, since the late nineteenth century, trade unionists had little desire to be cast in the role of machine-breakers or Luddites. As Professor Musson has written:

> Trade-union officials came to appreciate that 'Luddism' could not stop technological progress and that instead it would be better to try to negotiate manning and working agreements and to secure wage increases and reduced working hours, so as to control the pace of mechanisation and reduce its ill effects, such as technological unemployment, whilst also securing a greater share of its benefits through more pay and leisure.[53]

For the question of technological unemployment to be resolved Labour demanded that new technology had to be a creator of new jobs and a source of shorter hours of work. Apparently, a Labour Government would introduce a number of transitional benefits arising from mechanization: the forty-hour week without reduction of earnings, paid holidays and the regulation of overtime. It was hoped that these reforms would be a means of lessening unemployment and providing more leisure.[54]

It is true that after 1920 the TUC, hit by the problem of inter-union disputes and hampered by overtime working, failed to achieve additional major gains in the form of the shorter working week and the ratification of the International Labour Organisation's Washington Hours Convention of 1919.[55] Given the fact that the trade union movement was not at its strongest in this period, failure was to be expected. Nonetheless, overwhelming support was enlisted in the campaign for this particular demand. For example, when the employers tried to increase the working week in the early 1920s, the Labour Movement pledged united opposition to any such attempt. In the words of one trade unionist, Thos Savage:

> the present reduced working week is the greatest reform of this generation, and any attempt to enforce longer hours would, even in the present depressed state of the industry,

result in united and determined resistance from all sections of labour, as this is the one issue above all others where all would combine for one object.[56]

Up and down the country a similar resolve was shown by big and small unions, craft and general unions alike.[57] In fact, the Transport and General Workers' Union even went as far as involving the rank and file by running a great prize scheme, with a first prize of a motor cycle and side car, in order to attract funds to be used 'in opposing the employers' attack on hours'.[58]

Although union action was not always as concerted, united or as successful as it might have been, the call for reduced hours was established policy and was continually reaffirmed as such. Moreover, the desire for a reduction in the hours of labour was more than mere rhetoric. It was a sincere attempt to improve the economic and social position of the working class. Unions failed to extend hours reductions after 1920, not because of their own inertia, but because of their lack of bargaining power, the weakness of the economy and the intransigence of employers and Government. Despite the fact that in 1920 the Cabinet Committee on Unemployment was actively discussing the possibility of introducing work-sharing schemes – this was based on shorter hours and lower wages – by the mid-1930s official support for shorter hours had evaporated.[59] Hence, Walter Citrine's decision in 1937 to discontinue correspondence with the Prime Minister's office on the subject of the forty-hour week in State industrial establishments.[60]

Before the first world war, the idea of a paid holiday had not gained general credence. In a period when Labour was struggling for elementary economic, social and political justice, holiday pay must have been perceived as somewhat utopian. It was in the inter-war period that the representatives of the industrial working class first began to articulate the demand for universal holidays. There were a number of reasons for this.

At the top of the list must be the fact that holidays without pay brought social distress and economic hardship. Despite the existence of holiday savings clubs, especially in the Lancashire textile industry, as well as the provision and growth of facilities and services for the lower income bracket, the unions asserted that for the majority of working-class people the term 'holiday' was a misnomer.[61] As *Lansbury's Labour Weekly* protested, many thousands of workers had no chance to celebrate holidays, as this was a time without wages, when all that could be expected was activity 'in and about the streets in which they live'.[62] When all the expenses of travel, accommodation and amusement are taken into consideration, it is not surprising that many families could not afford a holiday away from home. In the words of *The Economist*: 'The cost of holidays is too high for many working people.'[63] There can be few doubts that the holiday habit spread during the inter-war period, though by 1937 only fifteen million out of a population of about forty-six million were taking a holiday of a week or more.[64] Even where there was an established custom of holiday thrift clubs, economic depression, short-time working and unemployment reduced the propensity to save. In Oldham, for instance, the money disbursed by the local holiday clubs fell from £247,804 in 1925 to £138,571 in 1933, due to a slump in trade.[65] The evidence for other textile towns tells much the same story. According to one local newspaper, this meant a fall in holiday making:

the number of people spending the Wakes at home was considerably greater than in previous years. Apart from the huge number of local unemployed, many workers of both sexes have remained at home because they felt that in the present unsettled state of trade they dare not spend their Wakes savings on seaside pleasures.[66]

Indeed, some of the holiday savings were used 'to buy clothing, to pay debts, to "straighten up things" . . .'[67] In this situation, some families borrowed money from special holiday loan clubs or pawnbrokers, and even resorted to illegality by dodging ticket inspectors to ensure a day at the seaside.[68] It is therefore hardly surprising that by the 1930s, 'the market for the traditional seaside holiday appears to have been stagnating, at least in the larger resorts'.[69] In order to increase holiday making, financial security was required – this eventually came with the introduction of holiday pay.

In appreciating that holidays without wages brought a great deal of hardship into working-class lives, the Labour Movement articulated a convincing case for paid leave. The engineering workers, for example, stressed the deprivation connected with the loss of wages, and in turn demanded payment for all statutory holidays:

> Workers have to live themselves and keep their families alive even on statutory holidays, and the loss of pay on a statutory holiday makes it impossible for them to take proper advantage of holidays, and drags down their standard of living . . . the worker should at least be certain of payment for wages.[70]

Shop stewards in engineering were close to the mark when pointing out that holidays were in effect lock-outs – days off and no pay.[71]

The case for paid leave was reinforced by the claim that it was unfair for groups of workers – white collar employees and workers in other countries – to receive this benefit whilst manual workers did not:

> We see no reason why the men who usually do the hard physical work of our community, and who are generally paid the least wages should be treated in this respect less favourably than are men who are usually much better remunerated, who are generally employed in more congenial work, and who live under more pleasant surroundings.[72]

Furthermore, the unions were the originators of a proposal that compulsory holidays with pay could improve the job situation by redistributing work from those on holiday to those unemployed.[73] Finally, it was pointed out that remuneration was important as a source of relaxation, rest and recuperation, a time for utilizing leisure for pleasure and health.[74]

Even though the overall case of the unions was difficult to repudiate, the majority of the employers managed to do just that. In the main, employers, particularly in the staple industries, based their opposition on the grounds that paid holidays would inflate labour costs, and so reduce international competitiveness, damage exports, squeeze profit margins, and ultimately increase unemployment. Although from the perspective of profit maximization this was a valid point, arguments relating to cost were continually used to pre-empt acceptance of even the most rudimentary of schemes. Under such circumstances a feature of paid holiday developments was trade union action.

In the two or three years after the end of the first world war, unions included holidays with pay in their collective bargaining strategy. As one Labour newspaper commented: 'The question of the payment of wages for holidays is one that has recently come very much to the front.'[75] Evidence suggests that union representation was made on this question in a variety of trades, ranging from transport services, coalmining and cotton to printing, and boot and shoe manufacture. In printing, for example, a national Hours and Holidays Agreement came into force in 1919 granting a week's holiday with pay after a year of service, later described as 'one of the greatest boons ever introduced'.[76] The growing demand for holiday pay was also taken up by the TUC who resolved in favour of payment for at least ten working days' holiday and all bank holidays.[77] It would be foolish to suggest a monocausal explanation of paid holiday concessions in this period, but a major reason can be traced to union action, bolstered by high membership and negotiating strength.

However, in the fifteen years after 1920 the campaign for holidays with pay was often neglected as economic depression, unemployment and falling union membership hindered the adoption of a forward-looking programme. It is therefore not surprising that organized Labour adopted an essentially defensive strategy of protecting existing agreements and conditions of employment. This is not to say, however, that the demand was abandoned entirely. Sections of the community debated the need for extra time away from work and a complete break from the rigours of the working day. The 1920s and early 1930s occasionally witnessed strong moves in the direction of paid holidays: at times the issue was a feature of official union negotiations, on other occasions the crux of rank and file discontent. For instance, workers in the distributive trade, engineering, building, and State industrial establishments all made positive moves in the direction of paid holidays, while militant workers in the NMM and communist factory groups recorded similar progress.[78] Whatever form the demand took, it brought the question of elementary working-class justice into the open and convinced many people of the legitimacy of the union's case.

In the lead up to the concessions of 1937 and 1938 organized

Labour played a crucial role. Ernest Bevin, the general secretary of the powerful Transport and General Workers' Union, had suggested in 1933 that there should be 'the organisation of a national movement for the purpose of securing a statutory holiday of at least two weeks in each year for all workers, with the payment of full wages'.[79] In his words, the campaign for holidays with pay was a 'vital issue'.[80] The main body of the Labour Movement agreed. In particular, the TUC pressed the demand at all levels of the political process. This included a meeting with the Prime Minister, Stanley Baldwin; although he both outmanoeuvred the TUC deputation by suggesting that a tripartite committee of inquiry be set up and was responsible for the rejection of a Parliamentary Bill on the matter, the union campaign continued to make significant inroads.[81] It is indeed interesting to note that during the summer months of 1937 the Labour Party launched a seaside campaign based on the demand for holidays with pay. This so-called seaside drive appears to have been a success, with over 150 meetings, the distribution of approximately one million leaflets and thousands of pictorial poster displays.[82] Further, with the upswing of the economy those militants who had been unemployed for years began to trickle back into the workshops, and it was they who nurtured the growing mass support for a paid holiday. For example, from its inception in 1934 the shop stewards' movement in South East London representing the workers of two electrical engineering firms, Siemens Brothers and Johnson and Phillips, had as its clarion call the demand for paid holidays. And in fact the same point can be made in the case of the rank and file in the aircraft industry, militant railway shopmen, and striking workers in Leicester and the Potteries.[83] In the light of these and other developments, many gains were made: engineering workers, railway shopmen, miners, iron and steel workers, and potters all signed paid holiday agreements. These gains had been achieved in spite of the publicity given to the departmental committee on holidays with pay; trade unionists had not waited for official reports or legislation, but had persisted with their own claims.

It emerges from the above discussion that holidays with pay (like the shorter working week) were introduced due to the actions and energies of organized Labour: the weight of evidence suggests that without trade union pressure concessions would have been delayed. As Andrew Robertson of the British Institute of Management has concluded: 'It was the trade unions who were largely responsible for making sure that the majority of British workers got an annual holiday.'[84] Not surprisingly, a similar verdict was given by the trade unions.[85] Although the major gains were made during times of trade prosperity in the immediate post-war years and in the economic recovery of the later 1930s, there is little reason to believe that agreements were introduced simply because of rising profits. Indeed, whereas employers remained intransigent during a period of increasing buoyancy between 1932 and 1937, they signed a number of agreements in 1937 and 1938, despite economic downswing and declining profits. If the demand for leisure was increasing during the inter-war years as is suggested here, then it is important to recognize that this was connected with trade union policy.

All this is not to argue that union pressure was the only factor in the extension of leisure. It certainly was the case that some employers, especially those in small-scale family businesses, were genuinely concerned about the welfare of their workforce and were willing to reduce hours and pay wages during holidays, even if this put pressure on levels of profitability.[86] As G. Cunningham, the chairman and managing director of the Triplex Safety Company, said: 'I should be ashamed to be controlling any company which showed a profit at all and denied its employees holidays with pay.'[87] Perhaps the most prominent of the enlightened paternalists, Seebohm Rowntree, thus refused to give evidence to the departmental committee on holidays with pay, as he thought the case needed no bolstering: 'I should have thought it was pretty generally accepted that a holiday of some kind is desirable, and that if a holiday is given it must be with pay.'[88] Some firms further stimulated the working-class holiday by providing information on travel facilities, maintaining a register of boarding houses and in some cases by actually organizing camps and tours.[89] The fact that the Establishment press, in the guise of the *Daily Express*, was a leading advocate of 'one of the greatest benefits ever conferred on the British people' is not surprising, since some influential leaders of industry were in favour of quite progressive social policy.[90]

It is difficult to deny, however, that increases in wages and paid holidays, as well as reductions in hours of work, were closely connected to the actions of organized Labour. It is also clear that increased leisure was perceived as a major achievement. Hence, in the pottery trade, holidays with pay were said to have 'reached both the hearts and the pockets of the workers, more than any other Award in the living history of the industry', while in the heavy steel industry, it was regarded as the 'biggest reform . . . since the eight-hour day was established in 1919'.[91] Elsewhere, many trade unionists and co-operators stressed that shorter hours and paid holidays were amongst the most significant improvements of the day.

2
Commercialization and the growth of the leisure industry

In the period before 1914 it is apparent that leisure had witnessed a process of commercialization. The operation of sports such as horse-racing and association football were based on prevailing commercial practices, while the music hall and holiday entertainments, having benefited from the introduction of limited liability in 1862, began to take advantage of significant capital investment, scale economies, and increasing division of labour.[1] Leisure became a business which involved the entry of entrepreneurs and shareholders, the establishment of a labour market and an administrative structure, capital outlay on facilities and equipment, and the generation of sales revenue and profits. Looking back from the inter-war years, it is possible to consider the 1890s as a watershed. As Asa Briggs has pointed out, 1896 can be regarded as a crucial year, with the arrival of Marconi in England, the founding of the *Daily Mail*, the first motor race held between London and Brighton, and the presentation of the first moving picture show in London. By the turn of the century the prerequisites for a modern leisure industry were in existence: urban markets, rising incomes, an increase in leisure time, transport systems and the application of technology to entertainment.[2] All this is not to say that the late nineteenth century can be viewed as the culmination of commercial leisure expansion. Capitalist enterprise had yet to enter all leisure activities: amateurism was still ubiquitous, regional diversity still great and the dialogue between entertainer and audience still important. The leisure industry of the late nineteenth century was therefore in its prototype stage, increasingly influenced by entrepreneurial activity, it is true, but still to experience thorough-going commercialism.

It is the purpose of this chapter to examine the commercial basis and growth of the leisure industry in the 1920s and 1930s. If by commercialization one means entrepreneurial interest in financial return rather than non monetary gain and an increase in the scale of merchandise being exchanged, there can be little doubt that the leisure industry underwent commercial expansion. Entertainment and leisure became big business as it was increasingly realized that a lot of money could be made out of people's spare time. It will be shown that in response to rising market conditions the industry became organized on a modern Capitalist basis, with greater employment, more investment, more managerial know-how and increasing concentration of ownership. Generally speaking, the working class benefited from commercial expansion, though there were notable exceptions.

Some general trends

There are problems encountered in defining the leisure industry. For instance, can cigarettes be regarded as a leisure good since they are smoked both in work and leisure time? Here the industry is regarded as those goods and services of an entertainment, sporting and spare time character, including cigarettes, which were provided in the market place. Unlike the traditional staple industries of coal, iron and steel, and shipbuilding, the output and structures of the leisure sector were, and are, varied and diverse. The main distinction to be made is between those concerns such as sports' manufacturers, film makers and breweries which were involved in production, and those concerns such as football clubs, cinemas and public houses which provided a service.

Aside from the problem of definition, there is also the problem connected with the paucity of data – there is simply insufficient information to make detailed estimates of the industry's track record. Indeed, given the diverse nature of the industry, it is very difficult to measure its importance systematically. Nevertheless, figures from the *Census of Production* returns, *Annual Statements of Trade* and other sources indicate that output, employment and exports followed the general fluctuations of the inter-war business cycle. As with other sectors of the economy, the leisure industry experienced a pronounced post-war boom and slump, followed by modest expansion for the rest of the 1920s; the industry shared in the downswing of 1929–32 and thereafter underwent a slight recovery, though given the profound economic nationalism of the 1930s exports lagged behind. To take just two examples from the data. First, output figures have been extracted from the *Census of Production* returns. Although precise inter-census comparisons are not always possible because of changes in classification, it can be seen from Table 2.1 that gross output increased considerably in the period after 1907, while there was a moderate decline in most trades after 1930 due to the overall fall in the level of economic activity. It should also be noted that the figures are in current value and therefore fail to take into account fluctuations in prices; since prices fell in the inter-war years the expansion of the leisure industry was greater in real terms. Second, the information contained in Table 2.2 for external trade tells much the same story. It appears that there was a marked increase in exports of sports goods in the years after 1918, though again a decline in the 1930s. Judging from the data, although the leisure industry was one of the 'new' trades of the inter-war years – an important part of the expanding tertiary sector of the economy – it was clearly not insulated from wider economic trends.

Table 2.1   *Gross output of selected leisure products*

| | Value of gross output (£,000)[a] | | | |
	1907	1924	1930	1935
Brewing/Malting	67,100	159,466	143,358	122,400
Film printing	–	686	1,053	1,439
Games/Toys	286	1,513	2,000	2,993
Musical instruments	1,867	8,301	11,428	4,312
Newspapers/Periodicals	13,237	46,095	50,993	50,772
Sports requisites	1,151	3,407	3,117	2,919
Tobacco trade	23,799	93,292	115,878	121,960

Source: *Census of Production*, 1907, 1924, 1930, 1935.
[a] In current value.

Table 2.2   *Total exports of sports and ancilliary goods 1920–39*[a]

	£		£
1920	1,339,056	1930	1,408,562
1921	1,107,902	1931	1,134,686
1922	1,326,644	1932	1,044,166
1923	1,362,945	1933	945,724
1924	1,325,363	1934	922,896
1925	1,435,713	1935	947,013
1926	1,544,160	1936	978,941
1927	1,513,618	1937	1,065,145
1928	1,528,126	1938	1,016,680
1929	1,566,096	1939	975,666

Source: Calculated from the *Annual Statements of Trade of UK*.
[a] Figures cover a range of sports goods from golf balls to rackets, fishing tackle and the like.

As was established in chapter one, consumer demand for leisure goods and services remained buoyant throughout the inter-war years. Increased purchasing power and more leisure time led to an increase in consumer expenditure on entertainment, sport, reading, smoking and so on. According to the somewhat conservative estimates of R. Stone and D. A. Rowe, annual spending on entertainment and recreation averaged between £200 and £250 million in the 1920s and 1930s, which was about 5 per cent of total consumer expenditure. The period witnessed an increase of 15 per cent in consumer expenditure on admissions to theatres, cinemas and sporting events: in 1920, expenditure was £56.2 million; by 1938 it had reached £64.9 million.[3] When examining specific industries, the results are even more spectacular.

Of all the leisure industries, the cinema was the most popular. Simon Rowson found that the total admissions to British cinemas in 1934 were about 963 million and the total gross box-office receipts were about £41 million.[4] It is therefore not too surprising to find that, despite American competition, the gross output of the cinematograph film printing trade increased from £686,000 to £1,439,000 in the years 1924–35 (see Table 2.1). A similar trend can be discerned in the other technologically based leisure industries, namely popular broadcasting and the gramophone. The number of wireless licences increased from 2,178,259 in 1926 to 9,082,666 in 1938, and although by the later 1930s radio manufacturing companies were catering largely for replacement demand, the industry had expanded considerably during the period in question.[5] The gramophone industry also expanded during the 1920s and, despite the shrinkage of demand brought about by the depression, the business continued to hold its own.

The sporting industry was no less affected by these trends, and it was spectator sport which expanded the most. For instance, in the London area the attendance on tracks licensed by the National Greyhound Racing Society increased from about 6.5 million in 1928 to about nine million in 1932, while annual attendances at the capital's five speedway racing tracks increased each year, reaching approximately 1.3 million in 1933.[6] Football crowds were also large, with total annual attendances in the four divisions of the Football League totalling 31.43 million in the 1937/8 season.[7] Despite the lack of concrete evidence, it appears that football attendances were high and increasing in the inter-war years. A comparison with some of the figures provided by Dr Mason in his book, *Association Football and English Society 1863–1915*, is revealing. In season 1908/9 six million people watched First Division matches, producing an average crowd per match of about 16,000; by season 1937/8 the comparable figures were approximately fourteen million and 30,000. Similar conclusions can be drawn from an examination of F.A. Cup fixtures. The third round of the Cup in 1913 was watched by a total of 661,381 spectators paying £23,154; in 1923 779,272 spectators paid £51,055, and by 1937 809,262 spectators paid £54,907. Taking the competition as a whole, in 1936 the sixty-three matches from the third round to the final attracted crowds of over two million, which compares favourably with the 1905/6 season when the same number of matches attracted crowds of 1.2 million. Furthermore, the attendances and receipts recorded at the final itself increased markedly in the years after 1918. The quantitative evidence therefore supports Dr Walvin's claim that 'English football on the eve of World War II . . . was certainly watched by more people than in 1914.'[8] Undoubtedly the sport was a large-scale financial undertaking in the 1920s and 1930s which attracted millions of spectators each year.

The popularity of sport was clearly related to a number of other trades, especially gambling. Horse races, as well as the new forms of the tote, greyhound races, 'spot the ball' and the football pools, spawned a huge industry, thought by some to be the second largest in the country.[9] Despite the fact that there are difficulties in estimating gambling turnover, the total value of all bets staked more than trebled in the inter-war years, so that by the early 1930s annual expenditure was between £300 and £400 million.[10] Underlying this is the fact that there were between ten and fifteen million gamblers and the majority of the working class gambled fairly regularly. Furthermore, as a select committee of 1923 pointed out, there was scarcely a company in the country employing more than twenty workers where one was not a book-maker's agent.[11] As far as the football pools were concerned, it is evident from the social surveys of the period that the industry penetrated a vast number of homes:

A form of betting which has grown to enormous proportions in recent years is the football pools. . . . The extent to which people in York take part in them can be gauged from the fact that each week during the football season no less than 48,000 pool promoters' circulars are delivered throughout the post to houses in York.[12]

Finally, the holiday industry needs to be brought into the discussion. The seaside holiday habit developed in the nineteenth century, principally in the Lancashire textile district, and was extended in the inter-war years. Despite the fact that holidays with pay were not extensively provided until the end of the 1930s, the annual break from work was financed by some workers through thrift clubs and other forms of saving. It is true, of course, that many people could not afford a holiday, but as the social surveys of the period show a section of the poorer families went away to the country or the seaside, no doubt benefiting from the cheaper modes of transport. The period in fact witnessed the growth of holiday organizations and the establishment of many camps for the lower income groups – it was in 1937 that Billy Butlin opened his first luxury camp at Skegness, 'giving the greatest possible all-in holiday value at the lowest reasonable price'.[13] By this time many people had a holiday of one week or more, and even if a holiday could not be taken there was always the possibility of a day excursion to the seaside. In addition, thousands of tourists came to the UK from overseas, representing a significant contribution to the balance of payments. The tourist traffic to the UK increased from 432,239 visitors spending £18,368,465 in 1921, to 720,429 visitors spending £30,506,740 in 1938.[14] Consumers, whether from Britain or abroad, thus made substantial outlays at travel agencies, transport booking offices, hotels and boarding houses, shops and places of amusement.

From this overview of selected industries, it is clear that market demand for leisure was relatively high during the inter-war years. The statistics of gross output, consumer expenditure, admissions and turnover used in this section, though not always comparable, point to this view. Indeed, the commercial returns from the leisure industry were very attractive: gross trading profits from entertainment, hotels and other services were £88 million in 1920, rising to £108 million in 1928, falling back again to £88 million in 1932, and recovering to £106 million by 1938.[15] This is not to argue that the leisure industry was a particularly secure form of long-term investment as firms were often financially extravagant and 'boom' flotations were known to collapse, as was the case with greyhound racing and the cinema industry in the 1930s. Nonetheless, profits were certainly made by those enterprises dynamic enough to take risks.

It has been estimated, for example, that the total remuneration of the gambling industry in the mid-1930s was about £50 million, leading *The Economist* to complain about 'unduly large "professional" profits'.[16] More specifically, as money spent on the football pools rose, companies earned high returns, especially as profits were computed at no less than 30 per cent of amounts staked.[17] A further indication of the money to be made is the fact that at several of the licensed greyhound tracks in the early 1930s as many as 200 or 300 bookmakers could be found.[18] Greyhound racing companies themselves also succeeded in establishing their businesses on a stable profit-earning basis. Even during the slump, the Greyhound Racing Association Trust, which controlled the operation of a number of urban tracks, increased its net profits from £87,519 to £131,867.[19]

Sports concerns also had a degree of commercial success. Football clubs, though not profit maximizers – the Football Association limited club dividends to 7.5 per cent before tax – sometimes made significant financial gains. As *The Economist* commented, the aristocrats of the game like Arsenal, Wolverhampton Wanderers and Everton had the opportunity to 'coin money hand over fist'.[20] For example, Wolves made a profit of £17,790 in the 1935–6 season.[21] Similarly, the salient theme of Howard Marshall's 'An Inquisition on British Sport' was that 'Money, in short, is the root of the trouble.'

> There is big money in boxing, and as a result many promoters are simply speculators, whose sole concern in the game is with the financial end of it. They make it their business to stimulate public interest, and to manipulate their boxers like puppets.[22]

By the 1930s, title fights at the White City, for example, attracted very large crowds.

Even those leisure concerns which did not fare so well during the economic downturn of the early 1930s were remarkably adaptable. The hotel and catering trades, despite having to spend additional sums on food and equipment, were able to secure larger profits by increasing turnover.[23] Moreover, although the consumption of beer stagnated, the brewing industry was still able to make high returns. The output of beer in the United Kingdom fell from approximately 35 million bulk barrels in 1920 to 24.5 million in 1938, but annual profits for roughly the same period increased from £29 million to £31.5 million.[24] The continued prosperity of the industry, as will be seen, was associated with greater efficiency.

Labour and capital investment

The supply side of the leisure industry also experienced considerable change and adaptation in the inter-war period. Entrepreneurs responded to the buoyant demand conditions by expanding output, so the question needs to be asked, how was this achieved? Production can be increased either by extensive or intensive means; that is, by increasing factor inputs or by improving productivity. In this section the inputs of labour and capital will be examined, to be followed in the next section by an examination of those variables which affected the productivity record of the industry.

During the inter-war years there was a substantial increase in the number of people working in the leisure and related trades. Although it is difficult to analyse precisely the employment pattern of the industry as the nature of the data makes comparisons difficult, the evidence clearly shows that there were large additions to the stock of labour. According to the estimates of A. L. Chapman and R. Knight, the number of workers employed in British hotels, pubs, restaurants and boarding houses increased from 415,500 in 1920 to 494,600 in 1938. Likewise, employment in entertainment and sport in Great Britain rose from 101,700 in 1920 to 140,100 in 1931 and 247,900 in 1938.[25] Detailed figures based on the population census are shown in Table 2.3.

Table 2.3   *Average numbers employed in leisure services*

	Entertainment and sport	*Catering, hotels etc.*
1920	101,700	415,500
1921	92,100	374,100
1922	97,000	326,300
1923	102,000	304,500
1924	106,900	316,700
1925	109,700	331,100
1926	112,100	344,400
1927	119,600	362,400
1928	124,900	378,100
1929	129,600	392,900
1930	133,700	397,000
1931	140,100	395,800
1932	156,500	413,100
1933	169,000	427,900
1934	182,300	449,200
1935	194,900	462,100
1936	213,500	476,500
1937	233,200	491,400
1938	247,900	494,600

Source: Calculated from A. L. Chapman and R. Knight, *Wages and Salaries in the United Kingdom 1920–1938*, Cambridge University Press, Cambridge, 1953, pp. 207, 210–11.

As with other trades entertainment and sport suffered from unemployment in the early 1930s. The percentage unemployed in Britain increased from 10.2 in 1929 to 19.5 by 1933, by which time it ranged from 9.4 in the South East to 25.5 in Scotland.[26] For the rest of the 1930s William Beveridge estimated that there was a dramatic increase in the number of males working in entertainment and sport so that this particular sector had the third greatest increase in employment of all industries between 1927 and 1937.[27] Elizabeth Brunner, using statistics compiled by H. Frankel, also pointed out that there was an increase of 48.7 per cent in the numbers occupied in the British entertainment and sports industry between 1931 and 1939.[28] Indeed, by the end of the 1930s *The Economist* was impressed by the size and the rate at which employment was increasing, having reached 140,000 insured workers by the middle of 1937:

> This is a surprising figure when it is remembered that this number of employees is larger than the 115,000 employed in electrical engineering, and not so far short of the 200,000 or so employed in cotton weaving. If we make an index number of the insured work-people in entertainment and sport, it has risen from 100 in 1923 to 233.7 to-day.[29]

Other leisure industries recorded similar increases. In the period 1924–35 the average number of persons employed in the games and toys trade increased from 4,992 to 10,907, and in the sports requisites trade from 6,775 to 8,253.[30] In fact, by the end of the 1930s the manufacture of games, sports equipment and musical instruments employed as many people as the fishing industry.[31]

The leisure industry attracted all types of workers, ranging from clerks and building operatives to stage hands and stable lads. Obviously the demand for labour increased as the demand for the product or service increased. Hence, with the expansion of gambling the number of persons professionally engaged as bookmakers rose from 2,897 in 1921 to 9,447 in 1931.[32] Also, high demand tended to bid up the price of labour, particularly in the case of top performers. The cricket writer, C. L. R. James, thus pointed to the example of George Headley, the West Indian opener, who received offers of £1,000 in 1934 to play for a Lancashire League team.[33] In contrast, the labour market in professional football was characterized by a number of rigidities, particularly the maximum wage and retain-and-transfer system, which meant that the maximum annual salary of a professional footballer in

1931 was only £386, compared with well over £1,000 for some cricketers. Having said this, the transfer market for footballers grew; the year 1928 witnessed the first £10,000 transfer fee, and thereafter the market expanded so that by 1939 £272,000 was paid out for players in the four divisions of the Football League.[34] Likewise, the growth of professionalism in rugby is indicated by the fact that between 1918 and 1939 forty-eight capped Welsh amateur union players were lost to the northern professional game of rugby league.[35]

Clearly then, the leisure industry was able to increase labour inputs and so raise output. Yet, perhaps capital investment was even more important in generating growth. The estimates of Professor Feinstein show that there was a substantial addition to fixed assets during the inter-war years, as cinemas, theatres, recreation halls and sports grounds were all constructed.[36] It is also true that many companies, depending upon market conditions, invested considerable sums in plant, machinery and equipment.

There was clearly an increase in the number of cinema houses, representing an important advance on the pre-war building programme. Some £15 million was invested in film exhibition by 1914 and this had increased to £70 million by 1929.[37] In fact, over 1,000 cinemas were built between 1924–5 and 1931–2, reaching a grand total of 4,305 by the end of 1934 and 5,300 by 1939.[38] In 1931–2 there were 258 cinemas in the County of London with a total seating capacity of 344,000, compared with ninety-four cinemas seating 55,000 in 1911; similarly, in Liverpool, there were sixty-nine cinemas in 1934, compared with thirty-two in 1913, and in Birmingham, 109 cinemas by 1939, compared with fifty-seven in 1913.[39] Many of the old cinemas were demolished and replaced by new ones, some of them luxury palaces big enough to seat 3,000 patrons, with 'plushier seats, richer decor and colour-lit Mighty Wurlitzer organs rising magically from under-stage in the interval'.[40] In addition, on the production side, as the film industry began to respond to American competition, existing studios were enlarged and new ones erected, floor space expanded, specialized organization introduced and up-to-date plants acquired.[41]

The experience of the urban dance hall also confirms this tendency. In the six years following the end of the first world war, there were about 11,000 dance halls and night clubs opened.[42] The local 'Palais', 'Mecca', and 'Locarno' were probably the only alternatives to the public house or the cinema in many towns. Dancing was popular in the 1920s and, although it declined in popularity in the following decade, the dance hall industry continued to prosper.[43] Indeed, purpose-built halls were opened which were similar in style to the super-cinemas. In Rochdale, Embassy Amusements Ltd opened the Carlton, which offered standards resembling those of the new cinemas opened in the town. It was far more glamorous than the smaller commercial halls and tried to entice dancers with its resident band and its restaurant.[44]

As far as sports stadia were concerned, expensive tracks, enormous grounds and elaborate seating arrangements were provided. Huge sums were invested in sports venues of all descriptions: greyhound courses, football and rugby grounds, speedway tracks and ice rinks. A grand total of sixty-two greyhound racing companies were registered in different parts of Britain in 1927, with a total capital of £7 million, and it was they who financed some of the most famous tracks – Clapton, Wembley, West Ham and Slough.[45] Football grounds had also been modernized and in some cases rebuilt. In the words of the sports journalist, Frank Johnston:

When many of the present day clubs started, almost any piece of ground would be welcomed as a playing pitch, provided there was not a quarry or a warehouse in the middle. Today minor clubs can boast up-to-date arenas.[46]

Not only was Wembley Stadium built at a cost of £750,000, but leading clubs such as West Ham United, Manchester City and Arsenal embarked on a major programme of capital improvements. Although some clubs held their grounds on lease and had a low level of capital formation, towards the end of the 1930s league clubs held assets of about £2.5 million, of which 82 per cent was in land and buildings.[47] This is not to say, however, that all sports facilities were improved, for in the case of race-courses, there was little modernization. Many 'racecourse amenities in the interwar years could rightly be considered inadequate and in a few cases downright primitive', but even this situation was being remedied to some extent through the financial assistance of the totalizator: between 1936 and 1938 over £76,000 was siphoned off for racecourse amenities and improvements.[48]

The holiday and related trades were also characterized by heavy capital investment. The expansion of the industry was associated with the growth of resort accommodation, public amenities and leisure concerns. Hence, in 1933 resort investment has been estimated at between £200 and £300 million.[49] More spectacular still, towards the end of the decade was the construction of several hundred permanent and semi-permanent holiday camps, some of which accommodated thousands of people.[50] The biggest were, of course, the Butlin's camps at Skegness and Clacton. Billy Butlin was a pioneer of the mass leisure industry, having introduced a number of novel amusements such as dodgems and the big dipper at fair grounds in the late 1920s, and with accumulated savings of £50,000, plus a similar amount from Barclays Bank, was able to finance the construction of a permanent camp at Skegness. This consisted of dining and recreation halls, club room, a gym and 800 timber and concrete chalets, as well as numerous entertainment facilities. Furthermore, additional capital was raised when Butlins Ltd went public; the business mushroomed and by October 1938 the total net assets of the company were about £876,500 and the year's gross profits nearly £121,000.[51] Thomas Cook & Son also diversified into the holiday camp business when they helped to set up British Holiday Estates Ltd with nominal capital of £250,000 to 'promote, organise, provide and manage holiday camps, amusement parks, lidos, entertainments, amusements, sports, pastimes, games and recreations of all kinds'.[52] Closely connected with the expansion of the tourist trade was the introduction of the milk bar: the number of bars throughout the country increased from 540 in 1936 to 1,475 in 1938, with total capital estimated at something over £1.5 million.[53] Indeed, policy advisers such as Hubert Henderson of the Economic Advisory Council began to recognize tourism as a factor of considerable economic importance, particularly as it was thought 'that the commercial opportunities of the future will be very largely in the development of services as contrasted with the mass production of commodities'.[54]

Lastly, it is important to note that there was a movement for public house improvement, led by Whitbreads, Mitchell and Butler, Ansells, other progressive firms, and also by Public House Trust Companies, whereby the structure of the pub was modified to make it spacious and airy, with tables and chairs, and amenities such as food, recreation and music.[55] This movement was especially popular in Birmingham, where the brighter, airier and loftier pub replaced 'the old, squalid, furtive, back-alley gin-palace, lurking in the shadows, afraid of the light'.[56] As a result there was a lot of investment, and even at the depths of the economic crisis in 1931 it was reported that the industry was still 'very well financed'.[57]

Productivity

Employment and capital investment in the leisure industry expanded rapidly during the 1920s and 1930s. It has been claimed, however, that for the service trades as a whole 'output did not keep pace so that productivity declined'.[58] Even though productivity is hardly measurable in leisure services, there is evidence to support this claim as far as some sectors are concerned. In the sports requisites trade, net output per person employed thus fell from £235 in 1924 to £196 in 1935 (see Table 2.4), the result of a failure to standardize goods, fluctuating demand and a slow rate of retail stock turnover.[59] Yet, this should not disguise the fact that there were some improvements in efficiency which undoubtedly increased output per unit of input. Despite the fact that data is not always strictly comparable, productivity gains can be seen by referring to the figures for net output per person from the *Census of Production* returns given in Table 2.4. It is true that output per person in some trades appears to have fallen in the first half of the 1930s, but the main reason for this was the downward trend in prices which the crude Census data does not take into account. The main sources of such productivity growth in the leisure industry were better methods of management, cost reducing innovations, and economies of scale. As the following discussion will attempt to show, there were notable managerial, technical and organizational developments which affected all levels of the industry.

Advanced managerial ideas in terms of business organization, quality control of the finished product and marketing ability were gradually accepted and became quite widespread. This was particularly true of association football. Although economists and

Table 2.4   *Net output per person employed in selected leisure trades*

	Current £s			
	1907	*1924*	*1930*	*1935*
Brewing/Malting	483	685	748	789
Film printing	–	289	539	555
Games/Toys	58	139	171	148
Musical instruments	104	222	296	228
Newspapers/Periodicals	190	542	518	476
Sports requisites	102	235	197	196
Tobacco trade	155	616	698	662

Source: *Census of Production*, 1907, 1924, 1930, 1935.

economic historians have argued that entrepreneurs of sport are not profit maximizers, it is likely that commercial considerations were of central importance in the running of a football club.[60] The best managers had to have the ability 'to keep a balance between a successful team and the club as a successful business concern'.[61] Indeed, management began to take the view that the club could achieve both championship and financial success. In the mid-1930s the role of team manager and secretary was sometimes the combined responsibility of individual officials, such as George Allison (Arsenal), W. H. Walker (Sheffield Wednesday), Albert Knighton (Chelsea), Harry Curtis (Brentford) and Robert Jack (Plymouth Argyle). As both Professor Korr and Dr Tischler have recently suggested, if a club was going to remain financially viable, especially in the long run, then success had to be achieved on the field of play.[62] One way of guaranteeing success was through the transfer market and the rise of professionalism, but probably a better way was through improved and more efficient management. Desire for success was translated into the very techniques of the game itself: coaching and tactics became commonplace. The new science, which even included the use of film and sports medicine, was thus used by Herbert Chapman in guiding Huddersfield Town from obscurity to success in the 1920s and in moulding Arsenal as one of the top club sides of the 1930s.[63]

Archaic social traditions were also broken down as the professional creed spread. On Empire Day 1926 a formidable social barrier was challenged. The Second Test Match between England and Australia, held at Lords (the spiritual home of first class cricket), featured the English amateur and professional players using the same dressing room and entering the field of play through the same central gate of the pavilion.[64] The distinction between the amateur and the professional thereafter gradually diminished. Although there was still a certain snobbish class element associated with the game, a characteristic not to be shed until well after the second world war, the tendency towards the emancipation of cricket corresponds with the diffusion of a more business-like approach.

A further way in which the leisure industry applied new managerial ideas was in the area of marketing. It has been estimated that in 1935 approximately £3.4 million was spent on advertising entertainment and amusement, which was about 3.8 per cent of total advertising expenditure.[65] Various kinds of media were used to advertise leisure goods and services, including press display, outdoor posters, direct mail and circulars, and film. Such publicity even gave rise to a degree of public concern. The Conservative MP for Newcastle, Alfred Denville, who had also had a theatrical career, argued that 'One of the scandals of the entertainment industry is the remarkable number of questionable posters which are sent round by exhibitors and firms to various managers in certain towns, with instructions that these posters are to be exhibited on the walls.'[66] Yet, clearly entrepreneurs did not view advertising in such a way; for them it was thought to widen markets, reduce marketing risk and uncertainty, and perhaps most important of all increase turnover. The holiday trades, for example, paid for advertising space in the specialist press, such as *The British Boarding-House Proprietor* and *Dalton's Weekly House and Apartment Advertiser*, in local and national newspapers, and in railway guides. *The Daily Express* thus carried more than 36,000 announcements of holiday accommodation in 1931, 'and scores of testimonials [were] received from satisfied advertisers'.[67] Likewise, about 55 pool promoters were advertising in the press during the 1937/8 football season, and according to one source, well over £500,000 was spent on such advertisements.[68] Even the film industry, which found it difficult to base its sales campaign on a trade mark due to the necessity of selling each film independently, was able to promote its product by excessive publicity and by generating interest in the well-known members of the production. Moreover, Oscar Deutsch, the leading figure behind Odeon Theatres Ltd, also made a trade mark out of the cinema' circuit itself, thereby popularizing the product. Lastly, adverts certainly helped to popularize drinking and smoking, especially among young people and women.

Perhaps an even more obvious way in which productivity was increased was through the utilization of modern forms of technology. Strictly speaking, it is difficult to differentiate between capital inputs and technical progress as such progress ultimately depends on the level of investment. Notwithstanding this, however, new technology was exploited in the entertainment industries. Certainly, broadcasting, the gramophone and the cinema relied on technical expertise for their effective operation. The BBC was engaged in continuous technical research from its earliest days, especially in the characteristics of radio wave propagation.[69] Remarkable advances were also made in receiving equipment. Writing in 1933 J. H. Williams, the managing director of the Marconiphone Company, thus commented:

> So great has been the progress in the design and construction
> of radio receivers that it is hardly credible that the
> cumbersome, complicated, and costly equipment of only seven
> or eight years ago is actually so closely related to the
> compact, reliable, and remarkably efficient receiver of to-day,
> with its pleasant appearance and lifelike tone quality.[70]

Moreover, amateur radio hams could build a crystal set for as little as three shillings, which was no doubt a factor in the rapid increase in the number of wireless sets between the wars. In the gramophone industry the major breakthrough came in 1925 when electrical recording was introduced: 'Perhaps more than any other, this advance in recording technique paved the way for the wider acceptance of the gramophone as a serious instrument for reproducing music.'[71] Technology in the cinematograph industry was particularly important in the production of films, and in fact it was a new invention, the talking picture, which was crucial in meeting the challenge of a trade slump in 1926–7.[72] Technological breakthroughs, particularly in the electrical field, were therefore the very backbone of the entertainment business. Indeed, it was these innovations which led to the setting up in Britain in 1936 of the first fully electronic television system in the world, a development which would again transform leisure habits after 1945.

Equally important in raising productivity was the growth in the size, concentration, and dealings of commercial leisure undertakings. The industry witnessed corporate growth as firms came together through mergers or restrictive agreements to take advantage of both internal and external scale economies. It is apparent that larger firms had a better productivity record than smaller ones. Figures of net output per person employed extrapolated from the *Census of Production* returns for 1935 confirm this. In the cinematograph film printing trade net output per person in firms employing between eleven and twenty-four workers was on average £452, while the figure for firms employing between 100 and 199 workers was £708. In the case of sports requisites, net output per person ranged from £165 in firms with fifty to ninety-nine workers, to £220 in firms with 200 to 499 workers. As far as brewing and malting was concerned, net output per person was £538 for the smallest firms and £905 for the largest firms, though at this point it is possible that diseconomies of scale were being experienced. Data for other leisure undertakings shows much the same pattern.

There was a considerable degree of concentration in the tobacco trade, with the Imperial Tobacco Company in a near monopoly position. As early as 1920 it controlled nearly 75 per cent of the trade, and over 90 per cent of the rapidly growing cigarette sector. Imperial's market domination was further consolidated in the inter-war years. The company acquired an interest in Ardath Tobacco and Gallahers, as well as the Mollins Machine Company which supplied cigarette machinery. In addition to its dominance of the tobacco trade, the Imperial Company therefore had interests in cigarette packaging and machinery. Not only this, the trend towards monopoly in the industry as a whole was further extended in the 1930s when the main tobacco manufacturers entered into a series of restrictive trading agreements.[73] Thus, according to information from the 1935 *Census of Production*, whereas the nine largest establishments (employing over 1,000 workers each) produced 78 per cent of the industry's total output, the remaining 109 smaller establishments (employing less than 1,000 workers each) were responsible for only 22 per cent of total output. Moreover, the productivity record of the larger firm was much more impressive than the smaller firm.

This process of concentration was also represented in the gramophone and broadcasting industries. From the beginning of 1927 to the middle of 1929, forty companies were formed to manufacture gramophones and records, yet by 1932 the trade was effectively dominated by the Electrical and Musical Industries (EMI) combine, brought about by the merger of the Gramophone Company and the Columbia Gramophone Company the year before.[74] Although the company had little central control over its subsidiaries, as Leslie Hannah has found, 'it nevertheless gave them access to the benefits of pooled overheads, risk spreading, the interchange of commercial and industrial methods, collusive pricing policies, and some degree of coordination of new investment'.[75]

In radio manufacturing there was also an element of oligopoly. One of the ways in which leaders of the industry responded to the losses of 1932–3 was through agreements on sales policy, avoidance of price cutting, and by building up contacts with the distributing trade.[76] It is also appropriate to recall that in the field of electrical sound and entertainment there was product diversification. The EMI group thus extended its interests beyond gramophone products into household appliances, television, radar equipment and even the bicycle trade, while E. K. Cole, the radio company, reduced its product dependence by developing a plastics business and acquiring interests in scientific instruments and electrical goods.[77] Elsewhere, the famous Distillers Company manufactured products from vinegar to solvents and plasterboard, and some of the pools companies reinvested a part of their profits in mail order concerns and retail distribution chains. In 1935 Vernon's Mail Order Stores Ltd was thus registered with a nominal capital of £10,000, and only three years later was a huge organization extending the length and breadth of the country.[78]

In the film industry there were similar developments as major companies sought to increase their profits by eliminating competition and encouraging rationalization. The dominance of family-run cinemas was undermined, so that by the 1930s circuits were the dominant mode of organization. Soon after the passing of the 1927 Cinematograph Films Act, which encouraged investment in the British film industry, four great groups emerged, concentrating on the purchase of the luxurious cinema and the vertical integration of film maker, film distributor, and film exhibitor. These groups, Gaumont British Picture Corporation, Denman Picture Houses, Provincial Cinematograph Theatres, and General Theatre Corporation, reaped a rich financial harvest by encouraging wide-spread combines and amalgamations. By 1929 the ownership of the latter three groups had passed into the hands of the Gaumont group, which also had interests in the music hall world of Moss Empires, itself a major combine.[79] Significantly, one of Gaumont's proprietors, Isidore Ostrer, was to have interests in a range of entertainments, including the Bush Radio Company, Baird Television, Radio Luxembourg and the *Sunday Citizen*. The process of capitalization and concentration of ownership was consolidated so that by 1933 there were three main controlling chains, Gaumont, Associated British Picture Corporation, and Odeon Theatres, and it would only be a few more years before the Rank Organization, with its interlocking directorships and shareholdings, arrived on the scene. In 1934 Gaumont British, with £6,250,000 share capital and £5 million new debenture stock, consisted of two production studios at Shepherds Bush and Islington, a film printing works, newsreel company, distribution agency and over 300 cinemas, whilst ABPC, with an authorized capital of £4 million, controlled studios at Elstree and Welwyn, the distributor Wardour films, and over 200 cinemas. In these and other cases, finance and industrial capital played a role through the activity of insurance companies, banks and industrial conglomerates. It was they who also financed the construction and use of some of the biggest studios of the period, notably Alexander Korda's London Film Production studios at Denham, with its 118,800 square feet of floor space, seven stages, eighteen cutting rooms, labs, film vaults and the rest.[80] Though in theory the consumer may suffer from such oligopolist tendencies, in practice film audiences benefited from cheap admission prices, improved cinemas, and access to some of the Hollywood and British spectacles of the time. Not only did the cinemagoing public have the opportunity to see Shirley Temple, Fred Astaire and Ginger Rogers, Clark Gable, Laurel and Hardy, James Cagney and other Hollywood stars through US domination of the distribution system, but also Gracie Fields, Charles Laughton, Robert Donat, George Formby, Jessie Matthews, Jack Buchanan and other British actors.

Despite the fact that it is difficult to estimate the productivity record of many of the trades in the leisure industry, it is not unreasonable to suggest that gains were made. Through greater expertise in management, new techniques, and scale economies, entrepreneurs were able to meet the demand for their products. By way of summary it is perhaps illuminating to note that the brewing industry responded to depressed demand conditions by introducing a number of productivity measures. A massive advertising campaign was launched to spread the idea that beer was better, even healthier, than anything else in life: 'Just What the Doctor Ordered' was William Younger's famous dictum. There were advertisements on hoardings, on rail and tram tickets, and even on hospital walls, so that conservative estimates had it that annual expenditure was £2 million.[81] In addition, there was a marked merger movement: in 1920 there were 2,889 breweries, by 1939 there were only 885.[82] The bigger breweries, among them some of the largest companies in the country – Guinness, Watney Combe Reid, Bass Ratcliffe Gretton, Mitchell and Butler – were able to maintain their profitability by enlarging the market area through the elimination and acquisition of marginal producers, as well as by the ownership of 'tied' public houses and joint agreements on the distribution of bottled beer. They also benefited from public house improvement, the use of motor transport, and the introduction of technical advances such as bottling, the application of electricity and more scientific analysis of materials.[83] As the *Financial News* reported in 1936: 'The installation of modern machinery, centralisation of production, elimination of overlapping distributive services and the improvement of the standard of comfort of licensed properties have been used to neutralise the shrinkage of demand.'[84] It was in these ways that labour productivity improved, with net output per person employed (in current values) increasing from £483 in 1907 to £685 in 1924 and £789 in 1935 (see Table 2.4).

Commercialized leisure and the working class

In exploring the leisure trades of the inter-war period it is apparent that there was considerable expansion. There had been commercialized recreation prior to the first world war and an embryonic leisure industry existed, but more fundamental change was still to come. In the inter-war period the leisure product was radically altered, if not transformed. After all, this period witnessed the advent of commercial amusements unthought of a generation earlier: popular broadcasting, cheap gramophone records, talking pictures and super-cinemas, Butlins, Wembley Cup Finals, speedway racing and new forms of gambling, including one pools win of £345,000. Given this growth of the leisure industry it is germane to explore the degree to which the benefits of commercial provision percolated through to the working class as a whole. As will be seen in the next chapter, it was inevitable that with commercial expansion the character and indeed the quality of working-class leisure would be transformed. Under circumstances where more and more people were attracted to the market, the ways in which spare time was spent were bound to change. It is not easy, however, to gauge subjective feelings such as pleasure and enjoyment, though it is possible to postulate that those workers who saw the silent movies of the 1920s or the great Arsenal team of the 1930s enjoyed their experience. This is at least the impression given by the social surveys of the time and by a number of other contemporary accounts: John Hilton, for example, found that the pools provided hope, excitement, relief from monotony, intellectual stimulus, and enjoyment.[85] It is also suggestive that even the so-called lumpenproletariat area of Campbell Bunk, North London, isolated 'from the normal social relations of civil society', had its 'zealous Arsenal supporters, its regular aficionados of the Empire music-hall, its up-to-the-minute dance-hall Saturday nighters'.[86]

Millions of workers were attracted to the pleasures of sport, exemplified by the 'varied orgy' of the big occasion – the FA Cup Final, the Derby, the Open Golf Championship, Test Match Cricket (which enjoyed a 'golden age'), Wimbledon. After all, sport was regarded as the Englishman's religion and was said to give more pleasure than religion itself, politics, literature, science, art, and other appeals.[87] It therefore seems a little surprising that one local newspaper should even attempt to urge that the Cotton Inquiry Report, the Report of the Simon Commission, and the virtues or fallacies of free trade or protection were more important than the pleasures of the cricket ground, the tennis court or the golf links.[88] Was such a plea likely to influence the supporters of sport? If Sir Herbert Nield was correct in asserting that the nation had gone 'recreation mad', then it had little chance of success.[89]

Sport was, of course, the tip of the leisure iceberg. The cinema with its concomitant attractions of warmth, privacy (especially important for courting couples) and escapism, was the archetypal palace of working-class enjoyment. In the words of one historian, 'By the 1920s, the cinema was truly an obsessional hobby for large numbers of the population.'[90] If an obsession, this was surely because it provided laughter, excitement and romance. A similar kind of observation can be made for broadcasting and drinking and, as implied by Robert Roberts' vivid account, for dancing:

> The great 'barn' we patronised as apprentices held at least a thousand. Almost every evening except Friday (cleaning night at home) it was jammed with a mass of young men and women, class desegregated for the first time. At 6d per head (1s on Saturdays) youth at every level of the manual working class, from the bound apprentice to the 'scum of the slum', foxtrotted through the new bliss in each other's arms.[91]

It has often been pointed out that recreation was a 'central preoccupation' of working-class life and there is little in the above evidence to suggest differently. In examining particular leisure activities, it seems that the working class derived real improvements in their leisure from commercial expansion; that is, with the growth of Capitalist entertainment came many benefits to the workers – more cinemas, more dance halls, and more radios. However, can it be claimed that the British people were unqualified beneficiaries of the commercial process at play? Whilst it is difficult to tell whether or not the working class benefited from these processes – even with oral techniques, it is a hard task for historians to judge personal impressions of the past, long since distorted by subsequent events – there is a need to probe deeper.

By adhering to the two nations theory of Northern depression and Southern prosperity, some historians, most notably John Stevenson and Chris Cook, suggest that with the exception of certain social groups such as the unemployed, the majority of the population participated in a new affluent society of rising real wages and living standards:

beside the picture of the unemployed must be put the other side of the case. . . . Beside the pictures of the dole queues and the hunger marches must also be placed those of another Britain, of new industries, prosperous suburbs, and a rising standard of living. . . . Above all else, for those in work, the thirties were a period of rising living standards and new levels of consumption, upon which a considerable degree of the new industrial activity was concentrated.[92]

As has already been suggested, the evidence of real wages seems to confirm this claim. However, quantitative indicators have to be supplemented by qualitative descriptions of human experience, if the affluence hypothesis is to mean anything. Hence, when considering the quality of life, it seems highly unlikely that even those southern workers in regular paid employment – the so-called new aristocracy of labour – suddenly became affluent. Migrant workers from Wales, for example, who found employment in the motor-car factories of Oxford left behind friends and relations, a way of life, a culture; the socially alienating world of the Midlands was not conducive to the retention of tradition.[93] It is difficult to compare material increases in living standards with reductions in the quality of life, but taking everything into consideration, it is apparent that the differences between the depressed North and the prosperous South were not as pronounced as sometimes claimed. As one detailed study has made clear, working-class experiences were similar in the towns of Burnley, Halifax, Ipswich and Luton.[94]

While in no way trying to suggest that the cinema or the radio did not bring real benefits to the working class, the full potential of such advances remained unrealized. There were many families on the poverty line, who had little enough money for food and rent, let alone for leisure. It is clear from a number of sources that the income of a significant proportion of the working class was insufficient to maintain the minimum standards of living. It is therefore probable that very large numbers did not share in the general expansion of commercialized leisure, a supposition borne out by the experience of two particular groups: the unemployed, of course, and the working-class mother.

Regional unemployment was a feature of British inter-war history. Since unemployment did not fall below one million between the early 1920s and the outbreak of the second world war, it is possible that there was a permanent residue of workless men and women who did not benefit from the leisure fruits of the commercial market place. Certainly, the out-of-work had plenty of spare time on their hands, but this was not a happy state of affairs, for leisure without money was restrictive. Unemployment benefit and assistance, especially as regulated under the notorious means test, simply did not stretch far enough to expend on leisure. Thus, a twenty-one-year-old contributor to the Carnegie Trust investigation, *Disinherited Youth*, pointed out that there was no way he could accept an offer of a week at a students' holiday camp for 5s: his unemployment benefit was only 29s a week compared with the national average weekly wage of 70s.[95] Unlike the experience of regular wage earners, the enforced leisure of the unemployed, although not apart from such activities as cinema-going and gambling, was spent in ways which were on the periphery of the Capitalist leisure industry, a point which will be returned to in chapter 5. The experience of the working-class mother was in many ways very similar.

The 1920s and 1930s have been popularly regarded as a period of female emancipation, characterized by a growth in female employment, especially in the service and light industries of the South and Midlands, the winning of the franchise and a decline in the burden of motherhood and housework due to a fall in family size (the gradual spread of birth control was important here) and the application of labour-saving devices in the home. Also, it has been claimed that there was greater social freedom for women, best represented by cigarette smoking, departures in fashion and music, and changes in tastes and conventions, all of which have contributed to the received notion of a 'Gay' or 'Swinging' twenties. For many women, however, there was a divergence between this picture and reality. If working-class women had to go out to work (a tradition long-established in the Lancashire textile industry) then it was usually out of economic necessity and not free choice. Indeed, women were often up against sexual inequality at work, receiving very poor wages in comparison to their male counterparts, or subjected to productive servitude as in domestic service, which actually grew during the inter-war period. As for life in the home, vast numbers of working-class women, often living in very bad housing, continued to have large families, without the comforts of household labour-saving devices (many mothers took great pride in their home and, in spite of all the difficulties they faced, tried to present as clean and as respectable a house as possible – blackleading the stove, whitening the hearth, scrubbing the kitchen table, polishing the brass, and washing and ironing the clothes were fastidiously carried out to keep the house filth free, exemplified most of all by the scrubbing of the front step and flags) and often with the added burden of outwork – laundry, darning, patching – or part-time work.[96] Under such conditions, working-class wives suffered from anaemia, headaches, constipation, rheumatism, bad teeth, indigestion, not to mention the problems of child birth – maternal mortality, stillbirth, neonatal mortality, maternal morbidity – and a host of other physical and psychological complaints.[97] Although the vast majority of women did have the determination to over-come adversity, it is likely that the majority at one time or another experienced the physical and mental strains of their material circumstances. The working-class mother with a large family, more than any other group, had little time or money for leisure, especially if her situation was compounded by the unemployment of her spouse. Hours would be spent in the home fending for husband and children, often in conjunction with marginal paid employment, leaving very few hours for recreation. According to Margery Spring Rice's study of working wives, the majority of women only had two hours leisure each day, and this was usually spent shopping, taking the baby out, mending, sewing and doing household jobs of an irregular kind which could not be fitted into working hours, such as tidying cupboards, repapering a room, and gardening.[98] As one St Helens woman has commented:

Mothers could do all the baking and cleaning and cooking, and just have time to go out with a clean pinny on in the evening to sit on chairs in the street and jangle. This was their whole life. They couldn't get ready to go out – there was no social life.[99]

Leisure for the working-class mother, if not spent in extra-work activities, often consisted of social intercourse with other women in similar situations or, in some cases, vicarious enjoyment through the family.

It can also be argued that the burden of holidays without pay fell on the working-class mother. If children could not get any 'change from their slum surroundings', then the tasks of the mother were that much more arduous.[100] Constance Harris found that Bethnal Green mothers had few holidays, only gaining vicarious pleasure through the activities of their children.[101] Easter, Whit or the summer holiday were times when the wife had to scheme 'harder than before because she has less money to manage on', or was forced into debt, with only the thought of the following week and 'Where's money for rent and rates and food coming from?'[102] Even when a mother enjoyed a holiday, it was never free from work – the children had to be cared for, washed and dressed each morning, and kept out of mischief for the rest of the day.[103] In overall terms it is therefore hardly surprising that some women complained that their biggest disadvantage was their lack of any leisure time.[104]

This argument, however, should not be pushed too far. The excellent work of Jeffrey Richards has shown that many sections of working-class women went to the cinema. A number of the social surveys and investigations of the period show that an important part of cinema audiences were composed of women. The Merseyside survey discovered that married women went to see films more often than their husbands, while the York survey reported that 75 per cent of the adult audience were women. A further investigation of cinemas in the East End of London found that women depended 'almost entirely for their entertainment upon the cinema'. In fact, in London many women, especially housewives, visited the cinema in the afternoon, between finishing shopping and before the children came home from school. One housewife, Mrs Edna Thorpe, gave the reasons why she and others like her enjoyed the cinema:

> Speaking as a housewife, I find a seat at the cinema one of the easiest and cheapest ways of getting a change from the daily round. It brings interest, amusement, education, almost to our doors at prices to suit nearly everybody.[105]

Possibly, women also went to the cinema because they could identify with some of the stars of the screen, particularly Gracie Fields. Aside from the cinema, it is evident that many women visited the local public house or dance hall. Still, the working-class mother was perhaps the least likely of all groups, young and old, rich and poor, to participate in the new leisure age.

The unemployed and the working-class mother were two groups in the community, to which might be added the low paid, the aged and the infirm, who did not derive a fair share from the expansion of commercial forms of leisure. Notwithstanding what has already been said about the rise in consumer expenditure on entertainment, it is true that the new leisure products were not distributed evenly throughout the population. Further, the novel outlets for recreation failed to compensate for the difficulties of unemployment, poverty and ill-health. In short, if it is to be concluded that working people benefited from the growth of the leisure industry, as many surely did, then this has to be qualified by reference to the everyday problems posed by economic and social deprivation.

3
Leisure provision in the voluntary sector

In the 1920s and 1930s leisure was also catered for by voluntary organizations. Groups of people interested in a particular leisure activity came together in a wide range of organizations which catered for anything from cycling to horticulture. For example, the protection of amenity and provision of outdoor recreation facilities was dealt with by many voluntary movements including the Commons, Open Spaces and Footpaths Preservation Society, Youth Hostels Association, Holiday Fellowship, Ramblers' Association, Council for the Preservation of Rural England, and a wealth of other groups. Such movements were organized at a national level with local branches such as the National Playing Fields Association or were firmly situated in the locality such as the Norfolk Naturalists' Trust. It is also true to say that voluntary organizations were differentiated along the lines of class, gender and age. Indeed, there were groups catering specifically for the working class, for women, and for young people.

In addition to well-organized voluntary provision, there was also informal provision. That is, popular cultural practices emerged out of working-class communities which were unorganized and characterized by spontaneity and inventiveness. The leisure time of ordinary people was not confined to a particular club or society. Many of the working class spent little time in organized leisure; they found the home or the street more conducive to relaxation. Social spaces outside the formal structures of a voluntary organization (or the leisure industry) were occupied due to financial and other reasons, providing yet another focal point for cultural expression. In this chapter the various forms of voluntary provision will be examined in some detail. The chapter will also consider the social and cultural impact of commercial leisure on the voluntary sector.

Voluntary organizations

Leisure interest groups have existed for many centuries. It was in the nineteenth and early twentieth centuries, however, that there was a proliferation of clubs and societies concerned with recreation. In the area of cycling, for example, the Cyclists' Touring Club, Clarion Cycling Club, and National Cyclists' Union were all formed prior to the first world war. The growth of organized recreation through private institutions was intimately related to the creation of a new industrial society. In very broad terms, the new factory masters required a stable, disciplined and industrious workforce and therefore promoted edifying and temperate leisure activities. This initiative came from above in the form of rational recreation and was offered to the masses through a host of clubs set up by the church, paternalistic employers, and other philanthropic members of the middle class. For instance, church and chapel offered a multitude of recreational services designed to promote orderly, structured and 'useful' leisure as an antidote to drunkenness and gambling. This is not to argue that rational recreationists in their attempt to fashion working-class behaviour were always successful. Boisterous activities survived until the end of the century and beyond, and perhaps even more important, the working class was resentful of patronage and was able to reshape middle-class provision to accord with their own tastes and predilections. The best known example is, of course, the way in which the working class took over the Working Men's Club and Institute Union from the Reverend Henry Solly and his attempt to impose middle-class ideology, above all temperance. Equally, the workers broke out of rational recreation through their own class based organizations such as the brass band movement.

By the inter-war period the attempt to inculcate the working class with notions of controlled leisure had faded into the background. Nonetheless, voluntary forms of leisure expanded in this period. There was a proliferation of voluntary agencies catering for leisure. As Alun Howkins and John Lowerson have stressed, 'great successes lay with voluntary organizations especially in relation to outdoor sports like rambling and cycling'. Cycling certainly experienced growth. In 1920, 385,000 bicycles were sold, which had increased to 1.61 million by 1935; and by 1938 the two main cycling clubs, the Cyclists' Touring Club and the National Cyclists' Union, had 60,000 members between them.[1] A range of clubs also catered for angling – one of the largest participant sports. Membership figures of various other recreational organizations in the 1930s also point to growth, as can be seen from Table 3.1.

Table 3.1 *Membership of selected voluntary recreational organizations*

	1930	1934	1938
Co-operative Holidays Association	22,900	26,259	28,872
Holiday Fellowship	28,241	32,704	39,439
Workers' Travel Association	18,000	25,000	48,000
Youth Hostels Association	6,439	37,285	79,821
Camping Club of Great Britain	5,450	6,200	12,859
Cyclists' Touring Club	25,720	31,794	36,609

Source: National Council of Social Service, *Holidays*, Oxford University Press, Oxford, 1945, pp. 30–1, *C.T.C. Gazette*.

To take a specific example, holiday-making was provided for in the voluntary sector. As a result of a high degree of organization and collective orientation a section of the working class was able to take a holiday away from home, though as already stated many did not. In a situation where for most of the 1920s and 1930s holidays without pay was the rule, the annual break from work was financed through thrift clubs. Judging from local newspapers, workers formed savings clubs through the medium of industrial establishments, the co-operative society, political organizations, public houses and various religious bodies. It is also interesting that the Industrial Welfare Society, which had broad support from the employers, was urging the establishment of holiday savings clubs at the place of work. At another level, the inter-war years also saw the burgeoning of holiday organizations which catered for workers. Amongst the best known of these non-commercial agencies were the Workers' Travel Association, Holiday Fellowship and Co-operative Holidays Association, but perhaps the most interesting was the Youth Hostels Association which started modestly at the end of the 1920s to provide cheap holiday accommodation for young people.[2] By 1937 it had 70,505 members, 275 hostels and received 461,711 visits during the year.[3] There were also local bodies which organized holidays for the poor. In Manchester, for example, it was the aim of the School Camps' Association 'to ensure that no Jewish child shall be deprived of a week's holiday in the country', and each year from the middle of May throughout the summer between 700 and 800 children benefited from a holiday in an open air camp.[4] Finally, it is appropriate to note that holiday organizations often co-operated with other recreational bodies, as was the case when the Workers' Travel Association placed its world-wide agencies at the disposal of members of the Camping Club of Great Britain who desired facilities for non-camping holidays or travel.[5]

Certainly there was an enormous growth in voluntary recreational bodies. However, this did not necessarily mean that there was a positive correlation between such growth and the growth of workers' leisure. Many of these bodies were not proletarian in composition, having been set up by the middle classes; a point made clear by the Manchester secretary of the British Workers' Sports Federation, Benny Rothman:

> When we entered the rambling field the rambling clubs that already existed in the North, apart from Sheffield which is one exception to the rule, were mainly middle class in origin and outlook. Not only were they middle class, they were specialists – botanists, zoologists and archaeologists. The ordinary working class ramblers were shunned, they were looked upon as dirt, they weren't wanted. We filled the gap, you see, this is why we were so successful. The same with camping – the Camping Club of Great Britain was more concerned with all the fancy gear they had rather than going out into the open air. When I came into camping I had to make my own tents out of bits of old cloth and so had our camping club. We hired gear, we borrowed gear and we pinched gear. We filled a need.[6]

The working class, on minimum levels of income, found it very difficult to afford the costs involved in active membership of a club or society: the subscriptions, the equipment, the travelling expenses. Glancing through such journals as *The Cyclists Touring Club Gazette*, *Camping*, *Out-O'-Doors* and the *Y.H.A. Rucksack* it is clear that, although not appealing to any one section of the population, they catered for those groups whose constituents had a surplus of time and money for recreational activity. Class prejudice was also a dividing factor – workers had a different set of values from their middle-class counterparts – creating difficulties of social mix, group solidarity and popular acceptance of aims and objectives, a common binding ethos. Moreover, as Martin Bobker, a waterproof garment worker from Manchester and a sports enthusiast, has claimed, workers found the protocol and formality involved in joining a club inhibiting and they would not go near establishment organizations for this reason.[7] Hence, the Merseyside survey found that country walking and cycling was largely restricted to non-manual workers; the York survey that members of the local Youth Hostels Association were confined to teachers, clerks and students; and the London survey that organized walking was mainly a middle-class activity.[8] Nevertheless, this evidence should not be stretched too far. There were obviously regional differences in experiences and no two branches of an organization would have exactly the same structure. Although there is a pressing need here for analysis of local membership lists and similar records, it is very likely that in some localities sections of the working class played a major role in voluntary recreational organizations, some of which had been set up by ruling *élites*.

At this point it is appropriate to make a brief digression. There has been a great deal of research into and debate about the emergence of an aristocracy of labour in mid-nineteenth century Britain; that is, a labour *élite* consisting of skilled artisans and craftsmen who took on many of the values of respectability, self-help, thrift and temperance. Generally speaking, it was this upper stratum of the working class who joined 'respectable' recreational and cultural organizations.[9] In contrast, at the other end of the working class 'disreputable', unskilled labourers were more likely to spend their leisure drinking, gambling or in other so-called irrational activities. It is not the place here to examine such divisions within the working class. Nonetheless, it does seem that by the 1920s and 1930s there were few significant differences in the ways workers spent their leisure. It is true that there was divergence based on gender or the simple fact of having a job or not, but even then proletarian mothers and the unemployed were drawn from all sections of the working class. Anyway, working-class leisure was a remarkably fluid milieu in which skilled, high status workers came into contact with all manner of unskilled, low status workers. Representatives from all groups of workers watched films at the cinema, drank beer at the local public house or visited seaside resorts. Equally, there is little evidence to suggest that as far as the working class was concerned club membership was differentiated along the lines of occupation or status. The main line of demarcation, as already suggested, was between classes, not within them.

Returning to voluntary recreational organizations, writing in the early 1930s, Thomas Middleton found that the Liverpool working class had access to numerous sports clubs – about 1,000 football, 500 tennis, 400 cricket, 200 hockey, 200 bowling and 100 cycling clubs, for example.[10] It is very probable that workers did compose the nucleus of some of these clubs. The same impression is conveyed by the various other social surveys: in Hull there were probably about 3,000 regular football players in the local leagues and 400 to 500 members of cycling clubs; in York 1,395 foot-ballers, 1,568 cricketers, about 1,000 tennis players and 1,530 bowls players were organized in voluntary clubs alone.[11] Despite the need for further research into local sources, it is fairly clear from the impressionistic accounts that the working class was not entirely divorced from club activity. Thus, in most London work-ing-class districts, drapers' shops were beginning to stock cycling kit to meet the demand created by the growth of cycling clubs.[12]

The church, through the YMCA, YWCA, Sunday Schools, Settlements, Guilds, Endeavour Societies and Missions, was also providing opportunities for workers' recreation. In addition to the annual religious celebrations such as chapel anniversaries and festivals, regular recreational activities were organized; there were garden fêtes, tea parties, bazaars, choir sermons, athletics and sport, lectures and dramatic performances. In working-class Becontree, for example, 10 per cent of the female population over twenty-five were active in the social activity of the church, and 33 per cent of the youth were members of the Sunday Schools.[13] In addition, many of the male youth movements of the inter-war period were closely connected with the church, specifically the Church Lads' Brigade, Jewish Lads' Brigade, and Catholic Boys'

Brigade and also the Boy Scouts. Although John Springhall has claimed that working people were deterred from joining the Boy Scouts and cadet corps because of the financial costs involved in purchasing uniforms and equipment, and the reluctance to acquiesce to the ideological notions of militarism and imperialism, there is evidence to suggest that considerable numbers of working-class youth were members of non-uniform youth movements, similarly associated with the church.[14] Although Manchester groups found it difficult to compete with commercialized leisure, such organizations as the London Federation of Boys' Clubs (and the Divisional Council of Girls' Clubs) were predominantly for the poorer classes, with an attraction of social, recreational and educational activities.[15] Furthermore, there was even scope for youth recreation within the structures of right-wing political parties: the Conservative Party controlled the Junior Imperial and Constitutional League – the 'Imps' – organized garden parties, cycling, rambling, photographic clubs and a host of social events, while the British Union of Fascists attracted young workers through the provision of gymnasiums, clubs, holiday camps, football teams, community singing and films.[16] Also interesting is the fact that by the end of the 1930s a 'Right' Theatre Movement had been founded 'to uphold constitutional Government and to oppose socialism, communism and Left propaganda', as well as providing plays having a social, educational and entertainment value.[17]

There were also a number of youth organizations catering specifically for girls' leisure. The National Council of Girls' Clubs coordinated the activities of those bodies providing recreational and social facilities for young women, namely the Federation of Working Girls' Clubs, Girls' Friendly Society, Girls' Guildry, Girls' Life Brigade and the Young Women's Christian Association. Membership figures are given in Table 3.2. The scope of cultural and recreational work under the ambit of the Council was very comprehensive – handicrafts, gymnastics, music, dramatics and even a club medical scheme. Close contact was maintained with the Girl Guides' Association, as well as a number of other groups with female membership such as the British Drama League.[18] There were, of course, many other women's organizations at local and national level which were not connected with the Council. The best known of these were the Women's Institutes with their vast array of amenities, lectures and classes, and The

Women's League of Health and Beauty which had about 166,000 members by 1939.

Table 3.2 *Membership of young women's organizations in England and Wales 1933–4*

	Units	Membership
Girls' Friendly Society[a]	2,256	158,000
Girls' Life Brigade	959	40,242
Girls' Guildry	125	5,200
Federation of Working Girls' Clubs	169	13,670
YWCA	175	26,653
Girl Guides	25,250	474,408
Camp Fire Girls	153	1,876
Christian Alliance of Women and Girls[a]	159	15,000

Source: M. Rooff, *Youth and Leisure: A Survey of Girls' Organisations in England and Wales*, Carnegie United Kingdom Trust, Edinburgh, 1935, p. 235.
[a] 1932–3.

Aside from the church and related organizations, employers were also major sponsors of workers' leisure. There is a lack of quantitative evidence on the number of industrial recreation and social clubs, but it is clear that thousands of British firms provided facilities for entertainment, the most impressive programme being organized by Cadbury Brothers with its numerous football pitches, tennis courts and so on.[19] Business histories have also shown that a number of firms in a variety of trades had sections for recreation.[20] It appears that a fair proportion of these pioneering firms were large-scale organizations able to bear the capital costs involved. Big companies in industrial Tyneside organized sporting, educational and music clubs, whilst two of the biggest companies in Oxford, Morris Motors and Pressed Steel, had all kinds of recreation clubs.[21] To take just one further example. Montague Burton, the Leeds clothing business, provided amenities for sport and the dramatic arts, organized one of the largest holiday savings clubs in the world, and even sponsored a Sun Ray Centre.[22] There were, therefore, many opportunities to participate in a range of leisure activities. A TUC memorandum on the subject of welfare work provides a useful summary:

RECREATIVE ACTIVITIES are the most usual and probably the most popular form of welfare. They may take the form of a sports club, with ground for cricket, football, tennis and club-rooms for indoor games and meals; sometimes there is a swimming bath and gymnasium; some firms run factory gardens, making certain departments responsible for particular portions of it, or an allotment association is formed to buy tools and seeds co-operatively and hold exhibitions; sometimes a holiday lodgings list is kept or camps and foreign tours are organised. Other recreative activities include hobbies club, handwork classes, debating society, folk-dance society, musical society or choir.[23]

Company recreation was obviously at its most prolific in the provision of sporting facilities, as was illustrated by an extensive survey of labour relations policy undertaken by the National Industrial Alliance of Employers and Employed.[24] A further inquiry made in 1935 found that of eighty-eight selected firms, seventy-five had their own sports grounds ranging from 3 to 82 acres. There were also a number of works sports associations in existence, the largest being London Business Houses with a membership of 300 firms.[25] In the larger provincial cities of the North active and enthusiastic associations had also been formed, for example in Hull and Liverpool. The Hull Association was set up in 1930 and after five years' work had a membership of fifty-two firms, representing 30,000 employees; by 1938 the number had apparently increased to sixty-nine firms. It catered for both indoor and outdoor recreation with sections for angling, billiards, ladies' golf, miniature rifle and whist, as well as the more popular sports such as tennis and cricket.[26] It is not known when the Liverpool Association was formed, but it is clear that sport was amply provided for. Business firms like J. Bibby and Sons, Lewis's and Crawford's had elaborate and comprehensive clubs with extensive grounds, and it was they who came together within the Business Houses Sports Association. Once again, a wide range of sports fixtures were organized, including a successful football league. For a small subscription, no more than about 3d a week usually deducted from the wage packet at source, employees/club members had access to a wealth of leisure facilities.[27]

The reasons why business and the church regarded recreation

as important are complex and far from transparent. It is difficult to categorize the motives behind this kind of recreational provision as leisure amenities were introduced to satisfy various objectives. If it is assumed that the main aim of business is profit maximization then worker recreation will be provided to stimulate productive efficiency and gain competitive advantages in the market. On the other hand, it is unlikely that profit is the only business aim: employers may be genuinely concerned about the welfare of their workforce and be willing to provide facilities for recreation even if this clashes with normal entrepreneurial rationale. Although this is not the place to rehearse the different interpretations of company welfare strategy, in broad terms inter-war industrial recreation was determined by the profit motive, but there were exceptions. As far as religious purveyors of leisure are concerned, once again there were a number of aims and objectives involved, though the main dynamic was to counteract such apparently irrational activities as drinking, gambling and even jazz, and to encourage the right use of leisure. Notwithstanding all this, an important point to stress is that recreational organizations ostensibly controlled by the middle classes were often run by workers for workers. A notable instance of this in the early 1920s was the Leeds Industrial Theatre which grew out of the welfare branch of the Simpson, Fawcett perambulator firm – the workpeople made their own scenery and also worked as voluntary door stewards, chocolate and programme sellers, and curtain and scene shifters.[28]

As well as middle-class institutions with working-class membership, there were many distinctly proletarian cultural organizations. First and foremost were the numerous working men's clubs, banded together in the Working Men's Club and Institute Union. As can be seen from Table 3.3, by the end of 1929 there were 2,626 clubs in the UK with a membership of 917,632 – nearly all of these in England and Wales, the vast majority in the North of England – and a number of others not actually affiliated to the Union. The working man's club was widely regarded as a drinking den, but it did perform a wider function in the provision of lectures, games, entertainment and even convalescent homes. The Union portrayed itself as efficiently administered, disciplined, democratic and a provider of rational opportunities for leisure.[29] Thus, in giving evidence to the Royal Commission on Licensing, the Union's secretary, Robert Chapman, argued that clubs were a force for improvement and independence:

> With the added attractions of indoor and outdoor games, concerts, lectures, participation and rivalry in flower and vegetable shows, glee parties, choral societies, and its many other amenities, the club provides something more attractive than the constant drinking which is the accompaniment of a purposeless leisure.[30]

Table 3.3 *The Working Men's Club and Institute Union in 1929*

	Number of clubs	Membership	Number of clubs which on Sundays had[a]		
			Lectures	Games	Entertainment
England/Wales:					
Metropolitan	190	68,960	65	171	174
Home Counties	227	63,576	56	150	181
Southern Counties	123	42,388	21	61	89
S. Western Counties	26	11,002	7	2	14
Eastern Counties	37	13,343	11	17	30
E. Midland Counties	165	68,152	50	69	151
W. Midland Counties	289	93,639	110	82	267
Lancs/Cheshire	368	104,628	181	151	331
Yorkshire	654	264,833	271	222	588
Northern Counties	380	140,440	154	56	341
Wales/Monmouth	158	41,822	120	16	125
Scotland/Ireland	9	4,849	6	6	9
Total UK	2,626	917,632	1,052	1,003	2,300

Source: *Minutes of Evidence Taken Before the Royal Commission on Licensing (England and Wales)*, HMSO, 1930–2, p. 1230.
[a] Particulars relating to the 2,608 clubs making returns.

In the majority of cases, clubs were fairly democratic, co-operative, and an expression of wider cultural and indeed political concerns: they were run by working men for working men. The Union regarded itself as democratic in character and closely aligned to the Labour Movement; there were long-established links with labour leaders, and the likes of Fred Bramley, C. W. Bowerman, Robert Richardson and Ben Tillett regularly spoke on club platforms.[31] Mr A. Temple, the educational secretary of the Union and a member of the ILP, thus regarded the club as a co-operative venture which endeavoured to eliminate Capitalist features and its ramifications.[32]

Closely related to working men's clubs were the miners' institutes. Under the Mining Industry Act of 1920 a Welfare Fund was created, 'to be applied for purposes connected with the social well-being, recreation and conditions of living of workers in and about coal mines'.[33] This operated throughout the inter-war years and was used to finance the building, modernization and improvement of miners' institutes (as well as other social schemes, such as pit-head baths) and to provide money for all kinds of leisure activities. Welfare institutions became the centre of mining culture with a host of indoor activities – socials, dances, concerts, plays, films, lectures, reading, billiards, drinking – in addition to facilities for outdoor recreation – sports fields, children's playgrounds, refreshment kiosks, gardens.[34] Indeed, as can be seen from Table 3.4, between 1921 and 1938 over £5.5 million, representing 32 per cent of the total Welfare Fund and 54.5 per cent of the District Fund expenditure, had been spent on recreation schemes. Designed as a 'liberal' experiment in employer-employee co-operation, miners' welfare was a focus of working-class consciousness. In Fife and Lanarkshire, welfarism, though never an unqualified success, improved the morale of miners by the provision of recreational and library facilities and by the funding of brass and pipe bands, and ambulance and sports competitions.[35] The Lumphinnans Welfare Institute Hall, which eventually had a left-wing management committee, 'served as the focal point of village life, with a reading room and a hall for concerts, socials and meetings. It was the headquarters for William Gallacher's parliamentary campaigns in West Fife and was used to welcome a delegation of Soviet miners to Scotland in 1929.'[36] Similarly, the Institute and Hall was the centre of social life in Mardy; it acted as an arena for leisure and a forum for education, politics and discussion of pit life – it was a microcosm of the local community.[37] The miners' institute with its colourful array of leisure activities, though dependent to some extent on State goodwill and employer patronage, was a force in local life and a clear expression of working-class culture.

Table 3.4   *Miners' welfare grants allocated for recreation 1921–38*

District	£ Amount	Number of schemes
Fife and Clackmannan	270,426	93
The Lothians	128,149	39
Lanarkshire	663,161	152
Northumberland	366,152	99
Durham	792,450	158
Cumberland	63,580	29
Lancashire and Cheshire	1,755	1
North Wales	115,725	28
Yorkshire	857,038	190
Nottinghamshire	296,762	55
Derbyshire	373,314	113
North Staffordshire	32,150	15
Cannock Chase	101,846	29
South Staffordshire/Worcestershire	32,822	11
Leicestershire	53,423	24
Warwickshire	121,171	58
Shropshire	29,996	13
Forest of Dean	27,818	34
Somerset and Bristol	29,278	36
South Wales	1,247,112	300
Kent	14,237	10
Total	5,618,365	1,487

Source: Calculated from *17th Annual Report of the Miners' Welfare Committee*, 1938, pp. 120–1.

Working men's clubs and miners' institutes show that the working class could organize leisure for themselves without having to depend upon the middle class or Capitalist leisure forms. If, in looking at the consumption of marketed goods and services it is concluded that there was unequal distribution, it should not be forgotten that on the periphery of the market ordinary working-class people banded together to provide leisure in associational form. The unemployed, the working-class wife, the low paid, the aged were deprived of their equal shares of commercial leisure, but it just might have been the case that compensation came through proletarian cultural activity. There were outlets for pigeon fanciers, jazz and brass band enthusiasts and artists, as well as the provisions made for sport, drama, film, travel, music and literature by activists and enthusiasts in the organized Labour Movement – a theme which will be returned to in chapter six.[38] Working-class cultural forms were varied, diverse and plentiful. However, although many leisure activities were organized by workers for workers, they were not exactly isolated from the Capitalist leisure industry. There were many points of contact and certainly there was no such thing as a hermetically sealed working-class culture. There were financial costs incurred in replenishing beer stocks at working men's clubs, providing amenities at miners' institutes, building lofts for pigeons, purchasing instruments for brass bands, and so an automatic link between proletarian types of culture and the market. It is probable that there is a blur between voluntary and commercial provision, a kind of grey area. To talk about working-class leisure outside the market is a misconception, yet perhaps the form of working-class cultural expression furthest away from commercialized provision is the spontaneous, the impulsive and the traditional.

Home and street

The main theme of the last chapter was the growth of commercialized leisure. If the accounts of Richard Hoggart are anything to go by, however, commercial forms of mass culture did not make an impact on working-class life until the 1950s. Indeed, the main thrust of Hoggart's now classic work is a comparison of the inter-war culture 'of the people' with the post-second world war urban culture of the masses.[39] In no way wanting to contradict the points made about the growth of the leisure industry, Hoggart's notable account of working-class culture in the 1930s has to be taken into consideration. Though failing to note the cultural significance of Capitalist leisure, in his evocative description of the working-class home and community he warns against exaggerating the degree to which commercialized leisure affected lifestyles. Central to Hoggart's analysis of working-class culture is the importance of the family and the neighbourhood.

The home was the central working-class institution: it was private, personal and protective, the centre of family life. The living room was the heart, providing gregariousness, warmth and plenty of good food, with the hearth the focal point: 'Much of the free time of a man and his wife will usually be passed at the hearth; "just staying-in" is still one of the most common leisure-time occupations.'[40] Leisure activity in the home, from all accounts, was varied, depending upon gender and age. It could be traditional such as family activity passed on from generation to generation, impulsive such as children's games, or merely restive such as relaxing in front of the fire. In addition to this, there would be purposive leisure pursuits – all kinds of spare-time occupations and hobbies from carpentry to household duties and, with the growth of Council housing estates like Norris Green (Liverpool) and Wythenshawe (Manchester), gardening.[41] As George Orwell observed in referring to 'the *privateness* of English life': 'We are a nation of flower-lovers, but also a nation of stamp-collectors, pigeon-fanciers, amateur carpenters, coupon-snippers, darts-players, crossword-puzzle fans.'[42] Any examination of working-class culture would have to take into account these activities, even if they are unrecorded. The home was not, however, entirely isolated from inter-war commercial developments. A great deal of domestic based activity was unrelated to Capitalist leisure, but as the years progressed more and more commercial forms were consumed in the home.[43] The cheap radio and gramophone, though not found among the poorer classes, were a feature of many workers' homes; cheap paperbacks, library books and news-papers were increasingly read, as were the various women's maga-zines – *Peg's Paper* (1919), *Woman's Companion* (1927), *Red Star* (1929), *Secrets* (1932), *Oracle* (1933), *Lucky Star* (1935), *Miracle* (1935), and *Glamour* (1938) all appealed to the ordinary mill girl – and children's comics, such as the *Wizard*, *Hotspur*, and towards the end of the period the *Dandy* and the *Beano*.[44]

In portraying the working-class home as the centre of warmth and pleasure there is a danger of romanticism. As Robert Roberts has made clear, poor housing and squalor were features of prolet-arian life:

In general, slum life was far from being the jolly hive of communal activity that some romantics have claimed. They forget, perhaps, or never knew of the dirt that hung over all, of the rubbish that lay for months in the back alleys, of the 'entries' or ginnels with open middens where starving cats and dogs roamed or died and lay for weeks unmoved. They did not know those homes that stank so badly through an open doorway that one stepped off the pavement to pass them by.[45]

If home was cold, overcrowded, poorly ventilated and dimly lit then it was very difficult indeed to enjoy domestic leisure activity. Constance Harris, looking at working-class Bethnal Green, found that it was 'almost impossible to have satisfactory recreation in the home owing to housing conditions', while the International Association for Social Progress protested that 'the cultural use of leisure in the working-class home is difficult'.[46] With little privacy and no private belongings, children in particular found the home restrictive, limiting its use to a place for meals and sleep. In areas where there was poor housing, the street, and not the home, was the centre of leisure.

Street celebrations, carnivals and parties were a feature of working-class life in inter-war Britain. On special occasions it was the street which became the stage for entertainment. Of special interest was the Jubilee of George V in 1935, and the coronation of George VI two years later. For both events, streets and houses all over Britain were adorned with all kinds of flags, flowers and decorations. And there were sit-down teas, games, music and dancing. An annual happening in the North West of England was the Whit Walk when processions drawn from the local churches marched through the streets, led by bands and floats. Press reports suggest that there were up to 20,000 participants in the Manchester Whit Walks of the mid-1930s. However, it is relevant to note that during times of trade slump, street processions of this kind were susceptible to attack. In 1931 the directors of the Manchester Chamber of Commerce made proposals that Whit week holidays should be curtailed, arguing that festivals and celebrations were inconsistent with the obligations of a trading centre, especially during a time when markets were being lost. With the support of a number of local commercial organizations, the Chamber requested that the City Council implement quite draconian measures – the banning of processions and other social or religious festivals. The idea was tried out and, according to a number of businesses, proved successful; it was considered 'that the experience gained during Whit-week, 1932, confirms the views of the Board of the Chamber that the trade of the City would benefit if arrangements were made for general opening for business'.[47] The recession had shown that businessmen regarded the problems of orders, deliveries and quotations more important than holiday festivals and traditions. In other words, economic and trading requirements were impinging on cultural practices.

On a more permanent basis, street entertainments were still an important part of working-class life, even in the 1920s and 1930s. People sang, whistled, jigged, danced and turned organs or engaged in local gossip. The street was the 'great recreation room' where, amid poverty and deprivation, banter and good-natured teasing was to be heard. Once again, however, money was not too far away, particularly in the case of drinking and betting.

It is true that with the growth of alternative leisure activities the public house played a smaller part in the life of the community than it ever did. Yet, despite the decline in beer consumption, the pub remained the focal point of neighbourhood leisure. As the Mass Observation study of Bolton found: 'In Worktown more people spend more time in public houses than they do in any other buildings except private houses and work-places.'[48] It appears from a number of sources that more women were using the pub. On a typical Saturday evening in the Fulham pubs of the mid-1930s, for example, over a third of the customers were women.[49] Also, in some areas heavy drinking was still common. In the South London working-class community of Bermondsey in the mid-1920s the local inhabitants apparently spent more on strong drink than on bread, milk, rent and rates all put together.[50] Even by the end of the 1930s the Women's Group on Public Welfare claimed that 'alcoholic liquor represents, either directly or indirectly, something so precious to the working man that he is prepared to pay very dearly, and much beyond his means, rather than do without it'.[51]

There were obviously different kinds of pubs according to the district in which they were situated.[52] Here the discussion will focus on the community pub, confined almost exclusively to the local inhabitants. The 'local' was frequented by a regular clientele, who used it as a kind of social centre. As far as can be made out from the various social surveys a range of recreations was on offer, though the Merseyside study noted that games such as darts and 'shove ha' penny' were practically never found. With public house improvement and the demise of the gin palace, as well as the fall in drunkenness, it is probable that more of the drink trades' resources were being diverted to social facilities. Aside from leisure the pub was intimately connected with the main concerns of local society; a place where people came together to talk and swap information about work, politics, religion, births and deaths and many more topics. In short, the public house was deeply rooted and continued to play a central part in the social and cultural life of the working-class community.

Of all street activities, gambling reigned supreme: groups of men played dice or crown and anchor, youngsters pitched coins or participated in card schools. Illegal gambling of this type was reinforced by business on a larger scale, with quite a sophisticated system of street bookmakers, croupiers and runners often operating through the local pub. Gambling not only brought excitement, interest and intellectual motivation, it also forged community links and produced feelings of group solidarity and mutual respectability.[53] It was therefore particularly important in the context of street life where the emphasis was less on the individual home and more on the informal collective life outside in the community.

For children and youth the street was their playground. In Bethnal Green, the immediate neighbourhood was the leisure haven for young people. Since there was little, if any, pocket money, popular sports were adapted to meet material circumstances:

> Down some of the quieter streets in summer, cricket is played with zest, often with no proper bat, but a piece of packing-case lid roughly shaped into a bat, and a pile of coats or chalked lines on the wall suffice for the wickets, whilst a bundle of rags tied into a ball (if no proper ball is available) complete the equipment.[54]

Although it is true that there was an expansion of municipal facilities for leisure, Allen Hutt in his social commentary on the working class came to much the same conclusion:

> The children in the central working-class quarters, as Dr Thomas of Finsbury remarks, 'have nowhere to play except in the dangerous streets' where 'they may be seen skipping, spinning tops, playing at soldiers, playing cricket with heaped

coats for wickets and a tied-up cap or newspaper for a ball, swinging and climbing over hand-trucks, baiting dogs or teasing cats'.[55]

Improvisation was the characteristic of young people's leisure, as finance stretched no further than the purchase of a sorbo ball, an old, second-hand pair of skates, a hoop, or a pennyworth of marbles. Under such conditions, leisure tended to be a combination of tradition and spontaneity. Ted Willis has recalled the importance of traditional pastimes – date-ogging, clay marbles and glass 'alleys', hoops and peg-hops, skipping – in addition to spontaneous group games such as 'release', 'knocking down ginger' and 'tip it and run'.[56] Though many of these activities seem to have a timeless quality, in the inter-war period they were an integral part of growing up for the working-class child. They were a class expression of community impulses and traditions, forced, it is true, upon working-class youth by material circumstances, deplorable housing, a scarcity of resources and shared experiences, but also a reaction against rational and regulated leisure time in school.

Leisure on the streets was a time of freedom, when feelings could be demonstrated in a variety of ways. Larking about, playing pranks, or practical jokes were popular ways of spending spare time. It was quite common for unsuspecting adults, seated in outside lavatories, to have their bottoms singed by a candle or stung by a nettle, and passers-by, having spotted an unclaimed coin, to suddenly discover that it was attached to a thread of cotton. This type of humour performed various functions: it was at the same time, witty, enjoyable, exciting and was also a form of identification and opposition to authority.[57] Working-class youth expressed their feelings and emotions, their hopes and aspirations in the informal leisure activities of the harsh, yet humorous, surroundings of the street. This was a further source of cultural richness, though it must be added that commercial forms, in the guise of the local flea-pit, were not too far away. It was possible to play street sport, games and pranks and still experience the delights of Tom Mix, Charlie Chaplin or Douglas Fairbanks. Indeed, it is likely that the street was the stage for the playing out of fantasies, be it in the role of a Western cowboy or the footballer scoring the winning goal in the FA Cup Final.[58]

The impact of commercialized leisure on working-class culture

Despite Hoggart's claims about the resilience of working-class culture, numerous commentators have pointed to the ways in which the 'mass', homogeneous and centralized culture of the leisure industry challenged voluntary and associational forms. Some historians have argued that as commercialized leisure penetrated deeper and deeper into people's lives, certain organic qualities of class and culture were undermined. According to Gareth Stedman Jones, the late Victorian and Edwardian period saw workers' interests in politics and education usurped by the pub, the race-course and the music-hall.[59] He views this development as a sign of political conservatism and a decline of class combativity. Apparently in the period after the first world war, with increasing numbers of people attracted by the commodities of the Capitalist leisure industry, the trends noticed by Stedman Jones were reinforced. Indeed, Eileen and Stephen Yeo have suggested that by the second decade of the twentieth century, leisure entered an imperialist stage of development, taken to mean here that the working class became subordinated to Capitalist cultural production in so far as they not only found it increasingly difficult to organize autonomous leisure activities of their own, but were also enclosed within an industrial leisure complex of controls, rules and regulations.[60] Despite the tendency for this school of thought to romanticize about the nature of pre-twentieth-century working-class culture, their argument cannot be discarded easily.

It has been stressed all along that the major characteristic of the period was the expansion of cultural production for the market and with it universal and homogeneous forms of leisure. Recreational and cultural pursuits became less differentiated by social group and region, though there were still important class differences. Through the mass communication industry – the press, radio, cinema – and the general spread of commercialized leisure, as well as the penetration of American cultural forms in the arts, music and dancing, people from all social groups and regions came together in their leisure. They listened to the same radio programmes and watched the same films, were attracted to the national sporting events, danced to the new popular music, and read the 'pulp' fiction of the age. The corollary of these developments, as noticed by a number of contemporaries, was the growth of a mass, standardized product, often in passive forms. F. R. Leavis wrote of the perversity of mass-produced leisure; Robert Sinclair of those 'mob amusements'; and J. L. Hammond of those 'mass pleasures' which failed to stimulate the intelligence or the imagination.[61] Equally, labour 'highbrows', echoing the Arnoldian cultural critique as then represented by Leavis and T. S. Eliot, feared that commercialized leisure would encourage over-indulgence and undermine aesthetic pursuits. Cultural luminaries 'adopted an attitude of aloofness' towards the cinema, 'sneered at it', and were openly critical of such things as 'sexuality in our entertainments' and the necessity 'to descend to the level of the American jazz exploiters'.[62] There were even fears about motor-car excursionists *en masse* who were said to vandalize country estates, and working-class day trippers who were said to abuse the opportunities of Epping Forest, preferring the 'mass' to 'the delights of solitude'.[63] Similar fears were also voiced about the growth of passive leisure which was apparently killing off active and creative leisure:

> . . . that the commercialisation of leisure was making ordinary people more passive in their enjoyment, receiving entertainment and culture rather than making their own, listening to canned music instead of playing darts or singing round the piano in the pub, silently goggling at the pictures instead of cheering or booing in the music-hall or joining in the hymns at church.[64]

Some of the critics of mass taste tended to be both elitist in their efforts to protect high culture, and ignorant of popular culture, yet there was a grain of truth in what they were saying.

The standardized commodity of the circuit cinemas or the 'Palais de Danse' challenged certain traditional values of self-provided leisure based on co-operation, association, solidarity, mutuality, shared experience, democratic control, political expression, creativity and innovation. With the tendency for leisure capital to concentrate, centralize and unify, consumers became divorced from the centres of cultural production and popular control was eroded except, that is, for the financial vote in the market place. Workers were remote from the decision-making functions of leisure entrepreneurs, and hence there was a limited commitment to and casual usage of the finished product. As Capitalist leisure diversified sections of the increasingly consumption-minded working class no longer needed to have a personal, familial, or communal stake in leisure provision. It is in this sense, then, that the commercial expansion of the inter-war years may have eroded workers' control over their leisure. All this is not to argue that the voluntary sector or associational forms withered away. As has already been suggested, workers showed a continuing inventiveness in their cultural practices, whether in clubs, home or street. Many working-class agencies for leisure continued to thrive, and certainly working-class culture as a whole was able to retain many of its qualities and adapt to external, material change. In brief, one is impressed by the remarkable durability of working-class culture.

The tendency for commercialized forms to replace associational forms, if true, should not be reduced to the level of overt Capitalist ideological penetration of working-class leisure time. Capitalist leisure was provided for the working class in response to increasing demand and in hope of a financial return, though advertising may have shaped consumer tastes in some instances. Leisure commodities and services were not provided as purveyors of Capitalist ideology, aiming at proletarian incorporation into the dominant social order. In order for the entrepreneur of leisure to succeed, he or she had to tap the likes, the wishes, the predilection of the consumer which meant, in some cases, appealing to those organic features of working-class life, not always in tune with the interests of Capitalism. If the leisure industry was to give consumers what they wanted, it could hardly ignore working-class tastes, even if bourgeois ideology was weakened as a result. In other words, cultural production was not necessarily commensurable with the ideological needs of Capitalism.[65]

Moreover, it is clearly not true to see the working class as 'a kind of empty bottle into which you pour culture, or a blank wall upon which you paint things', since the commercialized product was the outcome of, to use Alun Howkins' term, a 'negotiated culture', a mixture of Capitalist, proletarian, highbrow and other 'different, opposing and contesting cultural forms'.[66] Mass culture theory seems to miss the point that popular leisure can be received by the working class either in a creative way or in the way of resistance and contestation; leisure can be developed to express class identities. Indeed, commercialized forms were often reappropriated by the working class for their own use, or to express it another way, 'taken out of their original historical and cultural contexts and juxtaposed against other signs from other sources'.[67] Thus the public-house – part of a significant Capitalist industry – was the hub of working-class social life, catering for all kinds of activities. As the Mass Observation study pointed out, the pub was the focal point of quarrels and fights, trade unions, secret societies, sex, crime and prostitution, illegal lotteries and sweepstakes, and drunkenness – a fact hardly conducive to the stability of Capitalism.[68] Similarly, in football, the working class was not far from being organically linked with the industry itself. Even if football was run by the dominant groups of society, it would seem that the working class was able to colonize and make it their own. Grounds were built where the supporters lived, in among the factories and the workers' houses; players, managers and occasionally even directors came from the same class as the supporters, with similar experiences and ideas about life. Football was a tough game for a tough people, born out of a harsh yet solid community. Despite crowd disturbance in Wales, Scotland and England – violence, vandalism, fighting, stealing the ball – football entrepreneurs, though introducing methods of control, such as crowd segregation, better facilities and the use of regulatory agents, stewards and the police, were reluctant openly to advocate closure of the ground.[69] Such action would not only have brought financial problems, but also have alienated a considerable section of local working-class support. Social problems had to be tolerated if business was to continue as usual. Football, like other sports, was not subsumed under bourgeois dominance. Indeed, as Ralph Miliband has suggested, there is no reason why football supporters should not also be militant trade unionists.[70] Red Clydeside was thus a hotbed of soccer, as well as class militancy.

In the case of the cinema industry, a number of commentators have suggested that films acted as a conservative force in society. There was, for instance, the British Board of Film Censors which exerted a politically conservative influence over film content. However, in order for the cinema to operate successfully it had to reflect, at least some of the time, popular attitudes and ideas. This is one of the reasons why American films were popular in the 1930s. Towards the end of the decade Hollywood was even beginning to tackle reality and produce some films of social honesty.[71] By comparison, British films were often rather tame and failed to challenge social mores and conventions. This was to some extent due to political censorship, yet this should not hide the fact that film content reflected what people wanted. There was a huge demand for romance, comedy and escapism. The cinema was sometimes a dream house divorced from day-to-day existence struggles because audiences wanted it to be like this and not because of State direction. The last thing most of the working class wanted was to be continually reminded of their economic and social circumstances by drama documentaries depicting unemployment, poverty and poor housing – after all, life outside the cinema was a permanent reminder of social deprivation. If the working class had wanted British films to be more radical then surely the workers' film societies and the documentary movement would have been more popular. The simple fact is that the British people preferred 'our' Gracie, Will Hay and George Formby to the films made by Eisenstein or Grierson.

The spread of Capitalist leisure may have penetrated working-class culture with certain adverse effects, but to conclude that this was a conscious attempt to undermine proletarian beliefs with Capitalist ideology is to go too far in one direction. The commercial provision of leisure does not fit in with Althusser's notion of an 'ideological state apparatus' used to aid the exploitation of labour by capital.[72] Nor does it fit in with John Foster's idea of an ideological 'climate of opinion' – newspapers, radio, the church, education, government – designed during the 1920s to win over public opinion to the Establishment.[73] It is clearly wrong to see sport merely 'functioning as a means of political socialisation into the hegemonic culture', the cinema as a way of 'engendering consensus [and] fostering harmony and social integration', or art as 'the expression of culturally conditioned expectations'.[74] Cultural production has to appeal to the demands and dictates of the market. If the market points in the way of a commodity which has anti-Capitalist proclivities – a left-wing film or novel – then cultural production is not suddenly terminated – if it were, the profit mechanism itself would not be working; and when the market stagnated the leisure industry stagnated, it did not survive as a cultural propaganda machine. Also, commercialized leisure could be shaped and moulded by the working class into uses not always favourable to Capitalism. Therefore, the leisure industry was not run with the specific aim of eliminating proletarian cultural forms.

It is evident that working people provided self-created leisure, sometimes through middle-class patronage, but more so through proletarian organization and spontaneous or traditional pastimes in the home or the street. Some of the richness of proletarian cultural expression may have been tarnished by the commercial penetration of associational forms, but much survived. Capitalist leisure was not the purveyor of the dominant ideology, and in some cases was even appropriated for class-based activity. Although it is difficult to assess the subjective phenomenon of qualitative experience, by using one's historical imagination it is possible to suggest that the majority of working people, even those in poor material circumstances, were not entirely powerless in the face of external change to shape their own destiny and to gain a sense of well-being from their own spare-time experiences.

1 The demand for leisure: *Urban transport systems such as trams and motor traffic stimulated a range of amusements.*

2 The leisure industry: *Leisure was highly commercialized, involving much capital investment and the application of technology. Blackpool Pleasure Beach is a case in point.*

3 Urban pleasures: *The cinema was one of many working-class leisure interests. The Paramount cinema in the centre of Manchester can be seen flanked by ballroom, table tennis rooms, billiard halls, and Cook's Tourist Office.*

4 Association football: *The FA Cup Final was the climax of the English football season. The 1934 Final was between Manchester City and Portsmouth (and was refereed by Stanley Rous).*

5 Picture palaces: *Arguably the cinema was the main leisure institution of the 1930s.*

6 Dances and socials: *The dance craze spread during the 1920s. Dances and socials were held throughout the country.*

7 Theatres: *Despite the growth of alternative entertainments, the theatre survived as a centre of pleasure.*

8 Holidays: *The working-class holiday spread during the period, albeit unevenly. Many resorts benefited from the influx of working-class visitors, in this case the East coast town of Clevelys.*

9 Boxing: *The amateur and professional fight game was especially popular in many working-class districts.*

11 Cycling: *Cycling was enjoyed by men and women of all social classes. Here we have two members of the Clarion Cycling Club.*

10 Rambling: *Of all outdoor recreations in the inter-war years, rambling was perhaps the biggest growth area.*

12 Education: *Independent working-class education was regarded as a rational recreation by certain political activists. The Marxist Summer School held in Skegness from 31 July to 14 August 1937 had (according to the* Daily Worker*) a 'Good holiday programme. Bathing, Boating, Rambling, Socials, etc. Popular lectures and discussion.'*

13 Street entertainment: *The working class created entertainment in the informal arena of the street. Many British streets, such as this one at Salford, celebrated George V's Jubilee in 1935.*

14 Parks: *Public parks were provided by the municipal authorities, giving the opportunity for a variety of recreations.*

15 Open spaces: *A number of pressure groups stressed the need for open spaces, like Belle Vue Gardens (including speedway).*

16 Excursions: *The working-class outing was one alternative to a holiday away from home. The Nelson Labour Women's section organized such an outing in 1934.*

17 Leisure and politics: *The working class campaigned for access to the countryside. There were a number of protest rallies, such as this one in Derbyshire.*

18 Sport and politics: *The organized working class in London sought facilities for sport.* The Worker Sportsman *was the journal of the Communist-inspired British Workers' Sports Federation.*

4

State provision: the role of central and municipal authorities

In inter-war Britain leisure was also provided and regulated by organs of the State – by which is meant Central and sub-central Government, the administration, the police and the judiciary.[1] The scope of recreational services within the realm of the State was very wide. There were a number of legislative developments dealing with leisure activities and facilities and services for leisure were provided for the general use of the public. Furthermore, Central Government directly impinged on commercial and voluntary provision through a host of formal rules and regulations. The various agencies of the State had a network of official controls which performed a global role in channelling all kinds of recreational issues through the administrative process. It is indeed evident from the documents deposited at the Public Record Office in London that the State consistently intervened in the leisure province: relevant sources are to be found in the files relating to the Home Office, Metropolitan Police, Cabinet Office, Ministry of Education, Board of Trade, Ministry of Labour and so on. Also, at local repositories such as the Surrey Record Office evidence of an interest in sport and leisure can be found in judicial records, Local Government minute books and school log books.[2]

Perhaps an even more important form of State provision was the wide range of municipal services and amenities for recreation. During the 1920s and 1930s the municipal authorities played an increasingly important part in the recreational sphere. They provided opportunities for the local population to participate in a wide range of leisure activities. In the main, this came through free access to a large number of amenities such as parks, swimming pools and libraries. In addition, public buildings were frequently used by voluntary organizations for dances, musical recitals and other cultural events, and by entrepreneurs in the leisure industry for the staging of sporting contests such as wrestling or variety entertainment. This chapter will examine central and local authority provision and regulation of recreation. It will attempt to show that public provision expanded during the inter-war years and so contributed to the general increase in recreational opportunities, though there were still some shortages of public amenities and some areas of the country which lagged behind.

General trends

The origins of public provision and control of recreation can be traced back to the nineteenth century, if not earlier. Central and local authorities aimed to provide improved, reformed recreations to wean the working class away from the alleged degenerations of their own culture, though they were not always successful in doing this. More specifically, the Government regulated leisure through policing and judicial intervention, as in the suppression of street football and festivals. As Robert Storch has asserted: 'the state and its agencies became not only more willing to legislate in such areas but also proved willing to create and fund enforcement agencies.'[3]

In many ways such intervention clearly brought a number of benefits to the working class, such as public libraries and museums. For instance, swimming pools were provided under the Baths and Wash-Houses Act of 1846, whilst the Public Health Act of 1848 was used by town corporations to provide land for pleasure grounds or public walks. Also of note were the Museums Act of 1845, the Towns Improvement Clauses Act of 1847, and the Public Libraries Act of 1855 which all allowed the acquisition of powers for recreational purposes. By the second half of the century a number of urban public parks were also constructed, often a reflection of civic pride and philanthropic effort; these had a range of amenities for leisure and sport. In Bristol and Birmingham, for example, there was positive intervention by the municipal authorities in the provision of parks for the moral improvement of the population.[4] Public provision was at its height in seaside resorts. Municipal funds were spent on promoting local leisure industries and recreational schemes, as well as the contributions made to the economic and social infrastructure. It is interesting that this sometimes involved marketing campaigns through advertising and publicity. In addition, it was particularly important for the seaside corporation to regulate leisure and ensure that public order was kept at all times. Once again, municipal involvement was intimately related to notions of public welfare and civic pride, but as in the case of Bournemouth and Blackpool there was a further influence – support for the holiday industry and so the local business community.[5] Obviously, the State influenced the development of leisure in the nineteenth century, though this was not the end of the story. The role of the State in leisure was further extended in the twentieth century, with the first world war as a crucial period.

The Great War of 1914–18 was something of a watershed in British economic and social history. The State began to control and regulate many aspects of the economy and society. Most of all the full panoply of the governmental apparatus was brought to bear on financial and budgetary matters, together with intervention in industry and agriculture and the direction of manpower. Collective forms of action were also used to deal with leisure – sporting activities, drinking and holidays were severely curtailed.[6] State management of leisure certainly had an ideological side to it. In official circles, leisure was directly linked to war aims and objectives; so the provision of spare time facilities for munition workers was perceived as a way of increasing labour productivity by providing relief from monotony, a change of environment and a factor in the recovery from industrial fatigue. A fear of unorganized leisure also shaped official pronouncements: 'If opportunities of wholesome amusement, refreshment and recreation are not provided, the public-house and less desirable places of entertainment may benefit, but everybody else suffers.'[7] Rational recreation was therefore stressed as a contribution to the war effort, and indeed controlled leisure eventually recognized as important in retaining workers at the huge armament plants. It was further envisaged that one of the duties of welfare supervision would be to offer advice on and provide amenities for gardening, gyms, holidays and clubs. Initiatives of this kind, though not a new departure in State policy, represented an increasing tendency to intervention. Despite deregulation and the return to free market forces in the immediate post-war period, the collectivist trend was consolidated in the 1920s and 1930s.

Broadly speaking, the State began to play an increasingly significant role in economic and social affairs. Crucial developments were recorded in the field of economic and social policy-making and, after the gold standard had been abandoned in 1931, the government was less constrained in its ability to manage the economy: planned trade was rehabilitated, industrial rationalization encouraged, regional policy promoted and, somewhat fortuitously, expansionary monetary measures introduced. Furthermore, contrary to the generally accepted view that the Treasury retained a strict control of Government expenditure in the inter-war years, there was in fact a considerable expansion of the public sector. Measured as a proportion of Gross Domestic Product, total capital and current expenditure by the central and local authorities increased from 9.3 per cent in 1913 to 11.2 per cent in 1924 and 15 per cent in 1937. Interestingly enough, Local Government retained a great deal of autonomy in financial matters and had an important place in the growth of State activity.[8] Unsurprisingly, recreation benefited from the widening of the State's sphere of influence.

Alun Howkins and John Lowerson have claimed that, because of deflationary policies, successive Governments 'had little cash available to stimulate sporting and leisure activities'. When it came to spending, Governments were still dominated by Gladstonian financial orthodoxy. Economic and social policy-making, including the decision whether or not to increase expenditure on leisure, came up against a number of financial, political and administrative constraints. In particular, cabinet ministers, as well as public servants, had to decide on spending priorities within a balanced budget. However, the conclusion that leisure 'progressed . . . largely without government policy intervention' is open to debate.[9] The State was clearly involved in many facets of leisure, and the various agencies of the State increasingly interfered with and provided amenities for the recreation of the people. Although there were no institutions in Britain resembling the Soviet All-Union Physical Culture Council, Italian Dopolavoro, the Nazi 'Strength Through Joy' movement, or even the French Spare Time Committees, various direct and indirect controls of the nineteenth century were extended, overhauled and used as the basis of a fairly sophisticated system of regulation.[10] The State management of leisure was official in the sense that it received parliamentary consent; the most obvious form of control was legislative.

There were numerous parliamentary Bills relating to leisure and many of these were enacted. The Statute Book saw Acts aiming to control the cinema, drinking, gambling, camping, cycling, rambling and the rest. Let us take legislation dealing specifically with the film industry as an example. Legislative intervention first occurred in 1909 when the Cinematograph Films Act required the licensing of cinemas and the provision of adequate safety measures against fire. Due to American competition in the 1920s and the need for protection further legislation was required if the British film industry was to stay in business. The Cinematograph Films Act of 1927 required a small but annually increasing share of screen time in all cinemas to be reserved for British films, and placed an obligation on all renters of imported films to acquire a proportion of British films. It also established a Board of Trade Advisory Committee to administer the legislation and advise on matters concerning the film industry. Certainly the Act stimulated the production of British films, but perhaps even more important for the discussion here, it was a clear indication of public concern for leisure. As one historian has claimed: 'The British Cinematograph Films Act of 1927 is a sign . . . of the stirrings of collectivist concern in the matter of mass entertainment.'[11]

The most direct piece of interventionist legislation in the recreational field was the Physical Training and Recreation Act of 1937. It should not be forgotten that the State had intervened in physical education for some time and that the 1930s were 'exciting years for physical education, years during which it changed to meet the needs and aspirations of society'.[12] There was greater support for the notion of teaching sport, as illustrated by the funding of specialist physical education colleges at Leeds (Carnegie) and at Loughborough in the mid-1930s. Yet this piece of legislation must also be seen against the background of rearmament and the Establishment's disguised fear of war – physical fitness was essential if war was to be fought.

In essence the aim of the Act was to achieve a better standard of physical development in adults by offering more opportunities for recreation and by improving sports facilities. The scheme was to be very wide and 'embrace the whole field of physical culture and should therefore include arrangements for increasing the supply not only of gymnasia, but also of playing fields, swimming baths and other means of healthy physical recreation'.[13] The Act got off to a good start, with many organizations, including the TUC General Council, endorsing the terms of the so-called National Fitness Campaign.[14] Parliament voted £2 million and set up a National Advisory Council, under the chairmanship of Lord Aberdare, which in turn was supplemented by a number of local committees to allocate grants, encourage expertise and stimulate the growth of recreational bodies. Up until the outbreak of the second world war when the Council was suspended, the campaign gathered momentum and there was a clear increase in facilities, as well as help given with the coaching of games and sports, training schemes, research and the dissemination of new ideas. At the local level a crucial part was played by municipal authorities and voluntary organizations. Most important, the Government approved quite large sums of money for both capital and current expenditure on swimming baths, hostels, gyms, camp sites and playing fields. The relevant information for grants allocated is given in Table 4.1.

Table 4.1   Grants offered by the National Fitness Council (up to 31 March 1939)

Type of Project	Local Authorities £	Grants offered to: Voluntary Bodies £	Total £
Swimming baths	439,427	2,625	442,052
Clubs	–	289,297	289,297
Village halls	500	12,935	13,435
Other recreative centres	187,888	145,483	333,371
Gyms	3,200	3,070	6,270
Youth hostels	–	12,575	12,575
Camps and camping sites	5,050	17,900	22,950
Equipment	1,510	9,631	11,141
Playing fields	302,947	34,264	337,211
Total	940,522	527,780	1,468,302

Source: National Fitness Council, Report of the Grants Committee to the President of the Board of Education, HMSO, 1939, p. 8.

As the National Fitness Council remarked: 'The experience of a first year is encouraging as showing that interest has been increased, the appreciation of needs has been deepened, and the effort to increase facilities has been solid.'[15]

Aside from acts dealing directly with leisure, there were also other pieces of legislation, ostensibly concerned with other issues, which impinged on the recreational sphere. Public health legislation, originating in the nineteenth century, controlled camping. By the 1930s it was accepted that there was a need for a fresh appraisal of the regulations in force. After a great deal of discussion and compromise Public Health legislation was again used, this time in 1936, to regulate camps. A general licensing system was introduced whereby camping was allowed if campers and site owners satisfied the authorities as to the standard of dwellings. Once again, this type of legislation had a direct bearing on leisure developments.

At this point it must be added that quantitative evidence is rather thin on the ground, though the figures that are available certainly point to an expansion of services, particularly in the 1920s. Estimates made by the Royal Commission on Museums and Galleries, and the Committees on Local Expenditure, indicate that there was growth. Attendances at the National Museums and Galleries in London and Edinburgh rose from 4,382,419 in 1903 to 5,025,410 in 1913, and 6,463,178 in 1928. This involved a corresponding increase in State expenditure: £548,484 in 1903–4 to £1,201,257 in 1927–8. Institutions such as the Victoria and Albert Museum and the Tate Gallery in London, and the National Portrait Gallery and the Scottish Museum of Antiquities in Edinburgh, were clearly the beneficiaries of State backing. At another level, there was substantial public outlay on parks and other open spaces. Urban authorities in England and Wales spent approximately £5,217,000 on parks in the financial year 1929–30. This meant that expenditure per 1,000 of the population had increased from £93 10s in 1920–1 to £131 15s in 1929–30. Across the border in Scotland, local authorities' outlay on parks increased from £1,042,842 in 1903–4 to £1,996,528 in 1929–30; meaning that expenditure per head of the population had grown from 4s 10d to 8s 3d. Similar increases were also recorded for libraries and public baths. Between 1919 and 1939 191 new swimming pools where thus opened in England and Wales. Despite the lack of aggregate data, the information clearly points to a rise in State spending.[16]

Sub-central Government was therefore also involved in legislative developments. Relevant national legislation and local bye-laws all contained clauses granting powers to provide amenities for leisure. Although the principle of municipal interference in leisure was firmly established by the end of the nineteenth century, it is probably correct to see a far greater municipalization of leisure in the 1920s and 1930s. Certainly, local authority expenditure contributed to the growth of recreational facilities and services. There were indeed many spheres of influence ranging from sport and outdoor recreation to library services and tourism.

Evidence gleaned from the social surveys shows that most of the main British cities had a range of public amenities for sport. In Liverpool, for instance, the corporation provided facilities for all the main sports; there were 172 football plots, accommodating 344 teams, and 16 swimming baths by the beginning of the 1930s. Indeed, there had been a significant expansion in the 1920s, as Table 4.2 confirms. Similarly, the acreage of open space increased much more rapidly than the population: in 1913 there were only 1,000 acres of open space; by the mid-1930s there were over 2,000 acres. In all there were 110 public open spaces, as well as twenty-one parks of 11 acres or more, the largest being Sefton Park.[17] Likewise, progress was recorded in Manchester by the corporation's Parks Committee in the provision of playing areas and open spaces. Even the poorer working-class districts of Manchester such as Hulme had recognized open spaces and public parks.[18] The metropolis also followed these general trends. Speaking in 1927 the Minister of Health, Neville Chamberlain, claimed that there had been large additions to London parks, recreation grounds and open space during the past five years. A summary of parks and open spaces in London is provided in Table 4.3. By 1933 the parks of the London County Council (LCC) provided 783 tennis courts, 420 football pitches, 384 cricket pitches and 28 hockey pitches.[19] Moreover, at the beginning of 1935 Herbert Morrison, the new leader of the LCC, announced his intention to preserve a green belt of open space round the capital at the expense of £2 million; and by the end of the decade 70,000 acres had been earmarked for preservation, 110 square miles had been saved from the developers, and recreation areas had been safeguarded.[20]

Table 4.2   *Municipal facilities for recreation in Liverpool*

	Facilities in	
	1921	1930
Football plots	154	172
Cricket pitches	50	89
Tennis courts	172	400
Rounders pitches	26	59
Baseball plots	Nil	11
Bowls greens	Not known	53
Golf – 18 hole courses	Nil	3
9 hole courses	1	2
Putting greens	Nil	8
Boating – Lakes	5	5
Boats	100	105

Source: T. Middleton, 'An Enquiry into the Use of Leisure Amongst
the Working Classes of Liverpool', unpublished MA thesis,
Liverpool University, 1931, p. 117.

Although it is not the purpose of this section to examine the reasons for the extension of public facilities for sport and games, a major influence was the pressure exerted by leisure interest groups. In the early 1920s a number of voluntary organizations sponsored an Open Spaces Bill designed 'to extend the powers of local authorities with regard to the acquisition and use of land for recreation purposes'.[21] Despite the fact that the Bill did not progress very far, it was just one of many instances of pressure being brought to bear on the question of municipal amenities for recreation. Equally important was the establishment of the National Playing Fields Association in 1925, which had the support of groups as diverse as the royal family – the Duke of York was its president – and the TUC General Council. Not surprisingly, its aim was to increase the number of recreation grounds, and in this success was recorded. In the years 1927–33 the Association was responsible for the completion of 1,090 recreation grounds, many of them financed by public funds.[22]

It is also interesting to note that the inter-war period witnessed the start of a movement for municipal and public golf courses. In Scotland there were facilities for cheap golf – as little as 6d for eighteen holes. In England, however, golf was mainly a middle-

Table 4.3 *Parks and open spaces maintained in the City of London
and in each Metropolitan Borough by public authorities in
1927*

City or Borough	Area of land and inland water (Acres)	Approx. area of Parks and Open Spaces (Acres)	Approx. acreage of Playing Fields
City of London	675	4	Nil
Battersea	2,160	405	157
Bermondsey	1,500	74	33.5
Bethnal Green	759	99	98
Camberwell	4,480	226	79.25
Chelsea	660	5	Nil
Deptford	1,563	32	13.75
Finsbury	587	11	0.25
Fulham	1,703	71	28
Greenwich	3,852	429	70
Hackney	3,288	619	296.75
Hammersmith	2,286	277	127
Hampstead	2,265	408	60
Holborn	405	9	1.75
Islington	3,092	46	17
Kensington	2,291	60	Nil
Lambeth	4,080	258	161
Lewisham	7,014	358	173
Paddington	1,356	100	22.5
Poplar	2,328	87	5.75
St Marylebone	1,473	349	28
St Pancras	2,694	335	80.75
Shoreditch	658	10	0.25
Southwark	1,131	13	0.75
Stepney	1,766	34	Nil
Stoke Newington	863	55	67.25
Wandsworth	9,107	1,152	175.5
Westminster (City)	2,503	693	Nil
Woolwich	8,277	448	119.25
Total	74,816	6,667	1,816.25

Source: Hansard (Commons) 5th Ser. Vol. 203 Cols 553–4, 3 March
1927.

class sport, with a minority working-class following. Nonetheless,
Ben Tillett, the trade union leader, urged the need for the estab-

lishment of municipal courses, claiming that 'golf seems to be quite popular with all classes'.[23] By 1936 there were about fifty courses in England, most of them having been opened in the years after the first world war. In the Manchester area, for example, there were municipal courses at Bolton, Rochdale, Burnley, Altrincham and Heaton Park.[24]

All this is not to argue that the demand for municipal sports facilities was satisfied in the inter-war years, for there was still a shortage in many parts of the country. The social surveys of Hull and York both reported that there was a lack of playing fields. Notwithstanding what has been said about London, it is evident that facilities were still inadequate to cater for workers' leisure. In fact in the mid-1930s a considerable area of the open Hackney Marshes was hived off by the housing department of the LCC; and had it not been for the pressure brought to bear by such interest groups as the Commons, Open Spaces and Footpath Preservation Society, Metropolitan Public Gardens Association, National Citizens Union and the Hackney Marshes Defence League, even more open space would have been appropriated.[25] As the final chapter will demonstrate, a feature of recreational developments in the metropolis of the 1930s was the campaign for workers' playing fields and other amenities. Even in rural areas there was a remarkable dearth of playing fields. For instance, in 1934 only one parish out of forty-four in the North Riding had a playing field.[26] No doubt this was because local authorities outside the towns depended upon the altruism of the local landowners for access to open spaces or the provision of playgrounds.

Aside from municipal facilities for sport and outdoor recreation, local authorities also catered for cultural interests. In particular, reading benefited from an extension of library services. Robert Roberts has pointed out that by the 1930s more and more working people were beginning to borrow library books as a new generation established itself, 'better educated and growing more certain of its rights and needs'. Underlying this is the fact that in the ten years after 1926 the number of readers in the Lancashire library service increased from 8,000 to 167,000 and the stock of books from 20,000 to 297,000.[27] Nationally, the number of books issued by the public libraries increased from 54.3 million in 1911 to 85.7 million in 1924 and 247.3 million by 1939.[28] This evidence is supported by other sources. The social survey of York found that the annual issue of books never rose above 191,231 in the period 1893 to 1919, but by 1936 it had risen to 581,266 and at the end of 1938 to 724,000.[29] A similar finding was made by the Merseyside social survey, as can be seen from Table 4.4. In addition to libraries most of the major cities had museums and art galleries which, again, were well utilized by the public.

Table 4.4 *The use of public libraries in Liverpool*

	1900	1913	1930–31
Number of libraries	8	16	24
Total volumes in stock	213,000	350,000	510,000
Total issue of books	1,450,000	2,383,000	5,071,000

Source: D. Caradog Jones ed., *The Social Survey of Merseyside* vol. 3, University of Liverpool, Liverpool, 1934, p. 297.

As in the nineteenth century, local public provision of recreational facilities is best evidenced by seaside resorts, where both the tourists and business traders of all descriptions benefited from a number of projects. Municipalities were involved in the development of 'Dreamland' in Margate, 'Pleasure Town' in Blackpool and the 'Amusement Park' in Eastbourne, whilst Brighton corporation spent £180,000 on constructing the Marine Drive and £400,000 in building a promenade.[30] In more specific terms, the corporation of inter-war Blackpool played an increasingly important role in the development of the local leisure industry. The corporation was under the effective control of the main entertainment concerns and, as such, promoted publicity campaigns and offered cheap transport, admission rates and accommodation to holidaymakers.[31] It is interesting to note that, in addition to local financial provision, political representation was made in the House of Commons. MPs urged the Government to discriminate in favour of home seaside and health resorts and to develop a system of holiday advertising and publicity.[32] In fact, the Government supported the Travel and Industrial Development Association of Great Britain and Northern Ireland, which had been founded in late 1928 to promote the British tourist industry and encourage foreigners to holiday at British beauty spots and resorts.

Finally in this section it should be noted that there was a

considerable degree of co-operation between statutory bodies and other providers of leisure, particularly voluntary organizations. Most of all, the local education authorities set up Juvenile Organisation Committees which often had close links with local recreational and cultural organizations, and added their voice to demands for facilities and services. From 1937 the Jarrow Committee thus organized football and cricket matches.[33] The authorities themselves provided holiday camps, especially for young people attending continuation classes, centres and equipment for physical training, and playing fields. In addition, play centres for children of school age and evening classes all contributed to the stock of recreational amenities.[34] And as far as adult education was concerned, Government grants increased from £3,993 for 219 classes in 1913 to £89,003 for 3,004 classes by 1938.[35]

Government initiatives had a direct bearing on leisure, but this should not be seen simply in terms of legislative action and public funding. Recreation policy and resource allocation also had budgetary implications. The existence of an entertainment tax, for instance, not only contributed to the exchequer, but also affected the financial policies and economic structure of the leisure industry. Furthermore, the tax hindered the development of those smaller commercial concerns and voluntary organizations without the means to meet fiscal demands, as well as increasing the price of entertainment to consumers. As a result, many protests were made. In the words of the National Conference of Labour Women:

This Conference urges on the Chancellor of the Exchequer that he should abolish the tax on all entertainments where the price does not exceed sixpence, believing that the tax is a heavy burden on very poor people when visiting cinemas and other places of amusement, and that it hinders very seriously many philanthropic associations, youth or dramatic societies in their work.[36]

In the Manchester area there were a number of complaints made by cultural groups. The Manchester and District Dramatic Federation showed concern over the revised entertainments duty introduced in the supplementary budget of 1931; this was said to affect to a considerable extent the finances of amateur dramatic societies and would inevitably lead to an increase in admission charges.[37] Reg Cordwell, the secretary of the Manchester and Salford Workers' Film Society in the 1930s, has similarly recalled that the incidence of the tax was a serious problem – the Society sought exemption and after years of campaigning the Home Office eventually conceded to their demands.[38] Therefore a tax introduced as a temporary war-time measure influenced developments in and the mode of leisure provision.

From a slightly different perspective, there were also administrative, policing and judicial aspects to State provision and regulation. The existence of quasi-official bodies, such as the Racecourse Betting Control Board and the Board of Trade Advisory Committee on films, provided some kind of administrative control over a number of leisure pursuits so as to ensure that rules and regulations were not infringed. The police and the judiciary had a variety of legal responsibilities, from the control of crowds both inside and outside sports grounds, to the licensing of public entertainment. It was indeed quite common for these agencies of the State to play the role of overseer of a number of leisure pursuits, particularly street gambling, football and other entertainments.

State control and ownership

The State provided for and dealt with leisure, be it through public funding of facilities, tax collection, or administrative regulation. Yet there was perhaps a more fundamental influence at work: direct, public management or ownership of leisure concerns. Obviously, the State controlled a number of recreational and cultural institutions such as parks, swimming pools, libraries and museums. It was the various sub-agencies of the State which decided upon policy and the ways in which these institutions were run. In a different context there were pressures for the nationalization of leisure products and services. This was particularly true in the radical atmosphere of the immediate post-war period. Thus the National Conference on 'The Leisure of the People' in November 1919 resolved in favour of the idea that 'the provision of social centres for purposes of public refreshment, recreation and neighbourly intercourse, should be undertaken by the municipalities of the country'.[39] At the same time, Henry Oscar of the Actors' Association Council argued that, 'Together with the nationalisation of railways, mines and industry must come the nationalisation of the theatre.'[40] Indeed, the call for a National Theatre subsidized by public funds was one of the main policies of cultural organizations like the British Drama League. In addition, powerful individuals, such as Ramsay MacDonald, pressed for the municipalization of national art treasures.[41] All this is not to argue, however, that there were many significant inroads made by the State. The only permanent development of note, emerging at the end of the war, was limited State control of the drink trade.

The Government took the first tentative steps towards public control of the liquor trade during the war. The main reason for central control was, of course, the need to reduce the danger of alcohol abuse amongst the forces and munition workers. Therefore, a number of licensing restrictions were introduced; in 1915 the Central Control Board (Liquor Traffic) was set up to regulate the sale and consumption of alcohol, and a year later the State purchased licensed premises at Enfield Lock, Gretna, Carlisle, Invergordon and Cromarty – all areas of military concern for the Ministry of Munitions or the Admiralty. The new nationalized pubs were transformed under the aegis of disinterested management: back-street 'gin palaces' were closed down, public houses were redesigned with larger rooms and more seating accommodation, and food and recreation were introduced. The new public-house manager with his State salary did not receive any commission on drink sales and therefore had the time to concentrate on improvements.[42]

During the period of decontrol and a return to market forces the Liquor Control Board was disbanded in 1921. However, the successful experiments in the State direction of licensed premises continued. Moreover, when the war ended the demand for State control of the drink interest continued, so that by 1919 a Labour Campaign for the Public Ownership and Control of the Liquor Trade had been formally launched. Although the Campaign did not lead to an increase in State control or ownership, it is appropriate to carry the discussion a little further in order to appreciate some of the claims being made in favour of public provision.

The first secretaries were Arthur Greenwood and James Joseph Mallon, both prominent members of the Labour Party. It is clear that there was immediate support. In the correspondence columns of the sympathetic *Spectator*, for instance, leading Labour and trade union personalities, Fred Bramley, G. D. H. Cole, Charles Stitch and J. H. Thomas, expressed solidarity with the objective of public ownership.[43] Further, in the first few months of its existence, a great deal of effort was spent in the form of political lobbying, and favourable contacts were made with the Labour Party Executive.[44] It also appears that successful work was carried out in enlisting the support of trade unions, and trades and labour councils throughout the country. Hence, by the end of 1919 it was reported that 'the activities of the Labour Campaign Committee are now rapidly increasing'.[45]

The private ownership of the drink trade was seen as the major hurdle in the quest for sobriety. The profit-making objectives of the trade were regarded as inimical to social progress: 'The Brewing industry, in common with all other capitalist industries, has as its main motive, not public service, but private gain. It is concerned with obtaining the greatest possible return on the private capital invested in the industry.'[46] Breweries were Capitalist concerns run on the basis of self-interest and profit. According to the Labour Campaign it was the profit motive which stimulated excess consumption of intoxicants. In short, increased consumption would lead to increased profits; if the working class drank too much, there was little reason for the brewers and the publicans to feel guilty. 'Our Union is of the opinion that the Private Ownership of the Liquor Trade and the profit accruing to same is largely the cause of excessive drinking', is the way the shopworkers expressed it.[47] Not surprisingly, Labour provided political opposition to the brewers and quasi-trade organizations.[48]

British pubs came in for harsh treatment because they were presumed to emphasize drinking to the neglect of everything else. At their best, they were regarded as communal places of entertainment, at their worst, drinking dens, but on the whole, they were considered to be demoralizing places. Their sole aim was thought to be the sale of intoxicants, well reflected in their very design: 'Most public houses are in size and structure unsuitable for their purpose. They are often congested, malodorous and without amenities. The worst of them are unfit for use.'[49] Moreover, some commentators saw these circumstances as leading to new problems. Ernest Selley, a secretary of the Labour Campaign, referred to the public house habit among women. He suggested that, because of new feelings of emancipation and increased opportunities for drinking, more women were taking advantage of the pub:

> In almost every town I have found women drinking in 'bottle and jug' departments, or in alley-ways, yards, kitchens, and also in the street. I have found instances where women's rooms open on to the backyards and the back door is used as an entrance and exit.[50]

Though Socialist views of the English pub may have been biased, the conclusion reached was that private ownership was not conducive to improvement. Under State control, the pubs would revert to being social centres where a worker could 'sit at his ease and chat and smoke, where he can get a drink if he wants one, but from which he won't be ejected if he does not; where he can have a meal, or a cup of tea, if he prefers to a glass of whiskey; where he can take his ease with his wife, and perhaps listen to a bit of music.'[51] If drink shops were to be abolished and replaced by supervised centres for refreshment and social intercourse, then private interest had to be removed.

The campaign also had wider support. In particular, there were a number of religious interests in favour of public ownership. It was believed that the public house was a social necessity for the working class and therefore the way forward was through improvement under State direction, and not prohibition. The comments of the Dean of Manchester, W. S. Swayne, are suggestive:

> Temperance Reformers in general will do well to support the programme of the Labour Party. Organized Labour has the highest interest in promoting true temperance. It understands the conditions. It is dealing with a problem which vitally affects Labour. It is entirely futile to-day to suppose that any temperance legislation has a chance which is not supported by organized labour. It is earnestly to be hoped that the Labour Party will not relax its efforts until the reasonable and constructive policy . . . is brought to fruition.[52]

Even temperance organizations, such as the Temperance Legislation League, and Conservative periodicals like the *Spectator* added their weight behind the case for State control.

Undoubtedly in the early 1920s there was widespread support for the Campaign, and in anticipating the formation of a Labour Government the chances of progress appeared good. However, there was a failure to extend State purchase. The reason for this was not the weakness or apathy of those who argued for nationalization, but rather the opposition of the majority of the British people and indeed thousands of Labour supporters. There was very little political mileage to be made out of public ownership. Also, it has to be remembered that drinking habits were reformed in the years after the first world war, for with the growth of alternative leisure activities consumption fell, whilst spontaneous movements for public-house improvement by the private drink trade must have undermined much of the case for State control. Yet, this is not to argue that State control was without any success. The Carlisle scheme remained throughout the interwar years. By the late 1920s the State possessed properties worth about £900,000 and a trade yielding an annual profit of approximately £60,000.[53] Not only was the scheme commercially viable, but it was also an important piece of social reform, leading to a reduction of licences, favourable conditions of employment, increased sobriety and the improved pub. As such the Carlisle experiment was the citadel of the public ownership case throughout the 1920s.[54] In 1932 the Royal Commission on Licensing accepted the principle of public ownership, though only Lady Simon claimed that nationalization offered the main solution to the drink problem. It is true that apart from one or two contributions from the pen of J. J. Mallon the Campaign waned after 1930, but even then there is some evidence to suggest that other municipal authorities were keen to follow the Carlisle example.[55]

The British Broadcasting Corporation (BBC)

The most significant instance of public provision and management of leisure was in the field of broadcasting. The British Broadcasting Company was formed in 1922 as a cartel, consisting of a number of wireless manufacturers. It had a working capital of £60,000, with revenues derived from royalties on the sale of receiving sets, and half of the ten shilling licence fee paid to the post office by those with a wireless. Initially there were just five stations – London, Birmingham, Manchester, Newcastle and Cardiff – but gradually broadcasting increased in scope. Although the Company was a private concern, it was dependent upon the State. In the first place, the Government provided the Company with an exclusive licence to send out wireless programmes. But more important still, it was the Postmaster General who was the final arbiter when any question was raised as to what kind of matter was broadcast.[56] Despite this degree of public control, there were pressures to extend State involvement. The Crawford Committee on the future of broadcasting, though paying tribute to commercial achievements, thus rejected a free and uncontrolled system, and instead 'proposed that broadcasting be conducted by a Public Corporation acting as a trustee for the national interest, and consisting of a Board of Governors responsible for seeing that Broadcasting was carried out as a public service'.[57] Consequently, on 1 January 1927 the four-year-old British Broadcasting Company was transformed into the first major British public corporation, the BBC.

The State had ultimate responsibility for the management and effective operation of the Corporation. There were a number of indirect controls.[58] First, the Corporation was run by a Board of five governors, in effect appointed by the Postmaster General who was responsible for the BBC in Parliament. The Government thus had the opportunity to fashion the behaviour of the Board by its appointments policy. In the first years of existence it is perhaps indicative of Government aims and objectives that members of the Board were rather safe and conservative appointments. There was Lord Clarendon, a civil commissioner during the General Strike; Lord Gainford, a leading coal-owner; H. A. L. Fisher, an academic and architect of the 1918 Education Act; and J. H. Whitley, a Liberal MP and Speaker of the House of Commons. And the choices from the Labour Movement were hardly threats to the established order: Ethel Snowden, a temperance advocate and executive committee member of the Young Women's Christian Association, and Mary Agnes Hamilton, a journalist and daughter of a Professor of Logic. Second, the BBC was financially dependent upon the State. It was financed by licence fees again paid to the Post Office by the owners of wireless sets; and if the Government of the day was displeased with any aspect of Corporation policy or programme scheduling then presumably it could have threatened to reduce or delay increases in licence fees. This may well have been one of the reasons why programme builders and controllers had more power in the hierarchy than producers, particularly when it is considered that the State had the right to veto material to be broadcast. Third, there were facilities for review and no permanent licence to broadcast. The original royal charter provided a licence of ten years' duration. In effect this meant that the BBC had to be careful not to offend the Government of the day, or indeed any powerful interest groups, if it was to survive radical change when the licence came up for renewal.

Given the sources of State control it is hardly surprising that attention was drawn to the political bias of the BBC. The Labour Movement was particularly hostile. In very general terms popular broadcasting, in the 'dissemination of information, education and entertainment', was seen to discriminate against Labour. Trade unionists and members of all the main Socialist parties drew attention to the discriminatory policy of the BBC: a tool of the Establishment, an instrument of the National Government, the censor of working-class ideals and aspirations, and even the publicizer of Fascist events on the continent. In fact, although Labour came to accept broadcasting policy, there were still protests about the class bias of the Corporation in the post-1945 period.[59]

It does appear, however, that labour's claims were somewhat exaggerated. The State was always reluctant to impose sanctions on the BBC, even less to dictate programme content. In reality, the Corporation retained a great deal of autonomy, especially as the first Director-General, J. C. W. Reith, was staunchly independent. He insisted that broadcasting should be a public service, designed not merely for entertainment, but also for the preservation of the highest cultural standards. Moreover, political broadcasting, which had been restored in February 1928, far from being a form of discrimination, was as democratic as any of the other institutions in British society. In the campaign leading up to the 1929 General Election the (Conservative) Government and opposition parties were given equal air time. Indeed, the BBC itself regarded these broadcasts as contributing to the democratic process:

More political information from authoritative sources was, in fact, communicated by broadcasting to the mass of the people in the course of this election than on any previous occasion. Another effect of broadcasting on politics was observed in a new mood of close and silent attention at election meetings – a mood which Lord Linlithgow, in a letter to the *Times*, ascribed to the educational effect of the policy of the BBC. It would seem that the increased popularity of broadcast talks had fostered concentration and attentive listening, and this reacted upon political assemblages, making them much freer from noisy and irrelevant interruption than ever before.[60]

The BBC may have perpetuated the *status quo* and attempted to build a social consensus, but this is not the same as overt bias against the Labour interest. In fact, criticism of programmes came from the Right, as well as the Left. No doubt this was due to the fact that more time was devoted 'to the expression of new ideas and the advocacy of change in social and other spheres, than to the defence of orthodoxy and stability'.[61]

As far as entertainment is concerned, the BBC clearly catered for a range of interests. This is not surprising as the essential demand placed on radio was for entertainment. The share which radio took from the increasing leisure time varied according to socio-economic factors, but it is fairly clear that, apart from reading, it did not take people away from other amusements.[62] In fact, the Corporation found it difficult to cover all sport, as to take one example, the Football League frequently banned broadcasts of matches. Of those cultural activities covered there is much to suggest that the BBC did a lot to popularize music and drama. Radio drama achieved a fine professional competence, while a BBC symphony orchestra was created under Adrian Boult. Not only this, light entertainment programmes brought American dance music and popular songs into British homes, and towards the end of the 1930s made variety artists and comedians such as Arthur Askey leading personalities.

It has already been established that the number of licences increased. Even the poorer classes without a wireless at home had access to a set, maybe through listener groups which were proliferating at this time, or through other forms of collective provision – charitable bodies saw to it that miners' institutes in the South Wales valleys had radio sets.[63] In response to this rising demand the Corporation had to improve its service and increase the range of programmes on offer. Increased provision involved further recruitment so that the BBC staff rose from 773 in 1926 to 5,100 in 1938. A more efficient administrative structure evolved, and since broadcasting depended upon the services of engineers and programme builders efficient co-operation was essential.[64] All this points to the lengths to which the State would go to cater for people's spare time.

As with legislation and municipal provision for recreation and culture, State control of broadcasting helped to shape the development of leisure. State provision and regulation took many forms, but in general terms the main trend was for the extension of the State's sphere of influence. In short, the State made a greater impact on leisure than it had ever done before. Notions of social control and the desire to shape proletarian recreational and cultural patterns still had some influence on State policy, but more important was the broad collectivist trend of the time. General shifts in the relationship of the State to the economy and society inevitably had an effect on leisure, particularly the new forms of the cinema and broadcasting. In spite of the fact that *laissez faire* attitudes were still influential – the State was sometimes reluctant to provide official control machinery unless it was absolutely necessary – official attitudes and responses were increasingly collectivist. One positive sign of this trend was the call from many directions for the creation of a Ministry of Sport or Leisure. Some working-class leisure activities were constrained by State intervention. For example, there were restrictions on the workers' right of access to the countryside. Yet, despite some draconian controls, there were social reforms which undoubtedly improved the lot of the working class. There is a need to make qualifications for the shortage of public facilities in many areas of the country, but with protective legislation and municipal provision there is clear evidence of improvement. It is indeed a sign of the times that just before the outbreak of the second world war the first Access to Mountains Bill received the Royal Assent, while England's first National Forest Park was formally opened.

5
Work, leisure and unemployment

Probably the most significant economic and social problem of the inter-war years was mass unemployment. Although there is an absence of satisfactory statistics which makes comparison over time difficult, it is evident that unemployment increased significantly over the 1920s and 1930s. Whereas in the thirty years or so before 1914 the unemployment rate averaged about 4.8 per cent, in the years between the wars it averaged 14 per cent of the insured workforce. Moreover, by 1932 the unemployment rate reached a peak of 22.1 per cent, meaning that nearly 3 million were without work. What made the situation worse was that unemployment was concentrated in the so-called depressed regions of Central Scotland, the North East coast and South Wales, areas stifled by the economic decline of the old staples – coalmining, shipbuilding, and iron and steel. Those areas in the South and Midlands which benefited from the establishment of the new industries were less badly hit. It has therefore been claimed that on average in the period 1929–36 22.7 per cent of the labour force was unemployed in the North East, but only 11.1 per cent in the South East. Not surprisingly, there were also considerable variations between towns. In 1934, whereas 68 per cent of the insured labour force in the N.E. town of Jarrow was without work, the figure for Coventry was only 5 per cent.[1] One further important point is that superimposed on the general level of unemployment were more specific problems such as unemployed school leavers and prolonged or long-term unemployment.

Given this problem of unemployment, any study of leisure has to distinguish between consumers of leisure who were employed and those who were unemployed. It has already been claimed that the unemployed failed to enjoy all of the fruits of the commercial leisure boom of the period. Yet this analysis has to be taken a little further. It is appropriate to examine the ways in which the workless spent their enforced leisure. Was the leisure of the unemployed radically different from those in work? Were the unemployed able to use their time creatively or did it lead to feelings of social impotence? Was unemployment a threat to the established mores of society such as the work ethic? All interesting questions, but before they can be answered something must be said about the relationship between work and leisure.

Work and leisure

If we are not aware of the importance of work (or paid employment) in everyday life then it is virtually impossible to assess the significance of and the developments in leisure. After all, leisure may be described as that free time left over after work. As Denys Harding succinctly expressed it in the 1930s: 'Work, then, is what you do to get your living, and leisure is the rest of your time.'[2] Sociologists have carried out extensive research into the relationship between work and leisure. The studies of Stanley Parker are particularly suggestive. He has claimed that the work situation has an important influence on leisure, and that there are basically three forms of relationship between work and leisure. First, a relationship of opposition where there is a sharp distinction between work and leisure. In physically demanding occupations such as coalmining or deep-sea fishing work is regarded with hostility and there is a tendency for the individual to use leisure as an opportunity for escape. Second, a relationship of extension, where work is regarded as intrinsically satisfying and carried over into leisure activities. Third, a relationship of neutrality where leisure is neither a compensation for the inadequacies of work nor similar in content to work.[3]

As far as the inter-war years are concerned, it is of course very difficult to find evidence to test out Parker's categorization of work/leisure relationships. Nonetheless, it is certainly possible to suggest that the patterns of inter-war employment and work impinged on leisure. In very elementary terms, workers had to sell their labour power in order to earn a wage and so pay for the necessities of life. This imposed a number of constraints on leisure, not least of which was the length of the working day. As Gareth Stedman Jones has pointed out, 'Leisure time is clearly constricted by type and hours of work.'[4] From a Marxist perspective, Capitalist society is said to alienate or dehumanize individuals, in the sense that the objects that are produced are alien to them. Thus, 'because labour in capitalist society is alienated, "not-labour" appears as "freedom and happiness". As the worker becomes alienated of his labour, the activities outside it become more important to him.'[5] In other words, leisure is regarded as a compensation for alienated work. It is true that people have a great deal more autonomy at work than is sometimes credited, and workers are often able to use work time creatively for their own purposes. Consequently, their choice of leisure activity was not necessarily a negative response to the dictates, monotony and alienation of work. Yet, notwithstanding this, it may well have been the case that changes in the work process in the inter-war years, such as the introduction of conveyor belts, speed up, and new kinds of machinery, meant that workers retreated even further into leisure. Therefore, Parker's typology of contrast or opposition in work/leisure relationships may have some relevance for an analysis of the 1920s and 1930s.

Indeed, a study of the machine and the worker made by Barratt Brown in 1934 presented evidence to suggest that the content of work and leisure was deliberately different, and most important of all the main function of leisure was recuperation. As a worker in a mass production factory wrote: 'From talk and association with other work people, I would say that much of the lust for outdoor games, speeding on the road, and sensationalism of the films, is due to the desire to give vent to pent up feelings of monotony and boredom.' Second, the case of a miner:

My work incapacitates me for the full enjoyment of my leisure time. At the conclusion of my day's work I do not feel like indulging in much exercise, either physical or mental. Consequently, much of my leisure time, except for an occasional visit to the cinema, attendance at W.E.A. classes during the winter months, and occasional reading, is frittered away in lounging aimlessly about.

And third, the case of a smith's striker:

> I must admit that furnace work has sometimes compelled me
> to go to the cinema because I have felt physically tired and
> mentally indolent and wanted only to sink into a comfortable
> seat and be entertained with a minimum effort on my part.[6]

In a slightly different context, there appears to have been a strong
relationship between heavy manual work and heavy drinking.
Miners or steel workers working long hours, often in very hot
conditions, thus used to drink not only as a form of leisure, but
also as refreshment.

For those workers in typically extreme occupations such as
mining or smelting, it is possible that work activities inhibited
leisure during the week. After work, leisure was simply used for
recuperation, relaxation and sleep. However, at the weekends
there was a sense of freedom and more active use of leisure. This
was made clear by Herbert Mannion who was employed in a gas
works:

> It is a wonderful feeling when you wake up to realize that it
> is Saturday night. A thrill akin to exhilaration affects me . . .
> and when I put on my best suit I feel 'champion'. . . . The
> people are obviously in possession of themselves, and full of
> good cheer. Saturday night is the time to let themselves go:
> no work on Sunday to get up for, so a few extra drinks make
> no difference next morning, when the long Sunday-lie-in is
> their due after a week of attending to the factory buzzer.[7]

In such cases leisure was being used as a corrective to the work
situation, a time for rest, it is true, but also a way of asserting a
degree of independence in everyday life.

There is some foundation for believing that the quality of leisure
was influenced by the kind of work undertaken. The leisure of
both London and Liverpool dockers, Birmingham and Manchester
fitters, and Kent and Durham miners was dependent upon the
nature of employment, the permanence of contract, the casual
and cyclical aspects of the job, the hours worked, the intensity
and pace of work and a number of other factors. While the leisure
of the privileged classes was spent hunting and shooting, yachting,

sailing and cruising, ski-ing in the Alps, and in twentieth-century versions of the Grand Tour, the leisure of certain categories of workers was used for purposes of rejuvenation for the next period of work.[8] It does therefore seem that Dr William Boyd, a Scottish educationalist, was near the mark in 1937 when he asserted that 'leisure-time interests' were an escape from work, 'compensations for what is lacking in the regimented life'.[9]

There is, however, a danger of oversimplification in any argument which emphasizes a complete and sharp distinction between leisure and work. In the first place, during the years between the wars there was a decline in those occupations which were physically demanding and most likely to give rise to a relationship of opposition between work and leisure. Thus, there was a decline in the number of manual workers as a proportion of the total UK labour force. Inevitably, the demise of the old heavy industries brought with it a reduction in employment levels. In the period 1920 to 1938, the number of coalminers fell from 1,083,000 to 674,600, those in iron and steel from 527,200 to 342,100, and in shipbuilding from 282,200 to 129,100. On the other hand, in the same period the number of workers in the distributive trade increased from 1,773,200 to 2,438,200.[10] Such changes in the employment structure must have had implications for the work/leisure couplet.

Second, it is possible that the leisure pursuits of non-manual employees such as clerks or administrators had much in common with their work. That is, the work/leisure relationship was one of extension rather than opposition. Moreover, as the research of Ross McKibbon has demonstrated, many working-class hobbies, far from being a compensation for work, were actually an extension of work: carpenters and painters practised their crafts at home, and agricultural labourers even had their own allotments. In other words, 'the relation between work and hobbies is as likely to be "organic" as dialectic.'[11]

Leisure and unemployment

Despite the fact that many workers used leisure as a time of creativity and fulfilment, it is true that work was the foundation of working-class consciousness. Since the Industrial Revolution the British proletariat had internalized the work ethic which, rooted in the ideas of puritanism and Capitalism, exerted an all-pervasive influence on their thoughts, actions and experiences. The work ethic meant different things to different people and any generalization would have to take into account the complexities of age, gender, region and occupation. Nonetheless, eight hours plus in the hostile surrounding of the furnace, the dark of the pit or the intensity of the shop floor was bound to have significant repercussions on everyday life. It was not strange that work helped to mould personality and character, and produce attitudes of mind which dictated the particular nature of individual, family and community life styles. Work was, and is, the provider of social and cultural meanings, influencing the way in which people perceive the outside world:

> [the] work situation provides the most important set of
> conditions shaping the social imagery of industrial man for it
> is at work that relations and experiences of superiority and
> inferiority, of solidarity and separateness, of frustration and
> achievement are most persuasive, most viable and therefore
> most influential.[12]

Thus, in the mining novels of Lewis Jones, *Cwmardy* and *We Live*, work served as the central theme, providing form and reference points to the wider cultural milieu. The coalface was the focal point of Big Jim Roberts' reality. His place in the pit represented more than just physical energy; he had 'ripped it down and timbered it . . . risked his body and slogged his guts out to keep it tidy', it was his place, a part of his life.[13] Moreover, the masculinity of the working environment was all-important in the constitution of the family economy. Generally speaking, though there were exceptions to the rule, the division of labour meant that the husband was the breadwinner, a fact which subordinated the family, and especially the wife, to the authority of the male head of the household. The husband *worked* for the family wage, and from this simple fact a whole pattern of familial and social relationships emerged.[14]

If work provided meaning in life, life without work must have led to disorientation and social dislocation. For those imbued with the work ethic unemployment was a form of deviancy or moral condemnation. In other words, without work many in the community were lost and empty. As sociologists have informed us, a forced break from work 'is at least a deep personal shock and can assume the proportions of a national disaster in people's minds'.[15] This was certainly the case in the 1920s and 1930s, when unemployment was regarded as a stigma, particularly if friends, relatives and neighbours were in work. This is how George Orwell saw the problem:

> So long as Bert Jones across the street is still at work, Alf Smith is bound to feel himself dishonoured and a failure. Hence that frightful feeling of impotence and despair which is almost the worst evil of unemployment – far worse than any hardship, worse than the demoralization of enforced idleness, and only less bad than the physical degeneracy of Alf Smith's children on the P.A.C.[16]

Being out-of-work could undermine feelings of respectability, status and masculinity, and bring into disrepute the man's position within the family.

Unemployment meant dependence upon State benefits and these were often regarded as poor relief or charity, adding further to feelings of humiliation and shame. Moreover, the traditional role of the husband/father as head of the household was called into question, particularly if the female members of the family remained in work. Indeed, on balance, the actual number of women in gainful employment rose during the period. Only in the textile towns of Lancashire, where women had always composed a significant proportion of the labour force, 'was it more tolerable to let a woman be the principal wage-earner. But generally the loss of status and self-respect inevitably following from unemployment was more galling if wives or daughters remained in work.'[17] It is also appropriate at this point to stress that it was women who often bore the brunt of unemployment. Unemployment does not only present difficulties to those usually at work, but also to women in the home. As a number of the social investigations of the time made clear, it was the women who often had to do without in order to keep the rest of the family reasonably happy and well-fed. In addition, according to Kate Mourby's study of the wives of the Teeside unemployed, when a man became unemployed he was faced with the problems of a loss of occupation and responsibility, but precisely the opposite difficulty was presented to his wife. She was called upon to carry out her domestic responsibilities with less money (which inevitably meant extra work) and in many cases to find some way of earning money to keep the family.[18]

Prolonged unemployment in particular must have been very difficult to cope with. For those who had been out-of-work for a year or more there was little hope for the future, especially as they were unlikely to find work again. There were 480,000 long-term unemployed in Great Britain by 1933, concentrated in the mining, shipbuilding and cotton regions. After years of employment being jobless meant that the routine of daily life was disrupted. Most of all, long stretches of unemployment led to various kinds of nervous and psychological complaints, such as psychoneurosis. As the Pilgrim Trust pointed out:

Man, single, aged 40. In normal health until unemployed. After four years' unemployment complained of choking and pains in the head, but specialist reported no lesion. Later developed alleged throat trouble, but again specialist found no physical signs. Finally, had severe stomach pains for which there was no organic explanation. Only psychological explanation adequate.[19]

There was even a positive correlation between the unemployment rate and the incidence of suicide.

Returning to leisure. What can be said about the effect of unemployment on leisure? If leisure is that time left over after work then it would seem that the unemployed had more leisure than the average worker.[20] However, 'leisure is more than just a space of time: it implies relative freedom from constraint. Unfortunately, the unemployed are constrained in several ways: financially, socially, morally and in terms of the structure of their daily lives.'[21] Moreover, if leisure is only possible in relation to work, then the leisure of the unemployed is not leisure at all. What we are really talking about is the enforced leisure of the unemployed.

Arnold Shimmin, an economics lecturer at the University of Leeds, expressed it in 1936 in the following way:

> Leisure is usually regarded as the opposite of work: a period of spare time in which to enjoy hobbies – golf, bridge, fishing, motoring, and the rest. While it is common ground that leisure and idleness are not identical, we cannot escape the fact that there is much enforced idleness to-day. Unemployment is an unsought and unwelcome type of leisure that is definitely a disadvantage to the persons concerned.[22]

During the 1930s there was a continuing debate about the enforced leisure of the unemployed. Most commentators agreed that unemployment seriously impaired the quality of leisure. For instance, in an editorial headed 'Leisure That Kills', the *Morning Post* went to great lengths to show that the leisure of the workless was a word without meaning; even the cinema or wireless could not solve the problem of unemployment.[23] And an even more scathing indictment came from the pen of J. G. Patterson of the Industrial Welfare Society:

> Enforced leisure is an embarrassment which only those who have experienced it can possibly understand. It is an imposition, and should be treated as such. It represents a problem, the seriousness of which is tragic. Loss of skill and morale, physical and mental deterioration in the mass, cannot be viewed with equanimity. We do not realise how much we like work until we have none. The hopelessness and weariness of 'going after the job you know isn't there' imposes a stern self-discipline. The strain of keeping up appearances is not the best mental preparation for cultural occupation. The intrinsic value of leisure to the individual under these circumstances is almost negligible. . . . Work is fundamental, there is no leisure without it.[24]

Contemporaries agreed that the leisure of the unemployed was qualitatively different from that of the employed.

It has been argued that for the majority unemployment meant apathy. Certainly, there was a degree of fatalism and obvious signs of listlessness and low morale. However, to classify the unemployed as apathetic is unfair. Photographs and other signs from the 1930s have been taken out of context and used to sustain a number of durable myths. In some cases leisure spaces were filled by staying in bed late and going to bed early, standing on the street corner, queueing at the labour exchange or simply lounging about, but to characterize the unemployed as being completely idle is a grave oversimplification. Many of the unemployed were able to assert a degree of independence in their lives. For those temporarily out-of-work unemployment may have been perceived as a kind of holiday, a time of relative freedom from the restrictions of work and an opportunity to follow individual interests and hobbies. Furthermore, the longer-term unemployed did not necessarily resign themselves to idleness, or accept their condition with equanimity. Since unemployment was a regional or local problem, the jobless shared common experiences, which made life somewhat more tolerable. In Liverpool, the Pilgrim Trust discovered that, in spite of deplorable environmental conditions, the permanently unemployed were not stigmatized by lounging at street corners or in front of the pub.[25] A significant proportion of the working class were able to overcome the debilitating nature of enforced leisure by the qualities of optimism, no matter how muted, humour and camaraderie, and collective social strength. From a slightly different perspective, relationships within some families were often cemented. Unemployed fathers had time in which to see to their children, and this was sometimes used creatively in the playing of games, taking long walks, and other forms of support for wives and children.[26]

It is also true to say that the unemployed were not far removed from the products and services of the leisure industry. Notwithstanding the fact that unemployment benefit was low, and that the out-of-work had very little money for leisure, there is evidence of some conspicuous consumption. Orwell's well-known diet of 'fish-and-chips, art-silk stockings, tinned salmon, cut-price chocolate . . . the movies, the radio, strong tea, and the Football Pools' thus fell within the income range of unemployed consumers.[27] As Charles Mowat has concluded, life was sustained by indulgence in such cheap luxuries.[28] In particular, the unemployed were able to visit the cinema and they were able to bet.

The cinema was perhaps the most important leisure institution of the inter-war years, and was within the reach of virtually everyone, including the unemployed. In fact, it is true to say that cinemas were as ubiquitous in the North as in the South – there were more cinema seats per head of the population in depressed North Wales with its dying slate industry than there were in the London area.[29] The unemployed in particular were able to take advantage of cheap rates for matinees. In depressed Bolton, which had twenty-two cinemas by the late 1930s, there was even a price war with rates for matinees at 3d to 4d. Not surprisingly, managers reported that matinees did reasonable trade, and indeed, 'all Bolton's cinemas appear to have done well, afternoon and evening, winter and summer during the 1930s.'[30] Elsewhere, at least 80 per cent of the unemployed youth in Liverpool and Glasgow visited the cinema at least once a week, while in Cardiff 52 per cent went to the cinema once a week, and about half of these twice a week.[31] In general, cinemas did not witness a reduction in trade because of unemployment.

There were a number of reasons why the unemployed used the cinema. Most of all it provided amusement and enjoyable leisure. Westerns and comedies provided some kind of escape from everyday problems. As the American social investigator E. W. Bakke found:

'What attracts you to the cinema?'. . . . 'The picture helps you live in another world for a little while. I almost feel I'm in the picture'. . . . 'Pictures are my first choice, because they make you think for a little while that life is all right.' 'The pictures remind you that things do go right for some folks, and it really makes you feel that things will go right for you too, because you put yourself in the place of the actors'. . .[32]

The unemployed, like other sections of the working class, demanded the right to fantasize and to laugh. As well as being a distraction from boredom the cinema was, like the public library, a place to keep warm during cold winter afternoons. And finally, young unemployed couples found it provided a social space for courting purposes.

Gambling was also popular amongst the out-of-work. Many of the social investigations found that gambling was a feature of unemployed life, in spite of and perhaps because of lack of money. As many historians have pointed out, the Liverpool unemployed, despite their hardships, still managed to enjoy 'the all-pervading atmosphere of football pools, greyhounds and horses'. Apparently, they were immersed in the football pools, and even though they often found it too expensive to actually watch league matches, they did await with anticipation the Saturday evening football scores.[33] Small bets were placed to provide yet another form of distraction from boredom, as well as offering the hope of adding to the family income through incidental winnings. Most of all, they brought some colour and excitement into mundane lives. In the view of J. B. Priestley: 'there is the fun of deciding on his horse, greyhound or football team; there is the excitement of the race or the match, even though he is not there himself; and then there is the possibility of winning ten or twenty sixpences.'[34]

The unemployed were not, however, heavy drinkers. Whilst some of the workless took to drinking, in general the evidence suggests that enforced leisure was used in other ways. According to E. W. Bakke drinking among the unemployed did not keep up as much as betting.[35] The high price of a pint was probably the main prohibitive influence. Indeed, it has been suggested that drunkenness was more likely in times of prosperity than depression. Hence, in 1927 when unemployment was 9.7 per cent of the insured population there were 65,166 convictions for drunkenness in England and Wales, whereas in 1932 when the unemployment rate was 22.1 per cent there were only 30,146 such convictions.[36] Figures for the depressed areas show much the same trend. Unemployment thus led to less drinking, not more. Having said this, a man or woman, hit by unemployment, could hardly be blamed if they did turn to drink. This is how Joe Corrie expressed it in his poem, 'He Drank His "Dole" ':

> He drank his 'dole' and went before the Court
> All eyes were flashed on him, a scorching fire,
> 'Low wretch!' the judge declared, 'less than the dirt!
> Had I my way I'd hang you to that spire.
> And let you rot such rascals as you stink
> In decent nostrils. A nation gives you life,
> And yet you go and waste it all in drink,
> And burden more the nation with your wife.
> The jail's the place for you. Three months, and hard.'
> And down the steps he goes, a shadow man,

Thin clad, and cold, eyes furtive as a bird,
Long-haired and dirty. And the cold eyes scan
Him as he goes; that 'brute without a soul',
And not a one there thinks to blame the 'dole'.[37]

Aside from the cinema and gambling, it is also likely that some of the unemployed went to football matches or dance halls and had access to other forms of leisure. The workless were obviously not exactly outside the commercial system of leisure. However, they were principally occupied by the non-commercial activities of self-provided leisure; that is, organized activity at unemployed clubs of a social, occupational or political kind, and in the more spontaneous activity of a collective or individual nature such as street betting or illicit trading. It was this self-provided leisure at unemployed clubs which allowed for a certain degree of creative expression.

Unemployed clubs

With the Wall Street Crash of 1929 and the subsequent world economic recession, unemployment in all the major western industrial countries increased beyond politically acceptable levels. As already suggested, by 1933 the number of people registered as unemployed in Britain had reached nearly three million. Governments, including the Labour administration of 1929–31, were attached to the tenets of financial orthodoxy and failed to implement the reflationary ideas of Mosley, Keynes, the New Deal or, for that matter, of Macmillan and the other young Conservatives. The National Government did recognize that the distressed regions needed preferential treatment, hence the creation of the Government-assisted Special Areas of 1934, and the few concessions to programmes of public works. However, it appears that far more encouragement was given to charitable schemes for the unemployed. From the early 1930s charitable concerns increasingly provided opportunities for a range of activities, so that the unemployed would not idle their time away.[38]

During the 1920s voluntary attempts to help the workless were mainly carried out through the various Lord Mayor's funds which operated in a number of towns. There was little by way of a permanent, national and well co-ordinated scheme in existence. The real beginnings of voluntary provision for the unemployed had to wait until the last years of the decade, when the Society of Friends founded an educational settlement in the Rhondda, and the Joint Committee of the Carnegie United Kingdom Trustees and the National Council of Social Service (NCSS) began educational work among unemployed miners. Development was stimulated and further encouraged at the beginning of 1932, when a speech by the Prince of Wales, the patron of the NCSS, urged the need for voluntary social service.[39] The response was overwhelming, with over 700 schemes set up in the next few months, as well as a Government invitation to the National Council to act as the central agency in the co-ordination of local projects.[40] Thereafter, the movement grew rapidly, reaching the peak of its activity between 1936 and 1938 with a membership of about 200,000. Clearly then, the Council did achieve some success, but what kinds of opportunities were offered in order to keep the unemployed 'busy'?

The aim of virtually all the voluntary organizations was one of occupation, recreation and education. As far as occupation was concerned, the intention was not to compete with the production of those in work, but rather to provide work of an amateur character. According to *The Times*, 'the occupations most commonly practised were 'boot repairing and carpentry' and to a lesser extent 'the making of baskets, mats, rugs, toys and cardboard models, metalwork, simple tailoring, fretwork and linocutting'.[41] Recreational activities were similarly wide-ranging – sport, socials, physical training (especially after the Physical Training and Recreation Act of 1937), outdoor activities and general entertainments. Although recreation was circumscribed by a lack of money, a shortage of premises, and the fear of the 'dismal, smoky den where men play unendingly with a greasy pack of cards',[42] there were some notable achievements, especially in the organization of holiday camps for the workless. For example, in May 1934 *The Manchester Guardian* reported that 2,000 unemployed men from Lancashire and Cheshire were to be given a fortnight's summer holiday in camps arranged by the NCSS, at places such as the Lake District, Marple, Hayfield, Mold and Northwich, where recreation and guided tours would be the main features of interest.[43] The educational work of the National

Council of Social Service included academic subjects, as well as music, drama and art. Notwithstanding the point made by the Archbishop of York that there was a danger of education degenerating into mere entertainment, educational programmes were introduced.[44] For instance, in 1933–4 the LCC, in response to appeals made by the London Council for Voluntary Occupation, voted £5,000 for day classes for unemployed men and women.[45] As a result of this kind of work, as early as April 1933, there were 729 occupation centres, 636 recreation centres and 157 centres providing educational facilities under the auspices of the NCSS. Affiliated bodies such as the York Council of Social Service had a football team, a fishing club, a dramatic society and library, organized socials and concert parties, and received addresses on science, art and travel.[46] Some unemployed clubs and centres benefited from special BBC talks on industrial questions, sports and foreign affairs, while others benefited from the Library Association's national book appeal for the out-of-work.[47] The voluntary schemes were financed in two main ways. In the first place, there were charitable donations from organizations, individuals and the royal family – the king and queen donated £100 and £50 respectively in the later part of 1933.[48] Second, financial contributions were made by statutory bodies. Thus, between November 1932 and April 1935 the Council distributed more than £79,000 in Ministry of Labour grants, and £400,000 had been raised by voluntary effort.[49] The Council also received monies from the Commissioner for the Special Areas which in the year ending March 1937 enabled voluntary service groups to spend approximately £129,000 on school camps for boys and girls, £40,000 on adolescent welfare work, £20,000 on occupational clubs and women's holidays, £15,000 on education and so on.[50] By 1938 the total figure spent had reached £220,000.[51]

There were, of course, other unemployed organizations besides those under the umbrella of the NCSS. For instance, one body, the League of the Unemployed, had as its main objective the need for 'unarmed military technique', while another, the British Executive Employment Society, set up clubrooms so that unemployed black-coated workers could 'get away from that sense of isolation which they feel so acutely'.[52] Also interesting is the Over Thirty Association, founded in the early 1930s with support from a number of well-known public figures, including Lady Astor,

Margaret Bondfield and Ellen Wilkinson. Ostensibly, the Association aimed to help those women over thirty who had lost their jobs. A club was set up in London which provided sewing classes, wireless and gramophone concerts, travel talks, lectures and community singing, as well as facilities for meals, clothes at economical prices and an advisory bureau on employment.[53]

It would seem that unemployed clubs were sponsored by the middle classes as a way of solving some of the problems associated with enforced leisure, especially idleness, boredom and apathy. This did not mean, however, that the unemployed were not able to use club facilities for their own ends. Indeed, they were able to exert a degree of autonomy and independence in their recreational and educational endeavours. Many learned new skills and discovered new talents and interests. Others regained confidence and hope for the future.

Moreover, leading members of the social service movement stressed the co-operative nature of club work, where the unemployed themselves were in control and links were forged with the local community. Alexander Dunlop Lindsay, the Master of Balliol College, is a case in point. During the 1930s he held quite senior positions within the NCSS hierarchy, at one time serving as chairman of the Unemployment Committee. He strongly supported the idea of community service and, in this regard, promoted various occupational schemes. First connected with social service in South Wales, Lindsay was instrumental in setting up the People's Service Club in Lincoln which, by providing opportunities for the unemployed to use their skills, was able to help the community. Bedrests were made for old people at the Poor Law institute, children's boots were repaired and a voluntary nursery school for the children of the unemployed was set up, for which the club made all the equipment.[54] For Lindsay, the Lincoln experiment and others, though not solving the problem of unemployment, made a vast difference to the lives of men and women who joined: the unemployed were able to benefit the community and at the same time benefit themselves by occupying hours of enforced leisure. In Lindsay's opinion, this was not only right and proper, but was also an extension of humanitarian principles and, it must be stressed, the ideals of co-operation, fellowship and association. In essence, he wished to democratize voluntary service and make the unemployed club self-governing; in this way he hoped to emasculate the idea of voluntary help as a part of upper-class evangelicalism. His support for social service did not mean that he rejected wider State help, for he believed that the root causes of unemployment could only be solved by Government intervention. Lindsay suggested that voluntarism had a role to play alongside State action, by encouraging the unemployed to help themselves in as democratic a way as possible.[55]

The trade unions were suspicious of the voluntary schemes for there was a genuine fear that their occupational side would direct work away from the commercial market, help undercut union rates of pay and so maintain the prevailing levels of unemployment. In the words of Lewis Blackwood, the chairman of the Monmouthshire Federation of Trades and Labour Councils, there was a danger that the social service movement might 'break up all wage rates and trade union conditions'.[56] Trade unions also pointed to the palliative tendencies of social service, which, by excusing the Government from further intervention, were said to undermine the need for more positive measures of employment creation. As Ellen Wilkinson wrote at the end of the 1930s, the social service movement 'has not been concerned with a frontal attack on the problem'.[57] It is not surprising, therefore, that the TUC was reluctant to co-operate with the NCSS and officially refused to participate in what amounted to unemployment being assigned to a charitable organization.[58] Yet, despite national directives to the contrary, it is evident that various trades councils at grass roots level were quite prepared to offer assistance to the NCSS. In reply to a TUC questionnaire of 1933, out of 167 trades councils who replied, fifty-four were said to be 'directly associated with social service schemes'.[59]

Moreover, the unemployed were also able to use their time in some creative or constructive way within the structures of the working-class movement. During the course of 1932, in order to meet the increasingly demanding problem of enforced leisure, a number of TUC inspired Unemployment Associations were established.[60] Although it is no coincidence that these were set up at the same time as the ideas of voluntary social service were spreading, they also sought to keep the out-of-work in touch with the trade unions, and provide opportunities for recreation and education. The Associations initially numbered sixty-four in 1932, but increased to around 100 in 1938, by which time they were said to cater for about 400,000 unemployed workers.[61]

The TUC took up the call for recreation by establishing links with the National Playing Fields Association. In mid-1932, the Association had been invited by the TUC General Council 'to co-operate in the admirable steps being taken . . . to organize suitable facilities for the recreation of the unemployed', and this is exactly what happened, with forty to fifty county branches of the Association co-operating with local trade unions.[62]Help was given to the Unemployed Associations in the form of sports equipment – twenty-six sets of indoor games, thirty sets of cricket equipment and eight footballs in 1937.[63] Clearly then, the trade unions, through the Unemployed Associations, regarded the provision of recreational amenities as an important contribution in the fight against unemployment.

The Communist-inspired National Unemployed Workers' Movement (NUWM) regarded social service bodies as a despicable form of charity mongering, pacifying revolt and drawing the unemployed away from the militant fight for jobs. However, they, too, provided clubs and facilities for the unemployed, whilst continuing their struggle against the means test, poverty, and so on. According to Joe Norman, the Workers' Art Club in Salford was the headquarters of the Unemployed Workers' Movement, 'where the mass of membership were deeply embroiled in some kind of Socialist action'. Yet the club had its social side, with a bar (Tetley's best mild at 2½d per glass), a huge billiard table, a dance floor (the club had its own dance band), and a fully equipped gym for boxing and wrestling.[64]

From early 1933 the NUWM, under the pressure of the social service and trades council schemes, acknowledged that the 'movement must take up the question of sports clubs, libraries, etc., that we must compel the authorities to grant us halls to be used as headquarters and to be used, in every possible way for the social life of the unemployed. . .'[65]. A detailed memorandum was prepared, in which a plan was outlined to counteract the social service centres by means of the acquisition of club premises, the creation of a Social Committee to organize entertainments, the provision of libraries, the development of study circles and musical bands, and the creation of a Sports Sub-Committee to arrange physical training sessions, cycling clubs and sports days. As long as this was organized on democratic, working-class lines, the memo concluded, there was no reason to discourage social activity.[66] Although there was no desire for this type of work to become the 'predominant feature' of the NUWM – it had to be combined with mass activity on the streets – there does seem to have been some progress.[67] Perhaps the most popular and the most successful of NUWM leisure activities was the yearly workers' camp. These summer camps were designed to counteract the camps organized by the charitable bodies and the Transfer Instructional Centres, the so-called 'slave camps' set up by the Ministry of Labour, to act as a forum of discussion and recruitment, to provide political education and develop class understanding of society.[68] The first such camp was organized at Eastchurch, the Isle of Wight, and by all accounts it was a success. It lasted ten days, was very cheap (probably the most important consideration), with rambles, boxing, political discussion and the singing of revolutionary songs the order of the day.[69] Such camps were a hive of Communist politics, but, above all else, they made it possible for groups of the unemployed to enjoy at a reasonable price an annual summer holiday, an opportunity that they might not otherwise have had.

In clubs organized by the Labour Movement, as well as the social service movement, the unemployed were able to use their enforced leisure time creatively. Even the apolitical majority of workers may have responded positively to unemployment. In the North East of England, for instance, the out-of-work made a significant contribution to community spirit by banding together in jazz bands. Informal music provided an increasing number of unemployed men and women with an inexpensive hobby to occupy their time. The bands were a feature of cultural events such as carnivals and clearly brought colour and excitement into many people's lives.[70] All this is not to argue that unemployment did not bring with it physical and mental distress, but rather that a considerable section of the unemployed were able to resist adversity with courage, and use their enforced leisure constructively in recreation, handicrafts, educational courses and political activity. Further, established patterns of working-class life survived and communities did not break up.

A challenge to the work ethic?

With so many people out-of-work it is possible that dominant attitudes and ideas were called into question. In particular, there was some concern that the unemployed would become work-shy and that the work ethic would be undermined. Although the values associated with work were extraordinarily durable, there is some evidence to suggest that work was no longer regarded as the centre and meaning of life. Thus small groups of men and women chose to withdraw from society and 'do their own thing'. In a slightly different context some of the unemployed began to participate in what is now called the black economy, adding to their unemployment assistance by betting, keeping greyhounds, hawking, or crime. Most of all, the work ethic was critically examined by such writers as Delisle Burns, who suggested that 'the busy bee is no longer an adequate moral guide', and the puritanical attitude to work was an 'obsolete habit of mind which prevented our seeing that we are faced by a new form of the problem of leisure'.[71] The deeply held views about work were indeed being questioned.

If the status bestowed on work was to be modified, then some of the myths connected with the work process had to be dissolved. In advocating full employment, some commentators fell into the trap of sentimentalizing and, at least by implication, ennobling the activity of work. The coal faces, the shipyards or the factory floor were often regarded as the loci of human capabilities and skills. In brief, the predominance of a set of assumptions about the character of work made it particularly difficult to advance alternative ideas. There were signs, however, that some writers were prepared to call into question the widely accepted intrinsic value of work. It was suggested that men and women were not bursting to work at all, but that rather they were glad to be free from work. As Donald Fraser wrote: 'I can imagine coal-miners who are glad to get above ground at the end of a shift, factory workers who are glad to get out of the stink of machinery into the fresh air, even sailors who are glad to plant their feet on dry land.'[72] Far from work being a place to exploit individual potential, many believed that it was a dehumanizing institution and even a destructive one. Various groups, including the Labour Party, were denounced for insisting on employment as an end in itself – the onus of consideration, it was argued, should be shifted from work to leisure. The journalist, Minnie Pallister, stressed that people had 'almost forgotten that Man is not born merely for work, that he should naturally enjoy rest, sport, and the beauties of a world which offers him a hundred joys from which to choose!'[73] This line of argument may not have been particularly original – Ruskin and Morris expressed such views in the nineteenth century – and might not have had extensive support, but it is still important as an expression of disenchantment with the notion of work for its own sake.

Under Capitalism people were, and are, directed at work, not in order to maximize their own pleasure, but in order to satisfy certain profit-making objectives. This makes for the imposition of a whole series of direct and indirect employment controls, rules and regulations, ranging from time discipline and the division of labour to a plethora of production targets, which effectively restrict the freedom of the individual. The inter-war years witnessed the further development of capitalism with a human face – industrial canteens, improvements in health and safety precautions, recreational facilities – yet welfarism did not free the labour force from the restrictions of the working environment. It is, of course, simply not true that the working class have been passive, subordinate agents of Capitalist production for, as the research of Richard Price has shown, men and women have been able 'to resist and obstruct capitalist domination of the labour process' in a variety of ways.[74] In fact, it can be argued that leisure was taken in working hours in the form of conversation, practical jokes, horseplay, extra long breaks and so on. Even so, there was critical comment about the constraints of the work process. Even the moderate Union of Post Office Workers suggested that employers perceived men and women simply as labour, a commodity which could be bought just like any other factor of production.[75] Trade unions and other bodies thus argued that workers had to be given more control over their own lives – they had to be given more leisure. Workers were beginning to claim that the normal bargaining points of wages and conditions would not suffice. In the words of one member of the National Union of Railwaymen:

With all our mistaken ideas and our diversity of opinion on things pertaining to our daily lives as railwaymen, it behoves us all to recognise that we belong to a class that stands in economic subjection to the master class, and we have arrived at that stage when we should no longer be content to merely insist on our wages being risen to keep pace with the rise in the cost of living, and so on our present basis keep toiling from the cradle to the grave for a bare and meagre subsistence, but rather should we insist on the conditions necessary to enable us to live life more fully, and one of the first essentials is to secure more leisure.[76]

All this is not to deny that work was found tolerable, that work was preferable to unemployment and that people could enjoy themselves at work and find scope for their abilities. What is meant to be said is that certain groups in society were beginning to appreciate the fact that work was not above reproach and not something which could be accepted without critical appraisal. Although the provider of wages and some kind of material security, it was appreciated that work had the potential to restrict opportunities. Indeed, if work was repressive, then it was leisure which offered the one chance that people had to 'live life more fully'.

The fact that there were over one million people unemployed also stimulated the consideration of new ideas, often in a form highly critical of the work ethic. Those on the left argued that Capitalism had failed to provide the necessary opportunities for employment. If the economic system could not stimulate work, then alternatives had to be sought. There had to be a completely new emphasis: instead of the 'right to work' Labour was urged to concentrate 'upon the right to life and leisure'.[77] Since Capitalism was regarded as the cause of unemployment and, more significantly, the least likely answer to unemployment, Socialists shifted the emphasis of discussion from work to leisure.

The majority of the unemployed still took for granted the internalized logistics of work and its ideological ramifications, but there were some commentators, particularly within and around the intelligentsia, who, in searching for possible answers and solutions to unemployment, were forced to consider ideas in a new light. Bertrand Russell, in disputing the notion that work was the source of all virtue, suggested 'that the road to happiness and prosperity lies in an organised diminution of work'. To make this possible, he asserted, there must be sensible organization by which everyone could benefit from a four-hour day, with a consequent fall in unemployment, a decline in the burden of work and the possibility of ease and security for all.[78] Likewise, J. Edwards claimed that 'What you want is not the right to work, but the right to be lazy.'[79] This challenge to orthodoxy was more than just theory. Albert Knight, a lecturer for the National Council of Labour Colleges, ran a course for the unemployed in 1930 under the auspices of the Manchester Co-operative movement on the subject of 'The Right to be Idle'.[80] Unemployment had made Socialists and like-minded people reappraise well-developed ideas about work and leisure. If dignity and self-respect were to be returned to the out-of-work, so the line of argument implied, then attitudes had to be probed, overhauled and replaced by ones more appropriate to contemporary experience.

Organized Labour still accepted the work ethic, but not without dissent. The Workers' Union, for example, hoped that the future would see critical and intense thought on this question. It was hoped that the call for more employment would one day pass and 'that the object of the Trade Union and Labour Movement would be to make work the means to the end of an enjoyable leisure'.[81] This, at least, was the opinion of the Union's president, John Beard, who suggested that workers should not be 'wedded to work' or have to 'accept the curse of Adam for all time'. He was positively appreciative of the fact that benefits like holidays with pay, 'hit that stupid formula of the right to work in the solar plexus with a right to leisure blow'.[82] Outside the Labour Movement social reformers such as Kenneth Lindsay of the League of Nations Union asserted 'that the old gospel of work seemed to have gone by the board, and they would be having a doctrine of leisure instead of the dignity of labour'.[83] Equally, Henry Durant, in examining the diminution in the certainty of work, commented that 'Instead of being relaxation, leisure has become an effort to secure the meaning and justification of life itself.'[84]

Notwithstanding what has been said, there is a need for two qualifications. First, the vast majority of the British people did not wish to see the abolition of work as such. On the whole, the overwhelming desire was for the future time when there would be no 'superficial division of work and leisure', when 'the skill of men and women' would no longer be 'a commodity in the market', and when there would be equal liberty in work and leisure.[85] Workers desired greater freedom in work and more leisure time, yet they failed to struggle against productivist ideology in the same way as, say, the Parisian rank and file did during the period of the Popular Front, and certainly did not foresee a time when there would be no need for work whatsoever.[86] In fact, the Webbs went so far as to say that 'with the elimination of the capitalist profit-making and the competitive wage system, activities like coal-mining, sewing machine manufacture and dock work could become "truly an art" as distinct from an endless repetition of a purely mechanical task.'[87] Work was disparaged under Capitalism, but not in the context of an idealized future Socialist society!

Second, this particular issue was not at the centre of public debate and controversy. Oppositional values were located at the periphery of industrial, political and personal worlds. A challenge to the work ethic did evolve during the special circumstances of the inter-war years, yet this was not just because of a marginal ideological critique. It was also connected with the growth of leisure time and ways of using that leisure time, and with psychological responses to unemployment. It is difficult to deny, however, that ideas of an original and radical character were advanced as alternatives to the popular cry of 'The Right to Work'.

6
The Labour Movement and working-class leisure

No history of inter-war leisure would be complete without acknowledging the role played by the Labour Movement. It has already been noted that organized Labour played an important part in securing shorter hours and holidays with pay, as well as intervening in the debate about the enforced leisure of the unemployed. From its inception British Labour was concerned about working-class leisure. In the 1920s and 1930s, both because of and in spite of commercial expansion, a distinctive Labour approach can be discerned. Having recognized that leisure was an important part of working-class experience, the Labour Movement sought to improve the quantity and quality of leisure provision, and to provide an increased range of opportunities for cultural expression within its own structures. It is the purpose of this chapter to contribute to our knowledge of Labour culture by presenting a general overview of the Labour approach to leisure and by enlarging upon the cultural forms of the working-class movement. But first, a word about the composition of the Labour Movement.

The working-class or Labour Movement was a diverse entity consisting of trade unions, political groupings, co-operative societies and various cultural organizations. Since there were also regional differences in experiences, as well as changes over time, it is very difficult to make generalizations and to categorize the movement as a whole. One possible way to overcome these complexities is to separate the movement into the official sphere of influence – the Labour Party, TUC and like-minded bodies – and the unofficial sphere of influence – the Communist Party of

Great Britain (CP), and its supportive organizations. This institutional divide between official Labour and the Communists was based on important ideological differences. In this regard, the work of Stuart Macintyre is suggestive. According to him, the period between the end of the first world war and the early 1930s was characterized by two contrasting ideologies, one Labour Socialist, the other Marxist. Whereas Labour Socialism, the tradition embodied in the leadership of the Labour Party and TUC, was ethical, empirical, constructive, idealist/educationalist, corporate and reformist, Marxism, represented in the CP, was scientific, systematic, critical, materialist, oppositional and revolutionary.[1] Obviously, doctrinal contrasts of this nature are never totally clear – it is difficult to assimilate militant trade unionists, the Labour left, and many Independent Labour Party (ILP) members into either camp. Further, it is a matter of semantic interpretation what contemporary activists meant, and indeed historians mean, by such terms as Marxist, Labourist and Social Democratic. Nevertheless, the point to be stressed here is the general ideological differences between Socialists in the official Labour Movement and Socialists in the CP.

The doctrines of Labour Socialism and Marxism were dynamic, fluid concepts which were interpreted differently, according to the realities and aims of the time: the Labour Socialism of the early 1920s was adapted after the defeat of the General Strike in 1926 to the changed economic, social and political conditions of the 1930s; and the Marxism of 'Class Against Class' – a sectarian policy to show the Labour Party and trade unions as forces of the Establishment, even 'social fascist' – modified to the dictates of the united front against Fascism period. Although it is not always very helpful to characterize groups by ideological labels, especially over time, the divide between Labour Socialism and Marxism throughout the 1920s and 1930s is transparent enough for comparative purposes. Indeed, it is meaningful to look at the approach of the Labour Movement to leisure in terms of these two alternative ideologies.

Policy approach

Labour Socialists were all agreed that the working class should have more leisure time and more facilities in which to enjoy that leisure time. As discussed in the opening chapter, at the end of the first world war, organized Labour demanded more leisure, which led to reductions in the working week and paid holiday concessions. This set the tone for further hours and holiday demands, which even approached a marginal critique of work in favour of leisure. In 1920, the Labour Party Executive failed to accept an invitation to be represented at a conference on the 'Leisure of the People', but thereafter Labour was actively involved in the call for leisure.[2] Local Labour organizations advocated an extension of facilities for workers' spare time and tried to protect the recreation of the people from abuse: Bermondsey under Labour rule was famous for its beautification and open spaces; the Pontypridd Trades and Labour Council advanced a comprehensive recreational scheme for the town; both the East Ham and Sheffield Labour Groups improved town parks; the South Shields Labour Party and Trades Council campaigned against the encroachment upon open spaces by housing developments; and many other Labour Parties, such as Bolton and Rochdale, sought to extend local social and recreational amenities.[3]

Labour women were also calling for recreational places in rural communities, the ample provision of open spaces and safe playgrounds, and sun baths and paddling pools for children.[4] As one Labour woman pointed out: 'May the Socialist endeavour prove successful in obtaining more real leisure for all.'[5] Thus by 1937, it is not so amazing that one of the Labour Party's envisaged 'four great benefits' was leisure – a claim reiterated on the eve of the 1945 election victory.[6] Indeed, a general leisure programme, formulated in the 1920s, had already been put into practice during the period of the second Labour Government. The Ministry of Works, under George Lansbury as commissioner, drafted a number of enterprising schemes which, although opposed by the puritan lobby, sought to encourage healthy, active recreation by the introduction of bathing facilities (including mixed bathing), paddling pools, boating ponds, swings, roundabouts, and sand pits – a plan for a brighter and happier Britain.[7] As Margaret Cole has commented, such attempts to improve the leisure facilities of the metropolis established, in 'Lansbury's Lido', the best-known legacy of the second Labour Government.[8] It is therefore clear that in the years between the wars a Labour social strategy emerged which stressed the importance of leisure and claimed for qualitative improvements in cultural and recreational provision. Even so, the question still remains, 'What were the reasons for this?'

In some respects, Labour's concern for leisure was founded upon forces operating outside the movement. Labour certainly responded to the growth of the capitalist leisure industry. Chris Waters has shown that Socialists of the late Victorian period attacked the commercial organization of leisure.[9] With the increased commercialization of the inter-war period, the embryonic Socialist critique of the previous century was further clarified and legitimized. Perhaps a more concrete reason for Labour's involvement with the leisure question stemmed from the fact that cultural production was also the centre of work, and so a place for trade unionism – the Musicians' Union, National Association of Theatrical Employees, Association Football Players' and Trainers' Union. Trade Union representation in the cinema, on such issues as the entertainments tax, public safety in places of entertainment, the employment implications of sound films, and general conditions of workers, directly impinged on the form and content of the commercial product.[10] Yet, to understand fully the rationale behind Labour's overall intervention, it is necessary to consider the ideological imperatives of Labour Socialism.

Labour Socialists such as Frank Betts (the father of Barbara Castle) did not perceive leisure as part of a wider materialist world, but as an ethical foundation for joy.[11] Leisure was regarded as the chief outlet for individual choice, which, away from the dictates of work, was essential to the health of body and mind: 'It is the basis of the diversity in character and taste that makes human society alive, interesting and entertaining, like a pattern of many colours and lines.'[12] There were few attempts to see leisure in relation to the dominant mode of production, ultimately determined by the Capitalist order of society; the leisure question was never linked to a systematic overview of the Capitalist way of life as a whole.

In the opinion of many Labour Socialists, the role of the workers' organizations was to fight for a fair share of leisure, to extract benefits from the Capitalist system. The trade unions, in particular, were used as vehicles of constructive social reform, to campaign firstly for paid holidays, the forty-hour week and other leisure demands, and only then, if at all, to consider the creation of a society which could guarantee fair shares of leisure for all. Hence the arguments for the forty-hour week accepted that the role of Labour was to campaign for reform and not revolutionary change:

> This reform, long overdue, is imperatively called for as a means of giving the wage-earners a share of the benefits arising from mechanisation and scientific organisation of industry . . . and of providing more leisure and better opportunities of recreation, education, and enjoyment for the worker.[13]

Although not precluding the need for Socialism, the labour argument for the shorter working week was based on the reformist premise that, with Capitalist prosperity, benefits would percolate through the system into the palms of the workers – a premise to some extent evidenced by the increase in real wages, reduction in hours and expansion of Capitalist leisure forms for those in work. It was not the overt task of the Labour Socialist, so it appears, to overthrow the society that others on the left suggested restricted the quality and quantity of leisure, but rather to secure Labour its just rewards out of Capitalism. From a similar perspective, A. E. Ford, the Preston district secretary of the Amalgamated Engineering Union, felt that the problems of nervous tension, monotony and the pace and intensity of modern production should be mitigated by the 'wise use of leisure'.[14] Despite identifying these problems – presumably caused by advances in the modes of production – he did not offer a solution to challenge fundamentally the root causes; he, and others like him, merely desired the extension of opportunities for leisure to ameliorate the excesses of Capitalist employment. In this case, leisure was viewed as a palliative, not as something to be campaigned for in its own right.

The Labour Socialist aim of improving the quality of working-class leisure was accommodated within the logic and the constraints of the prevailing economic and social order. The Labour case for leisure was essentially reformist and social democratic in nature, seeking to work within the system and to prise out of the system as many leisure benefits as possible. If not exactly accepting the legitimacy of Capitalism – there was optimism about the Parliamentary road to socialism – Labour did accept the dominant institutions of society. The TUC president in 1938, Herbert Elvin, who had been concerned with the question of leisure for many years, felt that working people would be best served by creating an agency of the State directly concerned with leisure: 'I should like to see a MINISTER OF LEISURE appointed, who would have under his control, all problems of leisure time: recreational, educational and cultural.'[15] Agencies for improving the leisure of the workers were to be incorporated into the State, reinforcing the dominant structures of Capitalist society and perhaps making it difficult to challenge those structures.

The general approach of the official Labour Movement to leisure supports Macintyre's notion of Labour Socialism. It is true that many Labour Socialists complained about the long hours and holidays without pay, exposed the less endearing features of Capitalist leisure, and even related the issues of leisure and work to Socialism, but the overall thrust of policy was determined by a set of ideological assumptions concordant with democratic Liberal Capitalism. For the Labour Socialist a new economic system was not a prerequisite for real gains in workers' leisure: capital, if prompted in the right direction and reformed, could, it was thought, concede leisure benefits to the working class. To an extent, this was an admirable approach which, in fact, brought forth many gains without disrupting the democratic channels of worker influence. In contrast, the Marxist analysis depended upon ideological considerations antithetical to Liberal Capitalism.

The CP was not above the fight for social reform. Indeed, the demand for palliatives, especially the shorter working week, was to the forefront of Marxist industrial and political policy throughout the inter-war period. According to the Communist viewpoint, leisure and rest – the reward of labour – should be the right of all working people, a fact emphasized by professors and bus drivers alike.[16] Even at the height of its sectarian period of 'Class Against Class', the CP and the National Minority Movement still demanded an annual fortnight's holiday with pay and improved sport facilities – seemingly revolutionary posturing did not preclude the need for short-term expediency.[17] By the late 1930s, leisure reforms were firmly entrenched within Communist social policy: the Young Communist League called for more leisure amenities, including a Government grant of £5 million for sport, while local London groups at Southall, Finsbury and Westminster stressed the need for social and cultural centres, swimming pools, Sunday recreation, municipal gyms, more playgrounds, parks and open spaces.[18] The message was to organize to get more and better quality leisure, as Communist-influenced groups demonstrated in the struggle for paid holidays, and the British Workers' Sports Federation had pioneered in the fight for improvements in sport. The CP shaped a reformist leisure policy in the inter-war period, in many ways similar to that of the official movement, a development reflected by the articulate call during the 1945 electoral campaign for improvements in leisure.[19] Communists, unlike, say, the members of the extreme Socialist Party of Great Britain, were not against Capitalist concessions, but to say this is to state the obvious. In order to understand the overall Communist perception of leisure, the policy implications of Marxism have to be considered.

The most important principle, as revealed in so many policy statements, was a rigorous critique of Capitalist leisure in all its forms. To put it simply, sport, film or drama was viewed as a superstructural tool to aid the exploitation of the workers. Marxists also believed that leisure was an integral part of Capitalism, which could not be divorced from the materialist way of life. The dominant mode of production was said to have depressed the cultural level of the masses:

> Capitalism has seized on all pleasant activities, besides labour, and made them into sources of profit. It has made the people into consumers of culture, instead of partners in its production, and this division has impoverished both the practice and the enjoyment of it.[20]

Equally, the actual leisure time of the workers, in terms of hours free from work, was shown to be dependent upon the cyclical fluctuations of the Capitalist economy. In essence, Marxists were highly critical of leisure under Capitalism, reluctant to concede that short-term gains could serve as constructive models for the design of leisure under Socialism. Although it was acknowledged that improvements in leisure were possible under Capitalism – after all, Lenin suggested that a future Socialist society would preserve all that was best in the earlier forms of Capitalist culture

– this was heavily qualified by reference to the potential for leisure in a Socialist world.[21] In Edward Upward's surrealistic fable, 'The Island', there is a glimpse of the utopian future:

> Think what an island of promise is before you, what sunlight, what fields for athletic leisure, for sport free from all taint of professionalism, for that fulfilment of the body which was long ago the ambition of the Greeks, what paths for love, what satisfied evenings for discussion, for the arts, for literature, for music, what a chance to begin a new life of culture and vigour.[22]

By establishing a Socialist system of production, so the argument went, the leisure harvest of more free time, better recreational and cultural facilities and other improvements would be finally cultivated.

An editorial in the *Daily Worker* argued that industry could never guarantee workers their 'well-earned leisure', because, 'It is the capitalist ownership of the land, industries and banks which is preventing the development of wealth-producing power in order to provide wealth and leisure for all workers.' To rectify this situation, the editorial concluded, 'decaying, parasitic capitalism' had to be wiped out and replaced by a 'planned Socialist economy'.[23] Apparently, real improvements in the quality of working-class leisure had to wait until the collapse of Capitalism. In fact, according to many Communists, there was empirical evidence to support these theoretical ideas. A Socialist State, so it was rather naively claimed, had been established in the Soviet Union, supposedly bringing forth material and spiritual benefits to the working class – the reality was, of course, somewhat different. Throughout the inter-war period, the British Communist Party, though more autonomous than is sometimes credited, was closely aligned to Moscow. In contrast to and in accordance with the different kinds of views expressed by Labour Socialists, Marxists saw in the Soviet Union the model society – the society that really did promote the economic and social interests of the workers. Thus, Russia was cited as the only nation in the world which provided the opportunities and the facilities for leisure:

In the Soviet Union, where this capitalism has been destroyed, the workers have been able to achieve the seven-hour day, payment for holidays, and the creation of opportunities for healthy enjoyment, such as are quite unattainable under capitalism.[24]

The Communist press paid homage to the young Soviet republic and, in spite of its many setbacks, continued to endorse the Moscow line. In *Russia Today*, the organ of the Friends of the Soviet Union, there are numerous reports, articles and photographs depicting the qualitative aspects of Soviet-run leisure. The portrayal of sport, under such titles as ' "Everyone a Sportsman": Russia's Way to Health', 'Winter Sports For All', 'They Run Football Better in Russia', holidays with titles like 'Holidays in a Palace', 'Holidays – Not Lock-Outs', and culture, headed by titles such as 'Propaganda or Art – or Both?: The Soviet Theatre', 'Theatres, Concerts, Cinemas: Their Doors Are Kept Wide Open for Russia's Workers', all give the impression that Soviet leisure institutions were exemplary and, in some cases, the best the world had seen.[25] If only Britain followed the Moscow road, it was argued, the British working class would receive similar benefits. In the final analysis, workers' leisure could only be adequately improved, as one pamphlet inferred, by the revolutionary overthrow of Capitalism and the establishment of a Soviet Britain.[26]

Undoubtedly, many of the British Communist activists of the period sincerely and honestly believed that the Soviet Union had revolutionized the workers' standard of life and leisure. It is true that there were many improvements, but contemporary enthusiasm should not hide some of the realities, horrors and fallacies of Soviet power in the inter-war years. As well as overestimating the quality of Russian life, British Communists also failed to admit that workers in their own country had benefited from some of the changes in the Capitalist leisure industry, such as more cinemas, more radios, and more amenities in general. To neglect this fact and in failing to see that the prevailing culture was genuinely popular with the workers was to marginalize their own critique. There were, of course, many sections of the working class who suffered from a lack of spare time, purchasing power and facilities, but by exaggerating the richness of Soviet leisure and the poverty of British leisure, Marxists added little credence to some of their more persuasive arguments.

In comparing the official Labour and the Communist approach to leisure, certain similarities and differences are apparent. For both the Labour Socialist and the Marxist, palliatives under Capitalism were accepted – it was acknowledged by all those connected with the Labour Movement that paid holidays and other reforms could improve the quality of life, even under a so-called exploitative economic system. The campaigns and struggles for more and better quality leisure were supported by Labour Party followers and Communist Party members alike. However, the similarity in approach stretched no further than this. Labour Socialists stressed that leisure reforms brought forth incalculable gains to the working class; they argued that pragmatic methods of political and industrial persuasion resulted in piecemeal advance – perhaps ultimately to Socialism – so expunging some of the more unacceptable aspects of Capitalism. On the other hand, Marxists believed that it was impossible for working people to receive their fair share of leisure under capitalism; the emancipation of workers' free time was intimately connected with Socialism. Although short-term reform was not rejected out of hand, Marxist strategy was related to the eventual creation of the Communist society. Whereas official Labour was mainly interested in trade union agreements and legislative drafts, the CP emphasized revolutionary change.

Labour cultural forms

Between the wars there was a Socialist approach to leisure based on the doctrines of Labour Socialism or Marxism. This approach can be seen in terms of policy objectives, that is, the conception of leisure in Capitalist society and the aggregate design for improvement, be it social reform or the transformation of society. In addition to this, the Labour Movement was a provider of opportunities for leisure time activity within its own organizations. Besides the political and industrial wings of the movement, there was also a recreational or cultural wing, which catered for all kinds of leisure interests. If the overall Socialist approach to leisure is to be fully understood, then the recreational impulse within the movement itself cannot be ignored.

Labour cultural forms were prominent from the first half of

the nineteenth century, when the early working-class movement, working through their own institutions and often in their own premises, provided cultural forms and determined the shape that they took.[27] With the growth of the co-operative societies, friendly societies and other Labour organizations, an important Socialist recreational impulse had been generated by the end of the century. The Socialist League, the ILP and other political groupings, the trade unions, the Socialist Sunday Schools, and the Labour Churches all provided space and time for recreation as well as political expression, with the Clarion movement as the major forum for leisure provision, bringing recreation and Socialism together. Although Stephen Yeo has argued that, with the growth of a Labour Party machine stressing pragmatic politics, and the competition of a Capitalist leisure industry, Socialist forms of leisure were eroded in the twentieth century, the evidence for the inter-war period fails to substantiate such an argument.[28] It is true that commercialized leisure developed and Labour organization was strengthened, and that the overwhelming majority of workers opted for 'Capitalist' leisure, but this did not mean that 'Socialist' recreation was destroyed. If the sources are anything to go by, it appears that Socialist activity in the arts, travel and sport actually increased. Socialist involvement was both a response to Capitalist leisure – a desire to provide co-operative, associational, fraternal forms as an alternative to commercialism – and, as David Clark has pointed out, an integral part of Labour organization, sustaining earlier ethical values.[29] Indeed, in the 1920s and 1930s, social and cultural activity was a very important element in the local and national life of the Labour Movement, reflected in the proliferation of many Socialist agencies directly concerned with leisure – Workers' Travel Association, Workers' Temperance League, British Workers' Sports Federation, National Workers' Sports Association, workers' theatre, film, photograph and music societies, Unemployed Associations, and many more.[30] Certainly, some of these agencies had been inherited from an earlier period – the Clarion Cycling Club, for example, was rejuvenated in the 1930s – but even if they had, the empirical evidence points to the inter-war years, and not the late nineteenth century as Labour's cultural and leisure climacteric.

It seems that, as with policy approach, the ideological division between the official Labour Movement and the Communist Movement was all-important in determining the nature of socialist leisure provision. Although there were cultural bodies in the Labour ranks which were independent and transcended ideological types, Socialist cultural forms reflected both the doctrines of Labour Socialism and Marxism and were under the tutelage of either the official movement or the Communist Party. In the final part of this chapter, first the Labour Socialist and second the Marxist modes of cultural provision will be examined in some detail.

The industrial, co-operative and political wings of the official Labour Movement all had outlets and responsibilities for leisure. The trade unions, for instance, provided various opportunities for cultural and recreational expression. Reading through some of the contemporary union journals it is clear that at both national and branch level there were all kinds of union-sponsored leisure activities, from dances to football, from flower arranging to athletics.[31] The organization of youth in one particular union was described in the following terms: 'From reports received at Central Office, certain sections have displayed a considerable amount of activity, mostly on the social side. Football, cycling and rambling clubs have been formed, theatrical entertainments, debates and visits to places of interest have been quite numerous.'[32] This was indicative of wider trends. Milne Bailey was probably quite correct in suggesting that trade unions were not exactly 'omnibus' associations, providing all the social needs of their members, but it is nonetheless true that leisure provision was a function of trade unions and trade councils.[33] Indeed, by the end of the 1930s, one trade unionist could still write about the 'increasing development of social activities among unions . . . '.[34]

Similarly, it is apparent from the columns of *The Co-operative News* that many societies organized sports, concerts, plays, camps and other entertainments. The Co-operative Wholesale Society was one body which exemplified the range of leisure pursuits which were available to members: 'In making a résumé of present social and recreational facilities, the investigator finds himself almost overwhelmed by the variety and multiplicity of organisations which flourish in the widely distributed depots and workshops of the C.W.S.'[35] In addition, as some of the social surveys of the period clarified, working-class housewives were given the opportunity for social intercourse within the structures of the Women's Co-operative Guild.[36]

The Labour Party, too, in spite of the fact that many of its activities were mundane and routine, had a well-developed recreational and cultural life. In 1928, for example, it held a Festival of Labour at the Crystal Palace, which included sports, dancing, community singing, organ recitals, and many other events.[37] At local level, too, there were many occasions when Party members had the chance to participate in leisure activities. The records of a number of local Parties, recently available on microfilm, show that there was extensive provision for indoor and outdoor recreation. The minute books and annual reports of the Colne Valley Divisional Labour Party, for example, present a vivid picture of sporting, social and cultural participation. Building upon a wide network of Labour clubs, established in the 1890s, Colne Valley was characterized by a Labour cultural formation with Socialist brass bands, teas, rambles, excursions, whist drives and, most popular of all, the annual rally and carnival.[38] For most of the 1920s and 1930s, a rally arrangements committee was convened to organize such events as skipping races, egg and spoon races, hidden treasure, relays, side shows, which all took place at an annual gathering of Labour supporters. In 1933, for instance, the annual carnival was held at Slaithwaite, with political speeches, tea served in the Labour club, sports and competitions on the adjoining field and 'a very enjoyable day' concluded by dancing and music provided by the Milnsbridge Socialist brass band.[39] Other local Parties organized their own annual events, variously named field days, demonstrations, fêtes and May Day celebrations. These yearly occasions were a time for fun and merriment when serious political matters temporarily receded into the background: a May Queen, balloon competition and firework display at Swindon; side-shows, a dance troupe and a jazz band at Chadderton; a fair, games and a jazz band at Salford; and a gymnastic display, magic show and comic dress competition at Leeds.[40]

The social side of Labour activity, often ignored by historians, was an important part of the day-to-day existence of the movement. The majority of local Parties, at one time or another, had a specialist committee responsible for the arrangement and co-ordination of social activities: the Cambridgeshire Party, which had such a committee in 1920, placed it on a firmer, centralized footing in 1928; Sheffield tried to co-ordinate social activities and eventually introduced a diary of events; South Shields even had a casino sub-committee in the mid-1920s to organize whist drives, socials, galas and festivals, to deal with financial questions and to ensure that all musicians employed at Labour functions were trade unionists.[41] Indeed, according to the Tottenham Party, whereas in the past Labour activities were confined to political issues and the social side neglected, by the 1920s the situation had changed and there was greater interest shown in members' spare time.[42] As *The Cambridge Daily News* reported in the 1920s: 'Labour socials have become a familiar feature in many villages in the county', a remark echoed in many other areas.[43] It is also clear from the reports and advertisements which appeared in the Labour press of the North West that social, sporting and cultural activities were indeed an integral part of branch life.[44] In short, striving for the Co-operative Commonwealth within the creative patterns of social fraternity and fellowship was an admirable and enjoyable way to achieve wider goals.

The basis of Labour's social life was not just a matter of fellowship. There also had to be efficient organization and institutional representation – without premises, without finance, without political support there would have been little social life to speak of. Working-class halls, which first appeared in the 1830s, were a prerequisite for independence and cultural practice. As the Pontypridd Trades and Labour Council of the early 1920s continually stressed, there was an obvious need for a building of their own.[45] One way around the problem of premises was to create a labour club. During the 1920s and 1930s there were a number of clubs formed under the auspices of organized Labour. The Romsey Labour Club, for example, opened in October 1928 and, financed and built by Labour sympathizers, became the headquarters of the Romsey Ward Labour Party, three railway trade unions, the NUR women's section, ASLEF women's society and the Women's Co-operative Guild, who all enjoyed the club's range of social facilities.[46]

Some of these clubs combined in federations and unions. In the early 1920s, clubs in Leigh, Wigan, St Helens and surrounding areas – the heart of Labour club land – came together to form the National Union of Labour and Socialist Clubs. The clubs as social adjuncts of the Labour Movement were affiliated to and run by the local Party to strengthen Labourism and promote good fellowship via lectures, essays, handicaps, whist drives, billiards, and other devices.[47] While never the centre of political activism – Joseph Tinker MP, for example, was critical of the lack of Socialist propaganda – the clubs were both the pioneers of new kinds of commodity production and distribution, and associational forms designed to encourage participation and mutual self-help.[48]

Likewise, at the national level, the first real attempt to promote the social side of the Labour Party was made by Beatrice Webb in 1921. With the help of a number of close colleagues, she established the Half Circle Club, a kind of social platform for Labour women. Its main aim was to give the wives of Labour men, women organizers and the wives of Socialist intellectuals the opportunity for 'fastidiously chosen recreation' and social inter- course, by which they could be groomed and trained to take part in public life and to resist the attractions of 'London Society' and 'the onslaughts of duchesses and millionaires against their integrity'.[49] It was this experiment which led to the establishment of the Parliamentary Labour Club, a permanent central club with premises and social facilities. This was in turn succeeded by the National Labour Club and eventually the National Trade Union Club. The main Labour clubs were basically a way of making the leadership more accessible to the rank and file, encouraging the ideals of co-operation and fellowship, and of linking recreation to Socialism.[50]

Clearly, there was a Labour cultural formation in the inter-war period, but to give reasons for the growth and rejuvenation of Labour cultural forms is difficult. Socialist leisure, if such a phrase can be used for Labour's provision of leisure amenities, was to some extent generated by Labour's antipathy to commercial forms. It was far better, so it was thought, to encourage the provision of leisure activities within the Labour Movement than to leave such provision as the prerogative of Capitalism. In the words of a contributor to the *Leeds Weekly Citizen*: 'We should learn to play our own games, work at our own hobbies, choose our own associations and spare a little of our leisure . . . for the cause for which these heroes of the past gave their all.'[51] Indeed, beginning with the designs of Robert Owen in the 1830s, Labour cultural forms were characterized by an anti-Capitalist bias, that is, a tendency on Labour's part to discriminate against Capitalist leisure: Socialist brass bands, films, plays, football teams and even *Daily Herald* playing cards were preferable to the Capitalist alternatives. As George Hicks of the Federation of Trade Union, Labour, Socialist and Co-operative Clubs argued, Labour had to take into account the new developments of the wireless, the 'talkies', oil and electricity, the motor-car and the aeroplane if the working class was not to be saturated by Capitalist influences. In order to break 'away from the pernicious influence of the Capitalist Press and the Capitalist sport and social organisations' the workers had to 'provide themselves with ample opportunities for a fuller life and scope for self-expression'.[52] The Labour Club Movement, based on the principles of association rather than commercialism, co-operation rather than competition, democratic participation rather than Capitalist management, was a living, pulsating expression of such an aim.

In a similar vein, the trade unions wished to provide recreation, not so much to wean workers away from Capitalist leisure, though this was important, but to seduce workers away from paternalistic forms of leisure. The ubiquitous nature of employer sponsored leisure caused a lot of apprehension in trade union circles throughout the inter-war period. Company recreation was frequently evoked as a part of management policy designed to incorporate workers and undermine trade unionism. As one official of the Boot and Shoe operatives commented, in the case of those workers unconscious of trade unionism, 'welfare schemes and works councils have a very definite effect in retarding trade union development, rendering more difficult the operation of trade union principles.'[53] There was genuine fear that workers who took advantage of company recreation schemes would think that employers were not as bad as they might be imagined from their balance sheets.[54] If the main interest of the bosses was to pursue the half-yearly dividend, so it was argued, then the trade unions should ensure that 'no loopholes must be left whereby the employers can exercise any control or influence, direct or indirect, over the lives of our members.'[55] It is true that some trade unionists were more favourably disposed towards recreational welfare than others, but on the whole, welfarism was feared and countered by calls for union based recreation.[56] A section of the Transport and General Workers' Union, apprehensive about the tendency to regard those social and sports clubs under management control as a substitute for industrial organizations, thus pressed for trade union alternatives.[57] As a result of these pressures, the TUC General Council examined the question and, though concluding that welfarism was not open to objection if run in conjunction with trade unionism, exception was taken to those schemes which sought to replace the need for trade unionism.[58] Indeed, in spite of promises made by the Industrial Welfare Society, trade union suspicion of welfare and more specifically company recreation continued until the end of the 1930s.[59]

It is possible to regard Labour cultural provision, in all its different forms, as an alternative to both Capitalist cultural production and company financed recreation. This does not mean, however, that the leisure activities provided by the Labour Movement were part of a wider counter-cultural struggle – Gramsci's idea of an autonomous cultural intervention by the proletariat – for this was clearly not the case. Labour cultural activities were usually the off-shoot of the more fundamental needs of industrial and political organization. This is not to deny that Labour culture had anti-Capitalist implications, but that the primary concerns for the local Labour Party or trade union branch when arranging social functions were such issues as entertainment, finance, and recruitment, not the possibility of subverting the dominant social order. Sam Carey's scheme for a Labour dancing competition in Colne Valley was 'with a view to interesting the young people in the movement and raising finance for Party purposes'.[60] Trade unionists were similarly preoccupied with the organizational benefits of recreational provision:

> Concerts, dances, film shows of the non-flammable type,
> theatrical performances, cycling for the youth, boxing,
> running, athletics of every description could be indulged in for
> the purpose of making the union attractive to a very wide
> public. From the proceeds of these activities a fund could be
> built up in every district for the purpose of alleviating the
> distress in our ranks.[61]

Many local Labour Parties were enthusiasts for bazaars and jumble sales which, while a time for social intercoure and co-operative leisure, were held as public attractions and fund raising exercises.[62] In fact, as Christopher Howard has recently shown, Labour organizers made a conscious effort to integrate each local Party within the local community and 'mix politics with the social life of the people'.[63] Labour cultural activities were most obviously a recruitment device in the case of young people. The ILP Guild of Youth, Labour Party League of Youth and the youth organizations of the co-operative movement, especially the Juvenile Co-operators and the Woodcraft Folk, used outdoor recreation and sport as a way to disseminate Socialist ideas amongst the youth of the nation.[64] The League of Youth in particular was both a political and a recreational body which sought to recruit members by way of a radical ideology – in contrast to the boy scouts, it was anti-militaristic – and through a varied programme of social and cultural events.[65] The Leeds branch, for instance, had sections for sport, rambling, cycling, camping, drama and social events, as well as the normal political and educational activities.[66] In this way, so it was assumed, young people could be converted to Socialism whilst enjoying themselves in a spirit of fellowship, precluding the need for preaching and lecturing.

In their concern for questions of finance and recruitment, many Labour Socialist bodies were not exactly the agencies of cultural revolution. There were certain features of the Labour cultural formation which had little to do with egalitarian ideals – at social functions it seems that the task of preparing and serving tea and sandwiches was usually the responsibility of the Labour women and not the men.[67] Moreover, social events were not always characterized by class solidarity. The weekly dances in the Assembly Rooms, Burnley, organized by the local Weavers' Association, were sometimes the scene of unruly behaviour – probably the result of too much beer – and it was not unusual for windows to be broken. The Weavers, like their ILP comrades in Meltham, were therefore compelled to engage a policeman to maintain law and order.[68] Circumstances far removed from the spirit of Socialism meant that Labour was forced to seek the help of outside agencies of the State.

The official movement tried to organize the total environment of active supporters by giving opportunities for cultural expression. Although Labour cultural formation could neither match community generated organizations such as the village choirs of South Wales or the brass bands of the industrial North, nor compare with the extensive cultural activities found in the pre-war German Social Democratic Party, it was both a feature of grass roots Labour Socialism and an element in wider industrial and political behaviour. In some cases, it was a conscious attempt to subvert Capitalist leisure and company-sponsored leisure, yet more often than not it was simply part of a Labour political process which stressed the co-operative and fellowship ideal and linked recreation to Socialism. The fact that the frontage of the North Kensington Labour Club proclaimed 'Recreation' and 'Socialism' was thus a confirmation of the importance attached to recreation in Socialist circles.[69] In the main, the cultural forms of Labour Socialism were not a reflection of a rigorous political and ideological perspective, although they could be, but rather an integral aspect of a Labour totality generating recreational outlets for activists and marginal supporters alike.

The Communist movement in Britain between the wars cannot be seen solely in terms of the Party: there were industrial, political and cultural agencies of Marxist thought and practice, ranging from the Minority Movement to the International Class War Prisoners' Aid, the League Against Imperialism and the Negro Welfare Association. All of these agencies, at one time or another, organized leisure activities as part of a political and cultural education consisting of history, drama, ballet, art, literature, music, sport, and camps and outings. The journals and newspapers which came off the Marxist printing presses included features on popular culture – there were columns on all kinds of leisure interests, as well as advertisements revealing the extensive nature of the Marxist cultural formation. The Party even articulated a number of cultural demands in its programme for British soldiers: the right to form democratically controlled social clubs, study circles and sports organizations, and to associate freely and arrange fixtures with trade union sports clubs and other working-class bodies.[70] Throughout the 1920s and 1930s, the Communist movement stressed the need for cultural work, despite the critical response of some Party activists.

The CP also established workers' social clubs and organized annual celebrations, galas and festivals. Mick Jenkins, a young Party worker of the period, has thus recalled how cultural expression was an important aspect of Communist branch life: bands and music were a common feature of demonstrations and marches; socials, sports events and dances were organized to help strikes and Party finances and, of course, to provide entertainment. Even though Jenkins and his comrades were embroiled in revolutionary politics, they still had some time for the socials arranged by the NUWM and the Young Communist League, the films and plays presented by the workers' film and theatre societies, and the sports organized by the British Workers' Sports Federation.[71] For instance, at the Lancashire Charter Gala, held on 5 September 1931 in Haslingden, there were numerous sporting attractions, such as boxing, wrestling, and grasstrack riding, the Wall of Death ridden by daredevil Clem Beckett, displays by the Workers' Theatre Movement and film shows by the Workers' Film Society.[72] In other parts of the country, local Communist organizations were equally keen to impress. In spite of competitive church and chapel fairs, the first ever Sheffield field day was attended by 1,000 people, seemingly attracted by sports, baby shows, races, fancy dress and concerts. According to *The Daily Worker*, this was a great success: 'many workers expressed their appreciation of what we had given them to make life more happy, and said that they had seen that day the other side of the Communist Party, the social side, and that it was the best field day they had ever attended.'[73] As with Labour carnivals, Communist social demonstrations were, in Tom Mann's words, a time 'to forget for a few hours the serious side of the movement and to abandon [oneself] to enjoyment. . . '.[74] In fact, by the end of the 1930s, social activities of this kind, far from being an occasion to escape the realities of ascetic revolutionary struggle, were an integral part of such a struggle. John Mahon thus suggested that politics, entertainment and education had to be synthesized in order to give the people what they wanted: 'No more dreary, half-empty halls. No more dull and depressing speeches. Let's have Colour, Energy, Clarity, Confidence. Let's finish every meeting so that the audience wants to come back to the next one.'[75] Although one has to be cautious, even critical, of the sources, there is evidence to suggest that Communists provided outlets for cultural expression.

Moreover, in communities where the CP found a fair share of political support, Marxist cultural forms were pervasive. Places such as Lumphinnans (Fife), the Vale of Leven, and Mardy (Rhondda Valley) – the so-called 'Little Moscows' of inter-war

Britain – absorbed Communist-provided cultural activities. In addition to Marxist organized sport, musical events, socials and dances, there were many overt signs of a kind of counter-community: Communist representatives elected to the Lumphinnans Old Folks' Treat Committee, Children's Gala Committee, Welfare Institute Committee, and even the Ex-Servicemen's Association; the Vale of Leven Unemployed Workers' Movement band, with its tin whistles, flutes, triangles and cymbals; and Mardy's secular funerals, with red ribbons in place of black ties, wreaths in the shape of a hammer and sickle and not the cross, and revolutionary songs instead of traditional Welsh hymns.[76] Although the hegemony of Capitalist leisure remained and the great majority of people actually preferred commercially provided activities – Marxist inspired leisure never exerted a 'total' control over the spare time interests of any worker – Communist counter-culture supplemented the existing kinds of collective activity centred on the miners' institutes. Communists were implicitly and explicitly challenging dominant bourgeois values and making it possible to develop a proletariat aware of its own creative abilities and potential.[77]

In contrast to the cultural forms of Labour Socialism, Marxist cultural formation was essentially the antithesis of the commercialized product. The main reason for Marxist cultural activity was political – to further the class struggle and to disseminate the principles of British Communism. As one enemy of the Party remarked, 'the Workers' Theatre Movement puts Communism over the footlights, Kino puts it on the screen, and the British Workers' Sports Federation and the Spartacus Clubs disguise it as sport.'[78] Communist-inspired social activities were not to be mere copies of Capitalist forms, but 'new methods of genuine proletarian sociability and entertainment which, in the last analysis, also serve to develop class-consciousness and Communist training'.[79] Although the many Marxist-influenced cultural organizations responded to different political forces, they were united in their opposition to Capitalism. In the case of the British Workers' Sports Federation, for example, Capitalist sport was the target. The main aim of the Federation was to

> organise and direct the desire for clean and healthy sport
> amongst the workers of Britain along the lines of working

class solidarity. To conduct agitation against the anti-working class character of capitalist-controlled sport, and to win the workers away from such control into the ranks of the B.W.S.F.[80]

Hence, a simple sports festival was both a demonstration against war and fascism, and a fight against the Capitalist system 'for more adequate facilities and opportunities to take part in healthy, vigorous physical recreation'.[81] As Harry Pollitt suggested, cultural activity, especially amongst the young, was a serious form of revolutionary politics: it was a popular and direct approach which in its most attractive form appealed to the imagination, daring and audacious feelings of youth, and drew them from factory, club, sports field and street into the daily fight against Capitalism.[82] In spite of the tendency for leading activists to exaggerate the revolutionary potential of the working class, Communist notions of cultural politics were unambiguous. It was genuinely thought that Marxist sport, theatre or film could help to undermine Capitalism. Here, it would be illuminating to examine in more detail the Workers' Theatre Movement (WTM) which was clearly an overt attempt to counter Capitalist ideology and culture. The history of the WTM is now quite well documented, so what follows is a discussion of the more salient features of the movement.[83]

The WTM was first formed in the mid-1920s, having received encouragement from the Communist *Sunday Worker*.[84] Backing also came from the Minority Movement and, to a lesser extent, from the Plebs League and the National Council of Labour Colleges.[85] In the light of this support, a workers' theatre group evolved out of the Council of Proletarian Art, with Christina Walsh of the Glastonbury Players as its secretary.[86] The initial manifesto was quite open about the group's objectives: workers must write and act their own plays about the class war – strikes, lock-outs, revolution, Government policy, the problems of women and children – which could take the form of a satire, comedy or farce, and be performed at any trade union or labour club.[87] From the outset, therefore, the theatre was seen as a tool in the class struggle.

However, the group soon began to disintegrate and was only rescued by the work of the Hackney People's Players. The

Hackney Labour Dramatic Group, as the People's Players were originally called, was formed by Tom Thomas in 1926, with the support of the local Trades Council. It was initially designed to provide branch entertainment, but then moved closer to political theatre. Progressive plays were produced and performed at working men's clubs and Labour and Communist Party branches, culminating in the successful performance of Tressell's *The Ragged Trousered Philanthropists*, which had been adapted by Thomas.[88] As the nucleus of the new WTM, the Hackney group began to perform plays with a real political purpose:

> they chose really proletarian material, material of great
> simplicity, sincerity, seriousness and, above all, humanity,
> such as would appeal directly to the heart and mind of any
> British worker with thoughts and feelings for the situation of
> his class.[89]

Since a number of other groups were in existence, such as one in Manchester, the embryo of a larger organization had been conceived by 1929.

The early WTM, though not a formal Communist organization, was very close to the Party and consequently can be contrasted to Labour Socialist theatre groups. The new movement was to be, in Huntley Carter's words, a 'theatrical propaganda machine' which would 'throw every particle of the old capitalistic propaganda machine overboard'; Socialist plays were to be acted at factory gates, street corners or any other favourable place, in order to support strikes and the working-class ascendancy to power.[90] In fighting for Socialism, class struggle drama – legitimate drama was rejected as 'bourgeois' – was regarded as crucial. This meant that the propaganda side, rather than the recreational side, of drama was emphasized. Yet, drama was a form of recreation, no matter what political activists may have thought at the time, and many of the performances appealed to the workers' desire for entertainment. As Mark Phillips of the Manchester group wrote: 'It seems logical to assume that evolution in the workers' theatre must go in the direction of mass entertainment.'[91] Certainly, the productions of the Hackney People's Players, though politically generated, were also a time for enjoyment. Also, the Marxist approach was not as sectarian as it was to become. Where possible, there was co-operation with local ILP, Labour Party and trade union branches. Indeed, *Lansbury's Labour Weekly* allowed free publicity to all workers' theatre groups.[92] This kind of accommodation of views, however, was soon to change: the left turn in the Communist International in 1929 and its translation into 'Class Against Class' in Britain, effectively isolated Marxist forms of cultural expression from their Labour Socialist counterparts. Until about 1933, Communists were to develop the WTM as a revolutionary alternative to the established modes of Capitalist and social democratic provision.

During the period of 'Class Against Class', the arts side of the Communist Movement had a definite ideology – the idea that theatre could raise the aspirations of the working class and thereby stimulate the fight for a Communist society. Small groups of activists used drama with a kind of visionary purpose, a desire to improve the material and cultural conditions of the workers. Before 1929, class struggle drama was a part of the Marxist approach to the performing arts; with the onset of 'Class Against Class' it was the major part: 'Workers' drama which not only admits the existence of the class struggle, but shows it being fought, and being won.'[93] As David Leslie of the Edinburgh group asserted: 'The Workers' Theatre Movement showed the revolutionary way out.'[94]

As one would expect, the role of working-class drama was to portray Capitalism as the main cause of all economic and social problems: 'Our value as a means of exposing the capitalist system and its supporters in all their brutality, hypocrisy, lying knavery is undoubted.'[95] Moreover, in a rather deterministic way, cultural production was linked to the Capitalist totality and to Capitalist propaganda. In the words of Tom Mann's son, Charlie:

The professional stage is controlled by the same class that owns and controls the whole of industry and capital. It is not unnatural, therefore, that the professional stage is used in the interests of this class. Art being propaganda, it will be our purpose to expose the artful propaganda of the bourgeois scribes, who are perforce influenced in their writings by loyalty to the system on which they live.[96]

Members of the workers' theatre groups wished to use art in

order to further the class struggle and to expose and counter Capitalist propaganda. Yet, this was not all: not only was Capitalism to be vigorously opposed, but so too was Labour Socialism. Indeed, the official Labour Movement was characterized as an instrument of the *status quo*, the Labour Party as the third, Capitalist political party. In lampooning official Labour, the WTM was certainly, to use Raphael Samuel's phrase, 'uninhibitedly – even exuberantly – sectarian'.[97] In what ways, then, were such groups to use drama in the class struggle and in the fight against Capitalism and Labour Socialism?

The techniques used by the WTM were adapted from German 'agit-prop' theatre. Having toured Germany in 1931, a workers' theatre delegation brought back with them the idea that drama could be performed in the streets, on an open platform without any props. Subsequently, groups abandoned the curtained stage, footlights and floodlights, costumes and make-up, and started to perform on the streets: the theatre of agitation and propaganda became a way of reaching workers, involving them in political dialogue, and influencing them.[98] As Ruth and Eddy Frow have observed, these techniques were ideally suited to class struggle drama: 'plays were presented with little or no scenery and simple or symbolic costume to allow maximum mobility and participation in the activities of the working class movement.'[99] In the case of the Greenwich Group – the 'Red Blouses' – the living cabaret tradition of German 'agit-prop' was an important development:

> There was the same drive to go to the people rather than
> expect them to come to us. No catering for middle-class
> audiences in well-equipped theatres. We went to the streets,
> co-op halls, T.U. premises, factories, pits and labour
> exchanges. There would be no carrying of cumbersome
> lighting equipment, props, costumes. Truly 'a propertyless
> theatre for a propertyless class'.[100]

In this way it was hoped that by adapting the techniques of 'agit-prop' to indigenous British repertoire, workers' theatre would develop and perform its class struggle role.

In the early 1930s, it was estimated that there were about thirty groups throughout Britain, from Southampton to Dundee, with names like the South London Red Players, the Liverpool Red

Anchor Troupe, and the Sunderland Red Magnets.[101] They performed short sketches, mimes or songs in order to agitate for some kind of political demand. The groups had quite an extensive repertoire ranging from *Doctor Mac*, 'A political knock-about skit on MacDonald's cures for unemployment', to *Murder in the Coalfields*, 'A short, simple sketch, inspired by the recent colliery disaster.'[102] By using this material, it was possible to assist in all kinds of struggle. In London, help was given to the local Charter Committee to popularize their industrial demands; the Red Players 'lent effective support' to the Barkingside Tenants Associ-ations; and in the Lancashire area, the Salford Red Megaphones were active during the 'More Looms' agitation of 1931–2.[103] Thus, the WTM was engaged in a programme which was highly politic-ized – in January 1932 the South London Red Players performed in front of trade unionists, the unemployed, members of the Inter-national Labour Defence, co-operators, as well as the Barkingside Tenants Association and the ordinary working-class public.[104]

Furthermore, the WTM was to the forefront in supporting the policies and development of the CP and its constituent organiz-ations; it was the 'cultural shock brigade' of the Party, used as a crowd-drawer at meetings, demonstrations and social occasions.[105] It is indicative of wider activities that the tour of Scotland by the Red Pioneer Troupe – ostensibly a means to develop Scottish sections of the movement – was also used to disseminate the Party line and to help Communist candidates in the local elections. At one show given in front of the National Gallery in Edinburgh to over 5,000 workers (Tom Thomas has reckoned the figure to be 25,000), the political persuasion of the Troupe was clearly demonstrated when an effigy of a local 'Labourite' 'was burnt amid cheers'.[106] Electoral assistance was also offered South of the border. As Philip Poole recalls, the Red Radio troupe worked for Harry Pollitt during an election campaign in Whitechapel. They even composed a song based on a Gilbert and Sullivan tune, 'Three Little Maids':

> Three candidates for the boss are we,
> Liberal, Labour and New Party,
> You can vote how you like for one of us three-ee
> Candidates for the boss.

Three candidates who sing in chorus,
Well-to-do and quite decorous,
Capitalism's the best thing for us,
Candidates of the boss.[107]

This points to a further aspect of the Movement's politics – as already suggested, the Labour Party was treated with the same contempt as the Liberal and Conservative Parties.

The political climate of 'Class Against Class' changed when Hitler came to power in Germany. The British Communist Party, responding to the policy of the Communist International, gradually became more populist; the sectarian line was abandoned and Labour Socialists were increasingly tolerated. To counter the rise of Fascism, the united front strategy evolved, whereby co-operation was urged with rival left wing and social democratic organizations. This atmosphere of Socialist reconciliation favoured artistic developments and Socialist drama flourished. After returning from the Moscow dramatic Olympiad of May 1933, the WTM therefore began to broaden its methods.[108] The technical side of drama was increasingly appreciated; contact was made with sympathizers in the professional theatre, there was a gradual movement back to stage drama and a growing co-operation with social democratic and other groups.[109] The theatre director, André Van Gyseghem, for example, helped the Rebel Players by giving them technical advice about 'voice work, use of bodies, timing, well-spoken declamation, and a general feeling for the theatre'.[110] Joan Littlewood and Ewan MacColl also effected the transformation of the Salford Red Megaphones into the Manchester Theatre of Action, the change from agit-prop to more formalistic drama.[111] And it was not to be too long before the Unity theatre was formed. Unity theatre was Socialist creativity at its best: co-operation between famous professional artists like Paul Robeson and Sybil Thorndike and amateur actors, technicians and handymen in the production of socially progressive and entertaining drama like Odet's *Lefty*, the living newspaper sketch, *Busmen*, and the 'pantomime with a political point', *Babes in the Wood*.[112]

In many ways workers' drama was a source of 'proletarian creative ability'.[113] However, the act of politicizing the performing arts was not without its problems, particularly during the period of 'agit-prop'. The Marxist approach was, in short, subsumed in sectarian posturing. Not only were the activists blind to some of the qualities of bourgeois culture, but also unable to bring any understanding of popular culture that they may have had into public discourse. It sometimes appears from the writings of the revolutionary Communist, that the ordinary worker was the passive target of Capitalist ideological indoctrination. The views of Charlie Mann were somewhat typical: apparently, the workers were not free agents; their ideas and opinions were formed and suggested by every form of popular art, and their entertainment controlled by Capitalist interests, making it difficult for them to appreciate any new point of view![114] In fact, this kind of analysis left little room for working-class creativity. Generally speaking, the Marxist approach to popular art was lacking in subtlety; there was both a failure to understand the nature of the commercialized product and an unwillingness to accept some of the more progressive and autonomous aspects of popular culture.

In overall terms, therefore, the Marxist cultural formation was the outcome of an ideology which emphasized the need to overthrow Capitalist society. There were, of course, functional reasons why the CP decided to embark on cultural activity, the most obvious being that Communists, like other workers, needed opportunities for relaxation and recreation.[115] Questions of finance, recruitment and the propaganda value of Party entertainment were also important considerations.[116] Thus the Communist-inspired International Class War Prisoners' Aid in Fife used prize draws, dances, whist drives, raffles, concerts and parades in order to raise money and attract people.[117] It is also revealing that the organizational report of 1922, which led to the further bolshevization of the Party, noted the importance of socials as a source of 'real revolutionary activity':

> The purpose of 'socials' is to secure contact with outer circles
> of the workers with whom we would not otherwise become
> in contact. We must not cut ourselves off from the lives of the
> workers. 'Socials' are the means of drawing sympathisers,
> particularly from among women, youth and children, into the
> movement. For this purpose we will organise concerts,
> dances, plays, tea parties, outings and other recreations.[118]

It was envisaged that such occasions would provide the opportunity for political work: the Party paper would be on sale, speeches made, and revolutionary songs and poetry introduced. This was a serious attempt to establish political links with the mass of the people through recreational provision.

Recreational initiatives in the Labour Movement were the outcome of different organizational and ideological perspectives; one Labour Socialist with its reformist strategy, the other Marxist with its more systematic, revolutionary strategy. This does not mean, however, that the cultural agencies of Labour Socialism and Marxism were polar opposites. There were occasions, particularly at grass roots level, when Labour and Communist activities appeared very similar, and when there was a spirit of co-operation. As one writer pointed out, May Day was one time when unity should prevail, when Labour Socialist and Marxist alike should sing working-class songs together: 'We dislike Communist tactics as much as anybody, but when it comes to holding a united working class demonstration on May Day we shall be delighted to march side by side, in front, or behind our Communist friends.'[119] Moreover, there were also non-party organizations which overcame the limits imposed by ideological barriers.

In and around Manchester there were a number of groups which did not have any formal Party allegiance. For instance, the Stockport Labour Fellowship, which had its origins in the Labour church movement and wished to establish 'the Socialist Commonwealth', provided the local workforce, irrespective of their politics, with facilities for 'social contact'. It had drama, orchestral, rambling and educational sections.[120] Its central hall, as the focal point of all kinds of social activities, was offered to the workers during times of strikes and lock-outs: 'In times of Industrial Action or Political or Economic Conflict the workers looked to the Central Hall as a Citadel, and they had never been let down.'[121] Certainly the hall was not monopolized by one group. It is clear from the account books that the hall was let to numerous Labour organizations, including the Labour Party, ILP, CP, trade unions – farmworkers, builders, engineers, railwaymen, ironfounders, painters, bookbinders and so on – Women's Co-operative Guild, Clarion Cyclists, Workers' Educational Association, National Council of Labour Colleges and the Esperanto Society.[122] Furthermore, lectures were given by Labour figures as diverse in political views as Ellen Wilkinson on 'Europe, Limited', Tom Mann on

'Not a Revolutionist! Why Not?', William Paul on 'The Collapse of Capitalism', Oliver Baldwin on 'The Truth of Life', Mrs Dora Russell on 'Labour's Attitude to Birth Control', and J. H. Hudson on 'Labour and Liquor'. Also, debates were arranged involving different sections of the movement, such as the ones which took place between the CP and the Socialist Party of Great Britain.[123] It is, therefore, hardly surprising that the co-operative approach was expressed in the constitution: 'The Fellowship maintains an *Open* Platform for the expression of Socialist, Labour and Progressive thought.'[124] As one member claimed, 'not only could the Fellowship be of great service in the United Front movement, but that its future lay in the cultivation of that movement'.[125] In spite of financial instability, the Fellowship, like other non-aligned Socialist organizations, was able to lay the basis for peaceful co-existence between the various divergent Labour groupings. Indeed, the cultural role of the Fellowship was mainly responsible for the co-operative spirit. During rambles, lectures, play rehearsals, bazaars and dances, all kinds of politically motivated people had the opportunity to unite in social fellowship and so avoid or temper the stale bickering of sectarian politics.

This chapter has shown that the Labour Movement was interested in the question of leisure, and that this interest was shaped by the ideological dynamic of Labour Socialism and Marxism. Although there were similarities of approach, Labour Socialists campaigned for social reforms, Marxists struggled for revolutionary change. Further, Labourists and Communists had distinctive cultural formations of their own, though there were some Labour organizations which attempted to steer clear of political sectarianism.[126] Having said all this, the issue of leisure was never a primary concern of the working-class movement – wages, unemployment, and general blueprints for economic and social change were more important issues – and perhaps even more significant, the majority of workers paid little attention to Labour statements on leisure. It is indeed important to appreciate that only a minority of the British population were active in the campaign for holidays with pay and better sporting facilities, or were involved in the formation of ideas and policy; most people had neither heard about Socialist recreational organizations, nor bothered themselves with Labour's attitudes to the theatre or cinema. To put it simply, leisure for the British working class meant such things as the local pub, the Saturday afternoon at the football match or racecourse, and the plethora of activities centred on the home or local community; it had little to do with trade union action for shorter hours or the Marxist critique of Capitalist drama. Yet, notwithstanding this, the approach of Labour was part of the working-class cultural milieu of the inter-war years. Indeed, the actions of Labour brought forth various recreational benefits and shaped, if only marginally, working-class notions and aspirations of leisure.

7

The politics of leisure

The preceding chapters have mainly been concerned with the demand for and the provision of leisure facilities and services. The focus of the discussion has been on the quantitative and qualitative aspects of leisure. However, it is quite clear that leisure cannot be examined in isolation or divorced from the main economic and social developments of the period. There is no doubt that leisure was closely associated with changes in the economy, particularly the increase in real wages, social inequality, the collectivist trend, work and unemployment. Moreover, it is difficult to deny that leisure was, and is, intimately related to politics. Throughout, there have been many instances where leisure can be seen to have been influenced by and made an impact on political society. As far as the demand for leisure is concerned, it was stressed that the organized Labour Movement sought to increase spare time by a reduction in the working week and the introduction of holidays with pay. Not only did this involve negotiations with employers, interest group pressure and meetings with the relevant departments of State, but also direct Parliamentary representation. In the inter-war period there were a number of Private Members' Bills dealing with the issue of paid holidays, culminating in the legislation of 1938. Perhaps even more important was the fact that agencies of the State channelled recreational and cultural issues through the political process. As was noted, central and municipal authorities provided grants and facilities for leisure, as well as performing regulatory functions. And yet another example of the political nature of leisure is that the Labour Movement had a number of leisure related policies and a cultural formation of its own. What is known about Labour cultural initiatives shows that the Socialist approach to leisure was overtly political. The organizations catering for workers' drama and film, especially those on the Marxist left, aimed to use the performing arts as a weapon in the class struggle. Equally, the workers' sports movement regarded sport as a legitimate form of political activity.

Social scientists and historians have started to examine the functioning of working-class culture in Capitalist society. To the Marxist, leisure is an integral part of the superstructure of society and something closely connected to political life. In the opinion of Bryn Jones:

> Culture is a site of struggle, of conflict, of negotiations which constantly redefine (and usually reproduce in a new form) the existing relations of domination and subordination in the society. . . . The culture of the working class was and always has been a site of intense struggle for the control of their non-work time, what Marx calls a labourer's disposable time.[1]

At one level, because labour is said to be alienated under Capitalism, spare time or non-labour time appears as freedom and happiness; at another level, leisure has been regarded as a form of hegemony by which the dominant group obtains the consent of the working class, by, for example, ideological and cultural conditioning through the cinema or radio. Marxists and non-Marxists alike have used the Gramscian concept of hegemony in an extremely sophisticated and subtle way, stressing that contestation between dominant and subordinate groups over, say, recreational activities is in itself a dialectical process by which the ruling elite have to make concessions and search for new forms of dominance. Although the 'social control' versions of this line were questioned in chapter three, where it was claimed that the working class were able to insulate themselves from crude methods of political indoctrination into the dominant order, it is nevertheless evident that leisure is a political question. The cultural manipulation of workers may have failed, but this does not mean that ruling groups failed to perceive non-work time as a possible avenue for generating consensus and forging social harmony. Even those with a liberal democratic notion of and pluralist framework for analysing the State and society would find it difficult to refute the fact that leisure is firmly situated in the political domain. In this chapter a number of recreational issues which directly impinged on the political process will be examined. It will be shown that leisure is indeed a political question, inasmuch as it involves public debate about the meanings and use of leisure, as well as campaigns for adequate spare time facilities.

Leisure, education and religion

If the growing industrial leisure complex, the activities of voluntary organizations and State involvement affected the nature of leisure activities, as they surely did, then it was inevitable that there would be all kinds of political responses. Leisure was increasingly regarded as a social problem by many sections of the community. Social scientists, architects and town planners, hygienists, and historians all contributed to the leisure debate.[2] There was even a Leisure Society founded under the auspices of the Social Credit Movement, which had a number of objects:

1 To proclaim that leisure is a good and moral thing.
2 To urge the community to aim for the maximum of leisure consistent with a high standard of plain living.
3 To preach a wider and richer use of leisure; and to this end to encourage all art, research, scholarship, travel, crafts and sport.
4 To study currency and costing problems – with a view to discovering some means whereby our complicated and wasteful form of 'civilisation' may be exchanged for the simpler and more leisured way of life that the invention of labour-saving machinery has so obviously made possible.[3]

It is indeed interesting that A. R. Orage, the leading advocate of social credit, protested that unemployment was not a disease but a symptom of health. Although the details of social credit need not detain us here, it may be noted that the Leisure Society was little more than a dining club.

Educationalists also discussed and considered the recent trends in leisure. Concern was shown about developments in leisure, and particularly their relationship with a number of other social issues like Christianity, commercialism, and unemployment. For instance, one obvious claim had it that it was far better for the unemployed to be engaged in some kind of educational activity than to be standing on street corners. In more specific terms, it was suggested that there was a fundamental connection between education and leisure. With the extension of spare time and the growth of resources, there was increasing concern that leisure would be wasted; to counteract this education was to be used to promote the 'correct' use of leisure. As Ernest Barker, the principal of King's College, London, urged, education 'should be a training in the right way of using leisure, which without education may be misspent and frittered away'.[4] With the reductions in the hours of work in the immediate post-war period, it was similarly argued that through education the worker would not abuse 'his new-found leisure'.[5] In a different context, progressive thinkers believed that leisure would turn the workers away from political and social change unless accompanied by education. In the first instance it was asserted that with proper training in childhood the working class would use their leisure fruitfully, and to the advantage of good citizenship.[6] And once adulthood had been reached, it was essential to continue with education. In the words of one co-operator:

> The right employment of leisure is a problem to which co-operators are giving genuine attention. . . . Spare time ought naturally to be 'free' time, which the individual shall not be dragooned into using in any particular way. But on the other hand it should not be 'dead' time, wasted in empty amusements and listless loafing. Our co-operative guilds, circles, schools, and courses are examples of that right use of leisure which is one of the strongest weapons for the self-defence of democracy.[7]

In fact, throughout the 1920s and 1930s self-taught worker intellectuals were given the opportunity to study at classes arranged by the Workers' Educational Association, the National Council of Labour Colleges and the Plebs League. For the autodidact there was little enough time to absorb the principles of science or literature, let alone time for playing football or watching a Hollywood film; for them, a meagre leisure had to be spent profitably in education.

Some educationalists, such as Leslie Missen, Director of Education in Wigan, went so far as to claim that the employment of recreation was one of the most important parts of life.[8] It is suggestive of prevailing interests, that the main theme of the New Education Fellowship's first regional conference in Britain in 1935 was 'Education and Leisure'. Representatives of the Board of Education, Scottish Education Department, and Ministry of Education for Northern Ireland, as well as teachers, university lecturers and social workers, attended. A 25,000 word document was circulated which drew attention to the need for new attitudes and approaches. In addition, proposals were made concerning the facilities and training which the community should provide so as to enable the school leaver to make the proper use of leisure hours. The conference also organized some relevant discussion groups, exhibitions, and demonstrations of films, folk dancing, dramatic work and music. An attempt was being made to link leisure with education.[9] Furthermore, two years later, the National Institute of Industrial Psychology and the British Institute of Adult Education – at this time publishing its Life and Leisure pamphlets – with the support of delegates from more than 200 voluntary organizations, education authorities and industrial undertakings, set up a committee to examine the problem of the use of leisure.[10]

There were some educationalists, however, who were careful not to preach to the workers. This was the view of Joseph Findlay, Honorary Professor of Education at Manchester University and the author of many educational texts: 'It savours of impertinence for one man to tell another how to occupy his leisure time.'[11] A similar point was made by that great Christian Socialist, R. H. Tawney, himself a lecturer in economic history and sometime member of the Consultative Committee of the Board of Education:

No human being can educate another, unless, in some degree
at least, he has shared his life. Before a man offers advice
to a miner how to spend his evenings, he had better have seen
the inside of a pit; and the best preparation for an attempt
to improve the taste of shop assistants would be to stand for

a day or two selling expensive rubbish to rich fools. So far, in short, as adults are concerned, it is a question, not of imposing elevated standards on an uncultivated multitude, but of attempting to find new sources of enjoyment in company with people whom one likes sufficiently to feel justified in inviting them to waste their time with one.[12]

According to this more libertarian approach, an over-zealous advocacy of rational leisure was anathema. It was the right of individuals to decide for themselves the ways in which to use their spare time.

It is true that in the inter-war period 'the nature of debates about leisure provision and the moral purpose and moral usefulness of leisure, have a much more secular content than they had in the mid-Victorian period.'[13] From the beginning of the twentieth century there had been a decline in organized religion and with it a dilution of the church's role as arbiter of tastes and morality. By 1939 there was a great deal of concern about the decline of religious belief:

> Along with all this moral laxity [i.e. Gambling] is a growing indifference to religion. Every religious body is feeling the draught. Not only is church attendance declining, but Sunday School classes are melting away. It is becoming increasingly difficult to evoke interest in the things of the spirit. God has been forgotten.[14]

Nevertheless, with the expansion of new leisure forms the church and religious groups in general were still concerned about the rational use of leisure. There was, for instance, an element of doubt about the efficacy of the new means of mass communication, namely the cinema and the radio. One school of thought was apprehensive about the growth of leisure activities which were regarded as socially immoral, while others believed that misspent leisure time would prejudice the prospect of religious change and the acceptance of Christian principles. In very broad terms, the church is to be seen condemning many of the new recreational and cultural pursuits, though praising the judicious use of leisure. Yet, most criticism was still aimed at drinking and gambling.

Despite the fall in the consumption of beer the church continued to advocate temperance. It is true that the inter-war years witnessed the gradual demise of the temperance movement, but even by the end of the 1930s there were many organizations campaigning against the evils of drink. In particular, there were a number of bodies sponsored by the church: the Church of England Temperance Society, the Methodist Temperance and Social Welfare Committee, the National Unitarian Temperance Association, the Church of Scotland General Assembly's Committee on Temperance and so on. In addition, some of the main anti-drink organizations had religious figures as leaders; the Bishops of Norwich and London were presidents of the National Temperance League and the National United Temperance Council respectively.

As with church organizations in general, the temperance movement sponsored a number of recreational events. Undoubtedly this was part of a strategy designed to wean people away from the public house. To take one example from many: in the summer of 1928 the Bermondsey and Southwark Bands of Hope enjoyed one of their best street processions ever. There were fancy dress costumes and music from the Christian Mission brass band, followed by a park picnic and the presentation of prizes for the Temperance Truths' competition. Nearly 1,500 people were involved, and it was hoped that the event would 'have an appreciable effect in raising Bermondsey's quota towards the "Million More Abstainers" Movement'.[15] Despite the pull of the cinema and other commercially oriented activities, it is clear from newspaper sources that religion continued to play a part in the cultural milieu of the local community. It must be added, however, that the church was perhaps unsuccessful in its attempt at moral and social control.

More important than recreational initiatives were the political campaigns of the church. Throughout the 1920s and 1930s the church pressed for legislative reform of the drink trade. There was no such thing as a united approach by the various religious groups. Some believed in prohibition, others in local option or State ownership. In Scotland, for instance, the United Free Church and the Church of Scotland were in favour of prohibition, whereas the Episcopal clergy and the Roman Catholics were not.[16] There was even disagreement between members of the same denomination. Thus, in giving evidence to the Royal Commission on Licensing, the Reverend A. Courtney, a Wesleyan Minister, was critical of State ownership, while the Reverend G. Barwell Evan, another Wesleyan Minister, supported it. Nonetheless, there was a greater degree of consensus after the fusion of the Methodist movement in 1933, and the subsequent agreed programme of the forces of temperance – the United Kingdom Alliance (the main prohibitionist grouping), Wesleyan Conference and the Methodist Temperance and Social Welfare Committee (with its belief in local option).

There were also some positive legislative attempts to curb the drinking habit. Support was given to a number of Parliamentary Bills designed to promote temperance. The best examples are the Clubs Bill, Temperance Wales Bill, Liquor Traffic Prohibition Bill, and the Standardisation of Hours Bill. In retrospect it is justifiable to conclude that these attempts at reform were unrealistic. However, given the prohibition experiment in the United States, the demand for moderation in the use of, or even total abstinence from, alcoholic drink was still perceived as an important issue in inter-war Britain. Although there were many temperance supporters in the Labour Party,[17] it is true to say that there was still an affinity between the old nonconformist wing of the Liberal Party and those free churches advocating the need for restrictions. As the Reverend Sam Rowley expressed it, the Conservative Party had no temperance policy, the Labour Party was paralysed by the Club and Institute Union, but the Liberal Party had a constructive programme which would 'be generally approved by Temperance workers'.[18] It was through the support of the Liberal Party that the temperance arguments of the church received a political hearing.

The growth of gambling also concerned the church. Religious attitudes to betting were well summarized by the Reverend A. N. Boyle of Edinburgh:

There is its effect upon character so inevitably degrading; there is the crime it produces, for which the evidence is overwhelming. The path of this amusement, as some will call it, or vice, as others think it, is strewn thickly with ruined lives and unhappy homes. And the whole thing is a pitiful delusion for the man who bets – an organised business conducted by shrewd and unscrupulous men for extracting

money from those who have laboured for it. They follow a
will of the wisp of gain, and find themselves in a bog of loss.
But no loss ever cured a confirmed gambler. The only safety is
not to become a gambler. A bet may be comparatively
harmless but to love betting is to admit a poison into the
heart which will inevitably destroy all that makes life fine and
fair.[19]

Despite the fact that journals such as *The New Statesman* thought
that any attack on betting could not be based on the Scriptures,
religious opposition continued to have a moral, if not a theo-
logical, basis. Hence, Peter Green, the Canon of Manchester,
came out against betting principally on moral grounds.[20] With the
introduction and growth of new forms of betting, such as the
football pools, there was even more concern. As the National
Liberal, R. J. Russell, commented during a Parliamentary debate
on the pools: 'I am dealing this morning with an extraordinary,
an amazing and a sinister development which has taken place and
which has caused all thoughtful citizens much concern and not
a little alarm.'[21] Similarly, the Labour MP for Motherwell, the
Reverend James Barr, saw in the totalizator the antithesis of
'intelligent and disinherited citizenship' and 'a clean Democracy'.
It was not that he was against 'the socialisation of public utilities',
but that he was 'not in favour of the socialisation or nationalisation
of public iniquities'. He rejected the argument that control of
betting would bring a 'cleansed turf', for he wanted 'to see a
cleansed democracy and pure sport. I want the cleansing of our
great national sports from evils like this. I want to see for the
people, pure joy and clean recreation that will . . . give them the
love of virtue and an ardour for all noble pursuits and a desire to
avoid all the by-paths of vice.'[22] In short, betting was looked on
as an enemy of Christian morality.

Once again the church made representations to the various
committees of inquiry, including the Royal Commission on Lotteries and Betting of 1933, and of course lobbied MPs. Thus in 1928
the Conservative Home Secretary, Sir William Joynson Hicks,
received over 1,600 resolutions from religious and other bodies
calling for the State control of dog racing courses.[23] Having said
this, it is interesting to note that despite the church's public
position, lotteries and raffles were carried out at church functions.

Moreover, the mass of the British people were opposed to restrictions being imposed on their right to bet. This is apparent from the comments of Ted Williams, the Labour member for Don Valley, made during a debate on a Bill designed to curb the growth of the football pools:

> It is no exaggeration for me to say that I have had more letters from my constituents, threatening never to vote for me again if I voted for this Bill than I have ever had with regard to any Bill during the last 13½ years.[24]

Finally, it is also appropriate to examine the approach of religious organizations to Sunday entertainment. For the majority of workers Sunday was the main day of leisure, so consequently there was a demand for recreational outlets. Although the Sunday Observance Act of 1780 deemed that revenue stimulating public entertainment was illegal, this was largely circumvented by the licensing powers of local authorities. From the end of the nineteenth century, there was a growth in both public and private facilities catering for Sunday interests. In a typical London working-class district, for example, there were many opportunities for pleasure: the Sunday newspaper, the wireless, a bicycle ride into the country, concerts and organ recitals, boxing, the occasional greyhound meeting and the Sunday evening dance.[25] Furthermore, for the young working woman, Sunday was said to be 'the only day on which games are possible for the worker; she returns home on Saturday afternoon tired out after the week's work and often, even if she has the leisure or inclination to play, she is expected to help her mother with duties in the home.'[26] Not surprisingly, as we shall see later in this chapter, the Labour Movement sought to extend opportunities and facilities for Sunday sport.

The challenge to Sunday observance was obviously met with opposition from the churches and the Sabbatarian lobby. Organizations such as the Lord's Day Observance Society and the Imperial Alliance for the Defence of Sunday, supported by all the main Christian denominations, aimed to maintain the holiness of the Lord's Day. The church feared further secularization, and in the words of one protagonist, the possibility of the 'Devil taking over Sunday'.[27] In Birmingham, the Anglican and Free Churches opposed the Sunday opening of cinemas on a number of grounds, but the main concern was 'for the sanctity of Sunday and, implicitly, concern for church attendance'.[28] It is true that the church was modifying its position and was no longer strictly Sabbatarian; the Council of Christian Ministers on Social Questions thus had no objection 'to recreation in the usual sense . . . we are content to leave to the Christian's own conscience the decision as to the Sunday recreations which are suitable or unsuitable.'[29] Nevertheless, opposition to Sunday entertainment continued.

In January 1931 matters came to a head when the High Court of Appeal made it clear that revenue producing entertainment was prohibited by law. J. R. Clynes, the Labour Home Secretary, introduced a Sunday (Performances) Bill to amend the 1780 Act and grant local authorities the power to permit four types of entertainment – cinemas, lectures, speeches and debates. Yet, the Labour Government failed to draft a piece of legislation to actually repeal the Act, for they did not want to see prize-fighting, boxing, football matches, gambling or horse racing on Sundays. It is significant that the division was left to a free vote: the Whips realized that religion directly impinged on the question. For instance, the Reverend Gordon Lang, the Labour MP for Oldham, was representative of those Christians who feared the 'commercialisation and secularisation of the age'. For him, Sunday should be a day of peace and quiet rest, a time when the Christian church had 'the duty of rendering back to its Creator certain specific acts of worship and of dedication'. In his advocacy of the Sabbath, he recreated an image of spiritual enjoyment, long since tarnished by the opening of cinemas and other entertainments:

I can go back to the time when we gathered after services . . .
in a room with a piano or an organ and we sang simple
hymns and songs. They were quiet times, but we felt we were
fresh for the things that lay before us, more ready for duty,
more clear in conscience, more in tune with the infinite and
more sympathetic with our fellow men than some of the
crowded week-ends that we have to live.[30]

In the end, even though the Bill was read a second time, it was lost in committee.

The discord was relieved for a short time when, in October

1931, the Sunday Performance (Temporary Regulation) Act received the Royal Assent. Yet the controversy was renewed after the loss of the Sunday Performances (Regulation) Bill and the introduction of the National Government's Sunday Entertainments Bill. Because of religious differences of opinion, as well as the trade union's fear that Sunday entertainment would increase the working week from six to seven days, the issue dragged on. In all, two Parliaments, three Governments and four Bills were found necessary to deal with the matter. Eventually, the National Government imposed Party discipline, and on 13 July 1932 the Bill became law.[31] However, this was not the end of the matter. The legislation involved local polls and so all kinds of controversy and disagreements at the local level. Furthermore, the Sabbatarian bodies maintained their pressure. The Imperial Alliance arranged a deputation to the Home Office, while the Church and Nation Committee of the Church of Scotland urged the Secretary of State for Scotland to support legislation prohibiting Sunday games, and all forms of commercialized and organized sport and entertainment, notably aviation, football, cinemas and concerts.[32]

The stance of religious groups on leisure was rather conservative and more than likely alienated those workers taking advantage of the new leisure choices. Not only was there a certain antipathy shown towards drinking, gambling and Sunday entertainment, but also to the new forms of dancing and music, some of which had been imported from the United States. When the Charleston arrived in England in 1925 a Bristol vicar was led to say: 'It is neurotic! It is rotten! It stinks! Phew open the windows.'[33] This is not to say that all church groups were unresponsive to popular change and unwilling to modify traditional practices and attitudes. Indeed, many units of the church were primarily recreational organizations, competing against commercial and other forms of leisure. More specifically, the Conference on Christian Politics, Economics and Citizenship (COPEC) came up with quite a radical assessment of recent trends in leisure, admitting that under 'existing circumstances much can be done to improve the conditions and so the use of leisure time, and to develop leisure occupations'. They drafted a number of recommendations, including the demand for playing fields and holidays with pay, the recognition of the scope for vocation in the entertainment industry, and the need to free the Christian Sunday from negative rules and so enhance leisure.[34] Further, as Jeffrey Richards has found, there were a number of high ranking figures in the church who had an enlightened approach to recreation. In stressing that 'the right use of leisure is going to be every bit as serious as the problems of wages and industrial conditions', the Reverend E. S. Woods, the Bishop of Croydon, advocated the need for more leisure and amenities, not less:

> The Church should say plainly that Sunday is not an unsuitable day for some forms of recreation. With regard to the vast sections of the community who have very few facilities for Sunday outdoor recreation in summer time and who, in winter, are completely without a comfortable room and fireside, books and wireless, there must clearly be something in the nature of provided recreation. There are masses of young people in the streets of all big urban centres on Sunday evenings who literally have nowhere to go and nothing to do. I fear that with the great majority, it would not enter their heads to come to church. Is there anything that can be done for them? I should say open the cinemas and give them healthy films and it is a course which, according to many unmistakable signs, people are generally going to demand. The unwise people are those who try to block it, and, by blocking it, increase the demand until it reaches a point where it sweeps all obstacles away and becomes a revolution which cannot be controlled. . . . There are occasions when the Church must set itself against the whole world. This is not one of them.[35]

An examination of education and religion shows that leisure was related to and cannot be divorced from wider society. Educationalists and religious devotees were deeply concerned about recreational and cultural developments. Changes in leisure brought with them changes in tastes and meanings. Recreational change was perceived, rightly or wrongly, as a threat by those proponents of a regulated spare time designed to fit in with educational advance and/or religious custom. In turn this involved fierce debate over people's likes and dislikes, and the need to inculcate people with the 'right' attitudes and 'correct' approach to leisure. Again, debate of this kind exerted an influence over subsequent developments in the recreational and cultural sphere. Although the demand for rational recreation had faded into the background by the twentieth century, there was clearly an element of continuity. In brief, middle-class moralists and those proponents of rational recreation found in the new leisure activities of the inter-war years a further avenue for moral condemnation and reform. Educational or religious promulgations on leisure were of course controversial, and more than this they were highly political. At any rate, the fact that the meanings and use of leisure were contested by different social groups brought the question of gambling and Sunday cinemas into the very centre of political life, involving Parliament itself. The desire of the church to shape the recreational life of the nation necessarily involved pressure group politics, Parliamentary debate, legislation and even judicial intervention. Yet, leisure related issues were at their most political when originating from direct Government interference.

The Government and leisure

The relationship between leisure provision and the State has already been examined. The State provided sports grounds, and recreational and cultural facilities, especially at municipal level, made grants to voluntary bodies, and regulated many aspects of leisure. The fact that the State took an interest in and shaped the development of leisure meant that recreational and cultural questions were never far removed from the political process. As Colin Mercer and James Donald have pointed out, the British State has played an extremely active role in shaping leisure, a role which has had very significant economic, political and ideological implications.[36] Part of this was the decision of successive Governments to use leisure as a way of advancing certain political interests. In other words, there was a degree of overt governmental manipulation, whereby Governments used leisure in order to promote wider political and ideological objectives.

There were two very good reasons why Governments regarded leisure as politically significant. In the first place, there was the political pressure exerted by voluntary organizations. It has already been stressed that religious groups, worried about trends in drinking, gambling and Sunday entertainment, pressed the

Government of the day for appropriate legislation. More than this, many recreational and cultural bodies promoted campaigns and lobbied the administration on a wide range of questions. The Cyclists' Touring Club, for example, first made political representations during the 1918 General Election; by the mid-1930s it had embarked upon methods of direct action to counter the anti-cycling proposals of Mr Hore Belisha, the Minister of Transport.[37] As the *C.T.C. Gazette* expressed it:

> Our series of 'protest' meetings, in which cyclists of every kind have co-operated heartily, have been for the most part magnificently successful. . . . Nothing like this determined, continued and unanimous opposition to the Minister of Transport's proposals has ever been known before in the history of cycling, and the campaign will proceed with unabated vigour during the current month.[38]

In this it was joined by other cycling organizations, including the Socialist-influenced Clarion Cycling Club who complained to the Labour Party about Government plans to introduce cycle paths and the compulsory fixture of rear lights to cycles.[39] Even a small provincial journal such as *The Northern Cyclist and Athlete* felt it necessary and worthwhile enough to appoint a correspondent to the House of Commons to supply news of interest to cyclists, and to compile 'a list of all our friends in the House, who, if occasion arises, will defend and advance the interests of cyclists'.[40] Likewise, the British Drama League was involved in electioneering and lobbying political representatives – presumably Governments were seen as the political overseer of the arts as well as sport.[41] In more general terms, as will be seen towards the end of this chapter, central and local authorities were subjected to many demands for improvements in recreational and cultural facilities.

As a result of such pressure, which undoubtedly influenced public opinion and may have created new aspirations, it is interesting to note that candidates in both national and local elections began to consider leisure related issues in their manifestos and campaigns. The Labour Party thus advocated a number of leisure reforms. Despite the absence of Conservative Party commitments at the national level, Conservative Councillors and officials at the local level also considered leisure questions, and in some cases recommended limited reform. In the North Cheshire textile town of Hyde, for example, recreation was a salient theme of the election addresses of Thomas Middleton, a leading Conservative and a holder of the office of Lord Mayor:

> As Chairman of the Park Committee I have devoted time and effort to the improvement of the Park, the bringing of first-class music into the town, and the provision of Playing Fields and Open Spaces in various parts of the Borough. It was chiefly on my initiative that the Playground was provided for Kingston; the Werneth Lodge grounds opened as a Park for the Gee Cross end of the Borough; and the Tennis Courts at Pole Bank thrown open for the public. I am desirous of securing the provision of further playground accommodation for the children in Gee Cross and other parts of the town as soon as the finances of the town will permit. Safety and health alike demand that our children should not be compelled to play in the streets.[42]

Finance may have been a constraint on social policy-making, though it is apparent that Middleton played a not too insignificant role in the introduction of leisure amenities; and it was he who represented the Corporation at meetings of such national organizations as the National Playing Fields Association and the Council for the Preservation of Rural England.[43]

A second influence on the Government's approach was the quite popular view of the time that leisure was one of the variables which enabled the ruling class to pacify working-class militancy. Many employers thus believed that leisure activities turned workers away from political involvement and class conflict, and it was widely assumed that sport fostered understanding and moderation of feeling. Note the sentiments expressed in the following editorial from *The Ashton-Under-Lyne Reporter*:

> . . . it is generally acknowledged that football provides one of the finest antidotes to unrest in this country, and creates in the mass a sense of sportsmanship that no other games can possibly do. In such an atmosphere the possibilities of a settlement of Lancashire's cotton problems are considerably strengthened. Employers and operatives meet on common

ground as lovers of the winter pastime, and win, lose or draw, ill-will and prejudice disappear when both sides 'play the game'.[44]

This kind of assumption was reinforced by the views of many employers who expressed the notion of sport as a bulwark against Socialism and Bolshevism. In the opinion of H. Cropper, a coal-owner and the Mayor of Chesterfield Borough Council, speaking in 1922: 'One of the reasons why this country would never witness a political or social revolution or upheaval was because the average Englishman was . . . immersed in sport.'[45] For the employing class sport transcended class barriers; the playing field was said to be egalitarian, uniting king and subject, prince and workman. Thus, when Sir Robert Hadfield, the Sheffield steel magnate, opened his company's new sports ground he remarked that this was 'the best antidote to revolution and revolutionary ideas', adding that 'No one has ever heard of a good sportsman arising amongst the Socialists or Bolsheviks'.[46] Similarly, leaders of public opinion in South Wales regarded rugby union as a social healer during times of Labour unrest and class conflict.[47] From a different political perspective, a number of Marxists believed that sport 'was the best antidote to Bolshevism', a kind of 'dope for the working masses'.[48]

Although it is difficult to say whether leisure encouraged class collaboration rather than class confrontation, social stability rather than social strife, the fact that Governments perceived this to be so was a very good reason why they were not going to turn a blind eye to politically sensitive leisure developments. Thus during the industrial unrest of 1919 a Home Office report presented to the Cabinet on revolutionary activities in Britain placed sport near the top of a list of stabilizing factors.[49] Interestingly enough one Home Office report on revolutionary organizations in the United Kingdom advanced the view that the public house undermined militant activities:

My Glasgow correspondent reports that the revolutionary movement is certainly gaining ground, and he thinks that the strike threatened for next Monday must be very carefully watched. He thinks (and the same view is taken by correspondents in other parts of the country) that one of the causes for discontent is the liquor control and the high price of beer. The extremists support the present restrictions because they know that if men could congregate in public houses, they would not be driven to attend the revolutionary meetings.[50]

Presumably, both sport and drink were regarded by the Government of the day as ways of diluting social and political discontent.

Given that leisure was playing an increasingly important part in people's everyday life it was probably inevitable that the Government would take stock of the most important trends. Moreover, there was a tendency for an increasing range of activities within the State apparatus to become politicized; Governments were becoming more involved in these activities and more leisure questions seemed subject to political controversy. In effect, all Governments protected and indeed, whether by conscious effort or not, were a force in perpetuating the prevailing economic and social order; that is, the market economy, the legal institutions, royalty, the Empire, the dominant religious and moral values, and so on.

One of the main ways in which Governments tried to monitor leisure was through political censorship, particularly of films. Thus, according to the leading historian of inter-war cinema and society, Jeffrey Richards, film censorship helped to mould social consensus and maintain the *status quo*.[51] The content of films was controlled by the British Board of Film Censors. In spite of the fact that the Board was financed by the private cinema industry and was not an official agency of the State, it was, in effect, under the patronage of the Home Office which appointed the Board's President and Secretary. In fact, successive Presidents in the 1930s, Edward Shortt and Lord Tyrrell, had a considerable amount of 'political' experience between them in the fields of internal security, counter-subversion, counter-insurgency, political intelligence and overseas cultural propaganda. The main role of the Board was to advise local authorities – who had the right to censor and ban films – as to the suitability of film content. And indeed, due to the fact that some films contained controversial material, ranging from scenes of sexual depravity to scenes depicting hostile relations between labour and capital, there was a fair amount of censorship. By the early 1930s the Board actually vetted scripts before films were even produced. Moreover, in 1931 the State established a Cinema Advisory Council, consisting of representatives of local authorities, Chief Constables and Justices of the Peace, which advised and liaised with the Board. Though it was argued in chapter three that the cinema was not a form of social control, there is some evidence to support Nicholas Pronay's view:

> Instead of powerful, emotionally backed calls for taking matters into their own hands, for viewing their government as their enemy 'class' or otherwise, and their plight as the result of the system of government, they the cinema audience were encouraged to regard their economic and social condition as a personal and not a political problem, to take joy and pride in the institutions, historic and 'fair' of their country. In short, harmony and hope of better days, arising from the innate strength and justice of the system in which they lived, which was suffering only the temporary impact of a worldwide depression, were most successfully and effectively fostered. . . . Censorship ensured that dreams were not turned into nightmares of doubt and distrust and that there were no alluring visions of new orders.[52]

In particular, Governments were far from generous or sympathetic to Marxist cultural activity. It is likely that local authorities, using the guidelines laid down by the British Board of Film Censors, thought that Russian films were 'calculated and possibly intended to foment social unrest and discontent'.[53] Since the Conservative Party was also apprehensive about subversive propaganda – despite the fact that they used film for publicity purposes – it is not surprising that a number of Russian films were censored.[54] The Salford Watch Committee, for instance, banned the exhibition of *Storm Over Asia*, much to the dismay of *The Manchester Guardian* and the Dean of Manchester, Dr Hewlett Johnson (the film was eventually shown in Manchester).[55] Similar decisions were made by the Theatre and Music Hall Committee of the London County Council (effectively restricting the activities of the ILP Masses Stage and Film Guild), the Libraries Committee of the Liverpool City Council and the local Watch Committees in Sheffield and Cardiff.[56]

In addition to this, police intervention was commonplace. Alf

Williams has recalled how the police were always harassing the Manchester and Salford society and exerting pressure on potential exhibitors of their films: 'the police got us where they wanted us.'[57] The Communist-inspired Workers' Theatre Movement faced similar opposition. On one occasion, for instance, Nat Cohen, the organizer of the Stepney branch of the International Labour Defence, and five members of the Red Radio Troupe were arrested for obstruction; they appeared in the Old Street Police Court and were probably fortunate to be discharged with a caution – Cohen was bound over for twelve months.[58] For those Marxists active in cultural work, the restrictive actions of censors and police alike must have confirmed their rather crude conspiracy theory of Capitalist ideological manipulation; it was certainly not going to engender moderation of feeling or intent.

At this point it is appropriate to offer a word of caution. It needs to be stressed, once again, that the aim to promote the established order was resisted by many progressive social groups, often with a fair degree of success. The cinema was, after all, a collective institution, which, far from incorporating the working class into Capitalist society, may have been used to express and indeed reinforce proletarian values. It is difficult to imagine film censorship altering class boundaries and pulling workers away from trade unionism or some other form of class opposition. As already suggested, people were able to question and contest the social message of films. In other words, I am arguing that the Government and the ruling *élite* may have been able to censor films, but this did not necessarily bring with it the desired effect.

Government interference was at its height when leisure, and sport in particular, had international significance. If the index to the Foreign Office Archives is consulted it will be noted that there are entries for sport in every year between 1920 and 1945, some highly political in character.[59] Association football was certainly regarded as a rather sensitive area, for the Foreign Office thought it was essential for the English team to give a good account of themselves throughout the world. The British Government used football as an integral part of overseas cultural propaganda seeking to portray Britain as a nation of justice and fair play, and to support diplomatic objectives.[60] It would therefore be appropriate to use international football as a case study of the politics of intervention.

There were a number of occasions when the Government

meddled in the preparations leading up to matches between British teams and foreign teams. In 1930, for example, the Labour Home Secretary, J. R. Clynes, refused to grant visas to a Russian side from the mining area of the Don Basin to enable them to enter the country and play against English, Scottish and Welsh representative sides drawn from the British Workers' Sports Federation. The reason for the ban is clear from Clynes's speech in the House of Commons: 'In the absense of any evidence that the object of the proposed tour was for the purpose of genuine sport, I could not see my way to accede to the application.'[61] When a Foreign Office official dug a little deeper he found that the reason for the ban was 'that when a Soviet team went to France three years ago they entered the field of play waving the Red Flag and singing the "International" and that the authorities in the Home Office are doubtless apprehensive of all sorts of similar disturbances here'. Additional information was also produced: 'the reason for refusal was the prospect of trouble adduced largely from the places at which the team were to play and the backing of the project by the Communist party'.[62] Given the Labour leadership's vehement anti-Communism it is perhaps not too surprising that they took such a *political* decision. There is also a lot of evidence to substantiate the claim that the British Government played a leading role in forcing the English team to give the Nazi salute in the Berlin Stadium in 1938. This ploy was designed to foster smooth diplomatic relations between Britain and Nazi Germany. In simple terms, it was inconceivable that at the height of appeasement the English team would refuse to give the salute. Thus it is suggestive of the prevailing political atmosphere, that after the match the Foreign Office contacted the Football Association to show its appreciation of the fact that the government's 'pre-match request had been fulfilled to the letter'.[63] The politicization of international sport will now be taken up in more detail by examining the events leading up to the England versus Germany match staged at White Hart Lane, London, in December 1935.

When it was announced that a German football team was to visit this country in late 1935 many protests were made, particularly from Labour organizations. According to Sir Walter Citrine, the general secretary of the TUC, over 100 official complaints were received by 'branches of the Unions and so forth'.[64] Organ-

ized Labour was obviously against the match because of the anti-
semitism of the Nazi régime, and the fact that the German
supporters proposed to march through the Jewish residential areas
of Stoke Newington and Stamford Hill. It is also interesting to
note that it was estimated that about a third of the supporters of
Tottenham Hotspur (as already mentioned the match was to be
played at White Hart Lane, the home ground of Tottenham) were
Jewish.[65] As the South London Cab branch of the Transport and
General Workers' Union expressed it:

> That this 1/356 Branch of the T. & G.W.U. strongly protests
> against the projected International Football match between
> England and Germany on December 4 at Tottenham. We
> consider that the members of the German team will be
> specially selected from the most extreme anti-democratic and
> brutal section of the Nazis, and are sent here with the express
> purpose of strengthening the Fascist movement in Great
> Britain as well as propaganda in support of the Hitler regime.
> In the event of the match being played we shall call on our
> entire membership to boycott the 'Spurs' matches.[66]

In addition, plenty of protests were made by sports clubs, Jewish
groups, and voluntary organizations. In the light of this rising tide
of opposition, the TUC sent a deputation to the Home Office.[67]
It is apparent that the TUC, too, wished the match to be
prohibited. Sir Walter Citrine summed up their case:

> It will be known to you that the dissolution of the Trade Union
> and Labour Movement in Germany has produced many bitter
> feelings among wide sections of the people, added to which
> the general brutal intolerance displayed by the Nazi
> Government has called forth world-wide condemnation.
>   Great Britain is giving shelter to many of the victims of that
> system, who have been obliged to flee from the Terror. With
> these living examples of persecution among us, with the
> knowledge of inhuman cruelties still being perpetrated in
> prisons and concentration camps, great public indignation
> would almost certainly be manifested, leading possibly to
> grave disturbances of the Peace.
>   I appeal to you to prohibit the projected football match and

the visit to London of this large contingent of Nazis from Germany.

Their presence in London would undoubtedly be interpreted by many people as a gesture of sympathy from the British Government to a movement whose aims and methods have evoked the strongest condemnation from every section of public opinion in the country, including the Prime Minister and members of the Cabinet.

It will certainly arouse great resentment and will be an insult to democratic opinion if the proposed match is allowed to take place.[68]

Yet, despite a stream of protests the Home Secretary, Sir John Simon, declared the match to have no political significance what-soever. In fact, it was even suggested that the TUC were trying to import sport into politics. It is true that the campaign to ban the match was not very successful as there was still a capacity crowd of 60,000 at White Hart Lane to watch the International.[69] However, notwithstanding the fact that official pronouncements were seemingly impartial and non-political in tone, the decision of the Home Office to allow the match to take place had significant political implications. There were a number of factors in this.

In the first place it was clearly absurd for Sir John Simon to convey the impression that the match was not a political question. After all, there was pressure group intervention, and the fact that the Government had been drawn into formal discussions with the TUC and other bodies was in itself a political act. In reading through the appropriate departmental files it appears ironic that the Home Secretary continually denied that the match was a political affair when in effect he was actively engaged in the very dynamics of the political making process. Second, both the Home and Foreign Offices were apprehensive about the possibility of public disorder, and thus proposed that the number of Nazis coming to London should 'be limited to the strict minimum'.[70] Inevitably, this involved liaison with the police, and not surprisingly New Scotland Yard was called upon for advice. Moreover the Foreign Office, under its Permanent Secretary, Sir Robert Vansittart, advised the Prince of Wales to keep away from the match on the grounds that ugly scenes were anticipated.[71] Third and lastly, there were economic and diplomatic reasons why the

Government could not countenance a ban. After India, Germany was the biggest single market for British exports. Given the Nazis' trade policy of economic nationalism, there were sound economic and financial reasons why the British Government could not afford to strain relations between the two countries. Further, Sir John Simon let it be known that he did not wish to create a 'diplomatic incident', and that 'a decision not to intervene will need to be defended primarily on grounds of international policy'.[72] There was, therefore, a great deal of communication involving the British Embassy in Berlin and the German Embassy in London. Most fascinating of all is one memorandum suggesting that Adolf Hitler had become embroiled in the question:

> The German Ambassador called this evening about the Anglo-German football match. He said that Baron von Neurath had just telephoned to him personally to say that the Ambassador's report of his conversation with the Secretary of State had been considered in Berlin as had also been the recently published letter to the Home Secretary from the Trade Unions Congress. The Chancellor had personally considered the matter, and did not wish to cause any difficulties for His Majesty's Government. He therefore left it entirely to His Majesty's Government to decide whether, in view of the threatened difficulties, they thought it desirable that the match should be cancelled. It would, however, not be a feasible suggestion that the team should come without their supporters. If His Majesty's Government did wish the match cancelled, the German Government thought that the correct way to do this would be for His Majesty's Government to arrange for the Football Association to withdraw their invitation, which could perhaps be done ostensibly on non-political grounds – or it could be stated that the match was postponed.[73]

Sport, therefore, became the site of international diplomacy, involving heads of state, Governments, public servants, Embassies, and even the royal family. Both the British and German Governments were at the very least acquiescing in the subordination of sport to politics. What could be more political than this?

International sport was certainly regarded as a political issue by statesmen and diplomats concerned about Britain's wider role in world affairs. Sport was used as a device to support Government policy. It is true that interference in world football was determined by shifting ideological perspectives and commitments, but it is perhaps a reflection of political priorities that bans were enforced on football games with teams from the Soviet Union and Republican Spain, but not on games with teams from Nazi Germany and Fascist Italy.

The actions of Governments over film censorship and international football undoubtedly suggest that leisure was a politically sensitive area, used to try to achieve a wide range of objectives. However, an important amendment must be added at this point. In short, there were a number of areas in which Governments were reluctant to intervene. In late 1922, the Conservative Home Secretary, W. G. Bridgeman, decided to prohibit a boxing match between Battling Siki, the Senegalese light-heavyweight champion of the world, and Joe Beckett, the heavyweight champion of Britain. The reason for this decision according to one Home Office official was 'that contests between men of different colour are calculated to arouse bitter, and even dangerous, racial antipathies . . . we took the view that . . . the colour issue might awaken grave partisan passions and animosities among the spectators'.[74] This was yet another example of Government intervention for ideological purposes. However, this should not lead us to believe that the Government's position was rigid. With a change in Government and ministers came changes in ideas and objectives. Hence, when in 1932 the Home Secretary in the National Government, Sir Herbert Samuel, was pressed on the need 'to prohibit all boxing or wrestling encounters between men of white race and of coloured race in this country', he replied: 'I do not think that legislation on the lines suggested . . . could be justified. The question whether such encounters are desirable depends largely on the circumstances attending each individual case. The matter is primarily one for the organisations responsible for these contests.'[75] This *laissez faire* stance was reinforced by the financial orthodoxy of the time; that is, the Treasury, under its Permanent Secretary, Sir Warren Fisher, was committed to the balanced budget. Although there had been an increase in public spending on the arts, Keynes believed that the entrenched position of the

Treasury was an impediment to further progress: 'the Treasury view has prevailed. Not only in practice. The theory is equally powerful. We have persuaded ourselves that it is positively wicked for the state to spend a halfpenny on non-economic purposes.'[76]

The politics of outdoor recreation and sport

Since politics involves debate about and demands for greater resources it is appropriate to examine the ways in which leisure interest groups struggled for more and better amenities. More specifically, there were a number of bodies who campaigned for improvements in matters relating to outdoor recreation and sport. One of the salient issues of the period was the campaign for access to the countryside. Because private landowners often prevented ramblers or campers from using their land many organizations pressed for access. At the local level, there were many instances of groups taking direct action to remove restrictions. For example, in Little Hampden, Buckinghamshire, inhabitants attempted to tear down 'wire entanglements' which the squire had erected around the village common, and in Sunnymeade in the West Riding, rambling enthusiasts demonstrated against the closing of footpaths on land belonging to the Bradford Corporation Water Department.[77] Even the Conservative *Daily Telegraph* urged the need for 'Public Rights of Way', while the far from radical Commons, Open Spaces and Footpaths Preservation Society, 'realising the large amount of public support which has been given to the Access to Mountains Bill, urges that an effort should be made to secure the passage of a Bill giving the public reasonable access to uncultivated areas of mountain and moorland, subject to due protection being provided for private rights'.[78] In the view of another rambling organization, 'every opportunity must be taken . . . to see that every member of Parliament has before him all the arguments that can be employed in favour of the Bill.'[79] In fact, the Access Bill was presented to Parliament on numerous occasions, and it was only in 1939 that it received the Royal Assent. Aside from the question of access, recreational organizations put forward demands for more playing fields, sports amenities, open spaces, and the rest, as well as protesting about unfair and restrictive regulation. Yet, to appreciate the political nature of such demands or protests it would be revealing to take a more detailed look at the campaigns of one particular organization, in this case the Communist-backed British Workers' Sports Federation (BWSF).[80]

Probably the best known militant stand of worker sportsmen in the 1930s was the Mass Trespass, when hundreds of Northern ramblers trespassed on the area around Kinder Scout in Derbyshire. What is less well known is that the trespass was organized under the auspices of the BWSF. From its inception, the Federation had promoted the rights of the open air movement, including the demands and grievances of ramblers. In 1931 the Manchester branch formed a Ramblers' Rights Movement to fight for the 'opening to hikers of all parts of the countryside, including private property'. Even at this stage the 'Establishment' press, in the guise of the *Daily Mail*, were apprehensive about the determination of Communists to 'tramp our footpaths, careless of rural charm, musing only on the iniquities of the capitalist system'.[81] The truth of the matter was that a group of workers simply wanted to roam the countryside free from the fear of prosecution and the encroachments of the grouse shooter. The details of the trespass have been well chronicled and need not detain us here.[82] It is interesting to note, however, that the fight for ramblers' rights was a logical extension of the political commitment of the BWSF. It is difficult to assess the political effect of the mass trespass, yet along with a number of other similar actions, it awakened public consciousness and gave further momentum to a number of Parliamentary initiatives.[83]

In other campaigns initiated by the Federation success was more immediate. The London branch campaigned for more and better recreational facilities, as well as the right to Sunday sport. Michael Condon, one of the leading figures in the Federation, provided a lengthy indictment of sport in Capitalist society, and in particular the lack of decent amenities:

Thousands of workers who pack the big enclosures week after week only do so because insufficient facilities are provided for them to take an active part in sports, as distinct from being mere lookers-on. The amount of playing fields with proper equipment and dressing accommodation which is considered necessary and adequate for the worker sportsmen of this country is absolutely scandalous, and is a factor around which the thousands of worker sportsmen will unite with other workers in militant working-class action.

The streets are the playing fields of the working-class kiddies. Tired, overworked mothers must send their children outdoors, and are often haunted by the thought of their kiddie under the wheels of a lorry or a motor car. Scores of children are killed every year while playing in the crowded traffic-laden streets.

Many older children also have nothing better than a lamp-post for wicket, whilst they play their games with one eye on the ball and one eye on the possible arrival of a policeman. How many children are hauled up before the beak every year for daring to play games in the street – in many cases, their only playground?[84]

The picture he painted was a dismal one, with London boroughs such as Islington and Walthamstow especially susceptible to Capitalist economies in the recreational sphere. Clearly, the lessons drawn from such an analysis pointed to some kind of political action and this came with the Tottenham campaign for Sunday football.

Worker sportsmen and women feared that the decision of the Tottenham Urban District Council in 1930 to ban Sunday games in the local park would be extended through the activities of the religious and property-owning groups who sought to close down the Tottenham Marshes each Sunday.[85] The BWSF, therefore, helped to form the Tottenham Workers' Sports Association to fight the ban and to put forward more progressive demands. The methods applied by the Association during the campaign were wide-ranging. They held mass meetings with the local Communist Party, and open air debates, organized a petition, published a pamphlet written by Condon, entitled *Tottenham Sunday Games Ban* (which sold over 1,000 copies), distributed leaflets, lobbied the Council and, as the Conservative Councillor Miss Cox observed, one even 'saw pavements chalked on behalf of Sunday Sports'.[86] There was, of course, opposition to this campaign from religious groups like the Baptist Church, Primitive Methodist Church, Sunday School Union and the Salvation Army, who feared the secularization of the Sabbath, and were in turn supported by the Bruce Castle Bowling Club, Tottenham Temperance Association, and the Young Women's Christian Association.[87] Nevertheless, the arguments of H. W. Pearson of the Workers' Sports Association were very persuasive: 'Our Sunday games keep us healthy, and mean abstaining from habitual drinking, late hours, etc. The alternative to Sunday games is walking about the streets with little to do, which we feel is much more conducive to drinking, bad company and various other things which might lead a youth astray.'[88] The lifting of the ban by the District Council eventually came in May 1931.[89] It showed the BWSF that militancy and direct political action could be successful.

The BWSF was also influential within the London Workers' Football Council. The Council was open to all sportsmen and women, irrespective of Party politics, who agreed with the demands for Sunday League football, the reduction in the cost of hiring pitches and the provision of more playing fields.[90] The campaign for these demands was fuelled when the London County Council (LCC) decided to make the clubs connected with the London Workers' Council forfeit their annual deposits and be struck off the register of clubs for whom reserved football pitches were made available. All this for simply playing organized football on Sundays.[91]

The Workers' Football Council responded to this by sending a number of letters to the Parks and Open Spaces Committee of the LCC, stressing how orderly, disciplined and controlled organized football was.[92] In February 1933, the Parks Committee received a delegation from the Council. According to Condon, that the

> movement for organised Sunday football has the backing of thousands of young people in London is shown by the fact that the members of the deputation represent 585 teams, and that our movement has won the support of no less than 1,500 London teams. It is our intention to press forward our efforts, to broaden the movement along such lines as will convince the L.C.C. of the necessity for conceding our demands, and to this end we urge the support of all workers . . . of all progressive people who believe that the workers should be allowed to take part in organised sport on their one full

leisure day, under the best possible conditions, and at reasonable charges.[93]

The evidence presented was persuasive and bore immediate fruit when the Chief Officer to the Parks Committee reported in favour of organized sport.[94] Even so, the Parks Committee was still reluctant to concede that there was a legitimate case to be answered.[95] Consequently, football teams in the West London, North Kensington and Regent's Park leagues continued to act illegally and ignore the LCC Sunday regulations.[96] Furthermore, a Sunday League Football Campaign Committee was set up, and pressed for immediate concessions. In the end, as in the case of Tottenham, it was left to a Labour controlled Council to give effect to the demands. The newly formed LCC in 1934 had little hesitation in revoking the prohibition on Sunday football; the struggle started in 1932 had finally been won.[97]

Working-class ramblers in the North West and working-class footballers in London had sought to establish a number of fundamental rights, and improve amenities. To achieve this they had found the use of political pressure compatible with their leisure-time interests. The political implications of these struggles were also appreciated by campers and cyclists who were forced into action when their rights were infringed. A Campers' Council was formed in Manchester, with Martin Bobker of the BWSF as secretary, to oppose camping restrictions contained in the 1934 Movable Dwellings Bill.[98] Likewise, when the Alva (Stirling) Town Council closed Alva Glen to cyclists, it was the Scottish district of the BWSF who organized the protests.[99] It is therefore evident that the Federation was prepared to employ political methods of opposition to counteract the negative intervention of Central and Local Government. Moreover, the BWSF was a pioneer in the fight to improve the quality of workers' leisure. Campaigns initiated in the localities, in so far as they were successful, brought permanent benefits to all types of sportsmen and women.

The evidence assembled in this and other chapters shows that leisure was an important political question in inter-war Britain. Politicians and other leaders of public opinion dealt with issues which impinged on or were influenced by leisure. Ideological perceptions were continually changing, but no matter what the climate of opinion leisure remained a political fact of life. Indeed, leisure was as political as many other facets of civil society – crime, education, health – in so far as it involved contestation over a thousand and one factors which had a direct bearing on economy and society. Also, leisure certainly had an ideological side to it. Leisure activities such as the cinema and sport were regarded in some circles as ways of seducing the workers away from class conflict and radical ideas. Although there is no concrete evidence to show that leisure has ever been a successful means of class collaboration, the fact that leading statesmen thought it to be is nevertheless important. Additionally, Governments intervened in leisure to ensure that diplomatic objectives were achieved. This chapter has focused on the international politics of association football, yet this was not the only sport to be at the centre of political controversy. As is well known, the 1932–3 cricket series between England and Australia, which included the infamous 'body-line' or 'leg-theory' bowling of Harold Larwood, led to intervention by the National Government to heal Commonwealth relations. Interestingly enough in a completely different medium, that of film, it is likely that Alexander Korda, who had close links with the Conservative Party, produced such imperial epics as *Sanders of the River* (1935), *The Drum* (1938), and *The Four Feathers* (1939) so as to promote and solidify the Empire. In short, leisure was a central concern for all those actors in the politics of everyday life.

Conclusion

In this study it has not been possible to examine all aspects of inter-war leisure. The preceding chapters have inevitably failed to consider some important themes, and glossed over others. Since the leisure habits of the working class have been the main focus, very little has been said about middle-class leisure. Further work on the inter-war period would profit by focusing on the recreational and cultural pastimes of this substantial segment of the population. After all, it was the professional classes and the relatively new technical and administrative classes who imparted such a significant influence on the nation's leisure. The wealthier classes were able to spend a lot of money on all kinds of leisure pursuits, both inside and outside the home. It was they who benefited most from the spread of consumer durables. The middle-class home was almost sure to have a good quality wireless and gramophone, as well as the space and comfort for the enjoyment of spare time. Yet, there was still a large demand for outdoor pursuits, and here the motor-car was crucial. As the price of cars came down they were more readily available, and middle-class ownership grew. In 1922 there were 314,769 private cars registered in the United Kingdom; by 1937 there were 1,834,248.[1] It was the new Morris or Austin owner who now had the opportunity to visit places of interest, the countryside or the seaside resort. Further, the car made the middle-class family more mobile within their own district. Aside from this, it was the middle classes who were the very backbone of a number of sports, such as tennis, golf, and yachting, and even private aviation – the British Gliding Association was formed in 1930. National sporting occasions, like

195

Wimbledon, Cowes and Royal Ascot, were thus essentially for the middle class. On the cultural side, it is a safe bet that there were few working-class patrons of classical music, opera or ballet – not because of philistinism, but cultural orientation and lack of resources. As with proletarian culture, there was much that survived from earlier years. To take one example. In spite of economic recession, English fox hunting remained a fashionable activity in the 1930s, retaining its traditional function as a means of social climbing. In fact, the price of participating in field sports was falling, with obvious benefits. Prosperity is to be seen in the hunting photographs which appeared in *The Tatler*, and the advertisements for hunting clothes, saddlery and the like in Baily's *Hunting Directory*.[2]

Many of these leisure pursuits were not, of course, monopolized by the middle and upper classes. There was almost certainly a degree of social mixing in both urban and rural recreations. However, despite the emergence of a more homogeneous product and the greater uniformity in the nation's leisure, there was still a clearly defined differentiation along class lines. Another book would therefore have to consider middle-class influences. Here, middle-class interests and attitudes have been examined only in so far as they provide some understanding of working-class leisure.

Obviously in one book it is difficult to do justice to the breadth of the subject matter. As already suggested, there has been relatively little discussion of the regional experience or the differences between male and female leisure. Equally, little, if anything at all, has been said about the attitudes and responses of working-class audiences at cinemas or sporting contests. To some extent the subject has been rationalized by looking at three main forms of leisure. Although commercial, associational and municipal forms cannot be viewed as totally separate, they can place leisure within a more general context, and thereby help to isolate the most salient trends. Yet, even here it has been virtually impossible to cover all the main areas. For instance, when examining the commercialization of leisure it would have been appropriate to deal with the monetary side of athletics, the growth of motor-racing, as well as the demise of the music hall. And what of the labour relations side of the entertainment industry? Likewise, it would have been interesting to focus on the position of the aged and the ways in which they came together in the family, community and voluntary organizations. Lastly, more could have been made of the intimate relationship between certain voluntary groups and the State. For the enterprising student of leisure there is certainly a wealth of information in the Public Record Office, especially in the files of the Ministries of Education and Labour, on the Miners' Welfare Committee, National Fitness Council, National Council of Social Service, National Playing Fields Association and the Youth Hostels Association.

Perhaps one of the main omissions has been physical and cultural education. This was a major form of leisure for many of the younger groups in the population. Leisure was certainly taken in school hours, albeit in a regulated environment. Sports and drama classes introduced pupils to a variety of leisure activities. In addition, sports days, gymnastic displays, school plays, concerts, and art exhibitions were important community events. An examination of the educational system would undoubtedly provide the basis for a more detailed analysis of the role of the State. More than this, it would shed light on the ways in which educational socialization reinforced dominant social mores and sexual stereotyping. A start has been made. There are now a number of dissertations on the history of physical education, in the main covering the nineteenth and early twentieth centuries.[3] Furthermore, research findings are beginning to filter through into specialist journals such as the *History of Education Society Bulletin* and the *Physical Education Review*. As far as the inter-war years are concerned, however, there is insufficient published work to make a considered synthesis. But no doubt scholars will attempt this Herculean task in the not too distant future.

Despite its shortcomings, this study has made some positive claims. The main conclusion is that an understanding of the inter-war years is essential for any balanced interpretation of the social and economic history of leisure. In short, British pastimes were modified in a number of crucial respects in the 1920s and 1930s. The main trend was, of course, the expansion of leisure. Most important of all was the unprecedented commercialization of leisure, fed by rising real incomes and falling hours of work. But this was not the only point of change. The fact that the decline in beer consumption released money into alternative leisure activities was clearly a crucial development. Also, State spending on and regulation of recreation and culture appears to have increased, despite financial conservatism and attempts at retrenchment. There was also a growth in the number of voluntary organizations catering for leisure. Indeed, it must be stressed that newer commercial forms of leisure did not necessarily destroy older associational forms. Still, by the beginning of the 1930s, there were 12,999 clubs in England and Wales registered under the Licensing (Consolidation) Act of 1910, consisting of 4,096,637 members.[4] Leisure was not a very effective means of social control and the working class was able to maintain a considerable degree of independence in their spare time. It has been shown in some detail, for example, that the organized Labour Movement was able to establish, preserve and in some cases expand its recreational nexus, despite the incursion of the entrepreneur. The continuities in leisure may even have been as significant as the changes. It is not a contradiction to say that change and continuity can exist side by side. A dialectical process was at work whereby newer forms of leisure were able to present themselves as modern alternatives, yet at the same time accommodate older forms. This study has been, however, more than a sterile examination of change and adaptation. It has been claimed all along that leisure was, and is, a site of political discussion and struggle; and here the representative organs of the working class played such an important part.

The main argument of this book is nevertheless that leisure was recast, if not transformed, in the inter-war years. The leisure of the working class was very different in 1939 than it had been in the years before 1914. To appreciate the evolution of the leisure of the 1980s it is vital to examine the revolutionary changes of the nineteenth century. But, historians should not stop there; they have to place leisure within a changing economic and social context, be this in the 1930s or the 1970s. A proper sense of history and historical perspective is invaluable in any study of leisure. It is not enough to suggest that the leisure world of today is similar in context to the leisure world of the late nineteenth century. The economic, technological and social changes of the twentieth century have been so wide-ranging that inevitably the leisure of the people has been radically altered. This happened in the 1920s and 1930s, and has in fact continued ever since. It would therefore be appropriate to conclude by focusing on the salient trends of the post-1945 period.

As British Capitalism changed after the second world war, then so did leisure. Despite the general impression of economic austerity under the Attlee Government, leisure activities prospered; people flocked to cinemas, football grounds and holiday camps. Moreover, with the post-war reconstruction complete, the beginning of the 1950s signalled the start of a leisure boom. All sections of society began to purchase a wide variety of leisure products and services: television sets, record players, motor-cars, holidays abroad, and a plethora of household gadgets. The 1960s brought with them, in Arthur Marwick's phrase, a 'cultural revolution'. Presumably this is to be seen in terms of the 'permissive society', Beatlemania, the mini car, Twiggy, Mary Quant, and Wilson's 'white heat of technological revolution'.[5] The leisure boom itself was closely related to the rise in real wages, coupled with full employment (at least until the 1970s). Average real weekly earnings nearly doubled in the thirty years after 1950.[6] At the same time, annual working time has fallen. The reduction in the length of the working week and the proliferation of holidays with pay were also accompanied by a move towards earlier retirement. By 1983 the average basic weekly hours for manual workers was 39.2. In the same year 5 per cent of manual workers were entitled to between three and four weeks' holiday pay, 17 per cent to four weeks, 60 per cent to between four and five weeks, and 18 per cent to five weeks.[7] It is true that participation rates for women have risen since the 1950s, but on the whole, workers now have greater leisure time than they have ever had since pre-industrial times.

The leisure industry has again grown rapidly. By 1984 even the most conservative estimates reckoned that leisure spending was running at about £36 billion a year, accounting for about 8 per cent of gross national product. The number of jobs in the leisure sector increased by 36 per cent in the period 1960–80, the biggest increases being recorded in public houses, sport, gambling and clubs.[8] This leisure explosion has transformed the character of a number of businesses, particularly those under conditions of intense competition. Even the traditional working-class holiday camps have been forced to change their image. As families began to switch to foreign sunspots (by 1978 nine million Britons spent their holiday abroad, as against two million in 1951), Butlin's and Pontin's have introduced radical measures. As part of the huge

Rank and Bass organizations, they now boast health studios, aerobics, jacuzzis, adventure playgrounds, video TV studios and international cuisine – far removed from the knobbly knees competitions of the 1940s and 1950s. Also a sign of the times is the fact that while Butlin's have closed down camps at Clacton and Filey, they have opened a hotel in Torremolinos.[9] This is, of course, just one example of the changing leisure landscape. Rock and pop music has mushroomed since the 1950s, as has motoring, bingo, eating out, caravanning, ten pin bowling and the rest. An associated trend has been the phenomenal growth of sponsorship. Although the marketing of leisure can be traced to the inter-war years, it entered a new phase in the 1970s and 1980s. In particular, sports sponsorship has grown to new heights. The estimated sponsorship on sports in 1982 was £48,922,600. At the top of the list was motor sport with £19,450,000, followed by association football with £11,915,000, horse racing with £2,319,600 and cricket with £2,076,000. At the bottom of the list were curling, gliding, judo, and the martial arts, all with £2,000.[10] Sponsorship of cricket, for example, began in 1963 with the Gillette Cup, and was followed by the John Player League, Benson and Hedges Cup, Prudential World Cup, Cornhill tests, and Schweppes County Championship. Sponsorship has not ended there. It is interesting that at the beginning of 1985, companies like Kodak, Pearl Assurance and Peugeot Talbot entered the sponsorship arena with million pound deals in the amateur sport of athletics.

Within all this there has been a shift in the overall balance of the leisure industry. Here, the main development has been in home-based leisure. Both gardening and D.I.Y. are now billion-pound industries. But most crucial of all is the advent of television, and its powerful impact on consumer tastes and preferences. Since Independent television was launched in the 1950s, watching television has become the major leisure activity of the British people. The overall average weekly hours viewed by all persons aged five and over in the United Kingdom was 18.6 in February 1971, though falling back to fifteen in the summer month of August.[11] By the first quarter of 1984 the average time spent watching broadcast television in the UK was 21.75 hours among men and 25.5 hours among women.[12] Obviously, this has led to a great increase in the production of television sets, and since the 1970s in colour sets. The number of current colour television licences has increased from 6,824,000 in 1974 to 15,667,000 in December 1984, while in the same period the number of current black and white licences has fallen from 10,611,000 to 3,014,000.[13] Equally significant in the last few years has been the rise of the video recorder, which has, if anything, reinforced home-centred leisure. The number of videos in the UK has risen from 110,000 in 1978 to 685,000 in 1980 and 6,285,000 in 1983. By this later date, the UK was the largest market in Europe, with sales at 2.5 million, around 40 per cent of total European sales.[14]

As more and more people have retreated into the comparative luxury of their own homes, certain leisure activities have felt the draught. The cinema, in particular, has witnessed a decline in the number of attendances since the 1950s, though there was a slight revival towards the end of the 1970s. In the period 1974 to 1983 the weekly average attendances at British cinemas fell from 2.74 million to 1.26 million.[15] Inevitably, this led to the closure of cinema complexes: in 1971 there were 1,420 cinemas in Britain, but only 707 in 1983.[16] It is also possible that the growth of leisure in the home has contributed to the decline of football attendances. (Other explanations are said to be the dull and predictable state of the game, poor ground facilities, hooliganism, the rise of other forms of outdoor recreation, and wider changes in the community.) The record total of 41,250,000 attendances was reached in the 1948-9 season, but thereafter the figure fell, eventually stabilizing at around twenty-five million in the mid-1970s.[17] However, a note of caution. Despite the fall in attendance, it is apparent that films and football are still big business. Many more millions watch films and football on the television than is indicated by the above figures. Indeed, the early 1980s saw the renaissance of the British film industry, while in 1983 league football was being televised live on selected Friday evenings and Sunday afternoons. There is therefore every indication that films and football are as popular as ever, though viewed in a different way. Moreover, in the case of football, there is greater commercialization than there has ever been. The watershed occurred in the early 1960s with the abolition of the maximum wage and the introduction of greater freedom of contract. This in turn led to higher wages and a spiralling transfer market, which reached the million pound mark in the late 1970s. Football club finance may be perilous with little operating profit, inadequate working capital and liquidity problems, but no one can doubt that the sport is a huge commercial enterprise. In fact, a new trend may have been started by Tottenham Hotspur who recently became the first British football club to secure a full stock market listing for its shares.

The British people have also benefited from a vast increase in State spending on recreation and culture since 1945. With the acceptance of Keynesian economics and the growth of Government expenditure came a commitment to leisure. By 1980 a web of national bodies such as the Countryside Commission and the National Park Authorities spent £280 million, in addition to the £630 million local authority recreation spending.[18] Of particular importance has been the establishment of the Arts Council and the Sports Council which now channel considerable State funds into leisure. The Sports Council, for example, has promoted mass participation in sport, supported research programmes, and contributed to the funding of major amenities – indoor sports halls and leisure centres, outdoor sports facilities and equipment, swimming pools. The funds of the Council have therefore increased from £1.58 million in 1968–9 to an estimated £21.03 million in 1981–2.[19] The Government of the day has also been involved with all kinds of legislative developments, as well as the political side of leisure.

It may be thought that, with the unparalleled growth of consumer and State spending on leisure since the second world war, voluntary or associational forms would have been adversely affected. However, this is far from the truth. Despite the tendency of some commentators to portray entertainment as trivialized and increasingly uniform, there is still diversity and much autonomy in people's spare time. In fact, such recreational organizations as the English Bowls Association, National Anglers' Council and Football Association have all recorded an increase in membership. Leisure in the community has not faltered, and is still alive and thriving. As the Sports Council has commented: 'The work of voluntary groups is the mainstay of the performing arts, sport, gardening and the conservation of the national heritage.'[20] Most recently came the so-called English cultural movement, led by the Campaign for Real Ale, grass-roots cricket, Sunday league football, darts leagues, fell running, horticultural exhibitions, village fêtes and the rest.[21] In brief, there is still a variegated and dynamic popular culture; a culture in which, it must be added, class is the most pervasive influence.

Leisure has undergone radical change in the twentieth century. This is certainly true of the inter-war years, and perhaps more so of the period after 1945. It does seem, however, that leisure is about to be transformed in a more radical fashion than in any period since industrialization and the emergence of Capitalism. On both the Right and Left of the political spectrum commentators have claimed that leisure is a key to future economic and social development. In 1983 Mrs Margaret Thatcher suggested that the 'great industry in other people's pleasures', namely tourism, videos, hotels, and even McDonald's and Wimpy's, would be the generator of jobs and one of the foundations of Britain's economic recovery.[22] Yet more fundamentally, as Francis Pym has cogently argued, the present blight of mass unemployment, as well as technological advance, is 'the dawn of an age so momentous that it will force us completely to revise our attitudes'. He envisages that unemployment will be solved 'by reducing the number of hours worked by each individual in a working life', providing more leisure and opportunities for workers 'to lead much fuller and freer lives'.[23] A more systematic case for work-sharing has been advanced by the British and European trade union movement, in which leisure time is to be increased as a means of spreading employment more evenly throughout the labour force. The ex-leader of the TUC, Len Murray, thus proclaimed that, because there would be greater emphasis on leisure in the future, more collective agreements would have to be made on the patterns of work and leisure: 'Inevitably, we are moving into a situation where leisure is forming an important part of everyday life. So the issue is that in order to preserve living standards there will have to be an agreement about who gets what, and how work is divided.' He concludes, 'it is not good enough to say that if we reduce unemployment from 3 to 2 million, we will only have 2 million people out of a job. This is not a solution for unemployment. We must try to get a proper distribution of work and that can only be done by tackling the question of leisure as well.'[24] One may speculate as to the extent of hours reduction, but according to the French Utopian socialist, André Gorz, the productivity gains from technical change could be used to achieve a twenty-hour week plus longer holidays by the next century. All this involves the extension of leisure, the revolutionary freeing of time; no longer will man or woman be shackled by the restrictive working environment of Capitalism. Here Gorz cites a study made on *The Revolution of Choosing Your Time Schedule*:

> The freeing of time is a form of revolution or incitement to revolution insofar as it leads, almost automatically, to calling the productivist socio-cultural model into question. . . . To a greater or lesser extent, all attempts to find an alternative model of development turn upon the question of time. . . . Everything connected with ecology, decentralised sources of energy, conviviality, self reliance, mutual aid and social experimentation is based upon different modes of managing time.[25]

It is true that many experts have pointed to the fallacies of the shorter hours movement,[26] but if the advocates of work-sharing are correct and there is a considerable reduction in work time this poses all manner of questions for the future. Most of all, leisure and not work (paid employment) would become the individual's principal occupation and reference point. If the predicted diminution of work is realized, then it will involve the greatest upheaval in life and leisure that the modern age has ever witnessed.

Notes

Introduction

1 J. K. Walton and J. Walvin, 'Introduction', in J. K. Walton and J. Walvin (eds), *Leisure in Britain 1780–1939*, Manchester, Manchester University Press, 1983, p. 3.

2 H. Cunningham, *Leisure in the Industrial Revolution, 1780–1880*, London, Croom Helm, 1980, p. 14. See also H. Cunningham, 'Leisure', in J. Benson (ed.), *The Working Class In England 1875–1914*, London, Croom Helm, 1985, pp. 133–64.

3 S. Yeo, *Religion and Voluntary Organisations in Crisis*, London, Croom Helm, 1976, p. 185. J. Lowerson and J. Myerscough, *Time to Spare in Victorian England*, Hassocks, Harvester Press, 1977, p. 1. J. Walvin, *Leisure and Society 1830–1950*, London, Longman, 1978, p. 163. See also T. Mason, *Association Football and English Society 1863–1915*, Brighton, Harvester Press, 1980. J. K. Walton, *The English Seaside Resort: A Social History 1750–1914*, Leicester, Leicester University Press, 1983.

4 C. Critcher, 'The Politics of Leisure – Social Control and Social Development', in *Work And Leisure: The Implications Of Technological Change*, Leisure Studies Seminar 1980, Tourism and Recreation Unit, University of Edinburgh, 1982, p. 49.

5 D. H. Aldcroft, *The British Economy Between The Wars*, Oxford, Philip Allan, 1983, p. 123. See also A. Briggs, *Communications and Culture 1823–1973: A Tale of Two Centuries*, London, Birkbeck College, 1973, p. 14.

6 Cited in K. Roberts, *Leisure*, London, Longman, 1970, p. 1.

7 See D. Rubinstein, 'Sport and the Sociologist 1890–1914', *The British Journal of Sports History*, vol. 1, no. 1, 1984, pp. 14–23.

8 See A. Briggs, *The History of Broadcasting in the UK*, vol. 2, *The*

Golden Age of Wireless, Oxford, Oxford University Press, 1965. S. G. Jones, 'The Economic Aspects of Association Football in England, 1918–39', *The British Journal of Sports History*, vol. 1, no. 3, 1984, pp. 286–99. S. G. Jones 'The Leisure Industry in Britain 1918–39', *The Service Industries Journal*, vol. 5, no. 1, 1985, pp. 90–106. D. L. Lemahieu, 'The Gramophone: Recorded Music and the Cultivated Mind in Britain Between the Wars', *Technology and Culture*, vol. 23, no. 3, 1982, pp. 372–91. R. Low, *The History of the British Film*, vol. 4–7, London, Allen & Unwin, 1971–85. M. Pegg, *Broadcasting and Society 1918–1939*, London, Croom Helm, 1983. J. Richards, *The Age Of The Dream Palace: Cinema and Society in Britain 1930–1939*, London, Routledge & Kegan Paul, 1984. P. Wild, 'Recreation in Rochdale 1900–40', in J. Clarke, C. Critcher and R. Johnson (eds), *Working Class Culture: Studies in history and theory*, London, Hutchinson, 1979, pp. 140–60. G. Williams, 'From Grand Slam to Great Slump: Economy, Society and Rugby Football in Wales During the Depression', *The Welsh History Review*, vol. 11, no. 3, 1983, pp. 338–57.

9 A. Howkins and J. Lowerson, *Trends in Leisure, 1919–1939*, London, The Sports Council and Social Science Research Council, 1979, p. 57. Cf. W. J. Baker, 'The State of British Sport History', *Journal of Sport History*, vol. 10, no. 1, 1983, pp. 54–5.

10 See D. H. Aldcroft, *The Inter-War Economy: Britain, 1919–1939*, London, Batsford, 1970. B. W. E. Alford, *Depression and Recovery? British Economic Growth 1918–1939*, London, Macmillan, 1972. S. Glynn and J. Oxborrow, *Interwar Britain: A Social and Economic History*, London, Allen & Unwin, 1976.

11 *The Economist*, 17 April 1937.

12 Williams, op. cit.

13 L. Althusser, 'Ideology and Ideological State Apparatuses (Notes towards an Investigation)', in *Lenin and Philosophy and other essays*, London, New Left Books, 1971, p. 146. See also J. Hargreaves, 'Sport, culture and ideology', in J. Hargreaves (ed.), *Sport, Culture and Ideology*, London, Routledge & Kegan Paul, 1982, pp. 30–61.

14 Althusser, op. cit., pp. 147–8.

15 S. Macintyre, 'British Labour, Marxism And Working Class Apathy In The Nineteen Twenties', *The Historical Journal*, vol. 20, no. 2, 1977, p. 481.

16 This idea is borrowed from R. Williams, 'Base and Superstructure in Marxist Cultural Theory', *New Left Review*, no. 82, 1973, pp. 10–14.

Chapter 1 The demand for leisure

1 For further information on wages see A. L. Chapman and R. Knight, *Wages and Salaries in the United Kingdom 1920–1938*, Cambridge, Cambridge University Press, 1953. E. H. Phelps Brown and M. H. Browne, *A Century of Pay*, London, Macmillan, 1968. G. Routh, *Occupation and Pay in Great Britain, 1906–60*, Cambridge, Cambridge University Press, 1965.

2 London and Cambridge Economic Service, *The British Economy Key Statistics 1900–1970*, London, The Times, 1971, p. 8. For details of wage payments by the main industrial groups, see Chapman and Knight, op. cit., p. 22.

3 See K. G. J. C. Knowles and D. J. Robertson, 'Earnings in Engineering, 1926–1948', *Bulletin of the Oxford University Institute of Statistics*, vol. 13 (1951), pp. 179–200. R. Penn, 'The Course of Wage Differentials Between Skilled and Nonskilled Manual Workers in Britain Between 1856 and 1964', *British Journal of Industrial Relations*, vol. 21, no. 1, 1983, pp. 358–62.

4 G. Harrison and F. C. Mitchell, *The Home Market*, London, Allen & Unwin, 1936, p. 95. The Bristol Social Survey also noted that whereas those working-class families in poverty could only afford holidays, recreation, tobacco, drink and newspapers 'at the expense of the meagre allowances made for the basic necessities', the comfortable working-class families had a margin over and above basic necessities for holidays and other so-called luxuries. H. Tout, *The Standard Of Living In Bristol*, Bristol, Bristol University Press, 1938, pp. 19–20, 26.

5 H. Llewellyn Smith (ed.), *The New Survey of London Life and Labour* vol. 1, *Forty Years Of Change*, London, P. S. King, 1934, p. 136. Department of Employment and Productivity, *British Labour Statistics: Historical Abstract 1886–1968*, London, HMSO, 1971, p. 40.

6 Department of Employment and Productivity, op. cit., pp. 167–70. See also Routh, op. cit., p. 110. J. Burnett, *A History of the Cost of Living*, Harmondsworth, Penguin Books, 1969, pp. 309–11. F. Capie and M. Collins, *The Inter-war British Economy: A Statistical Abstract*, Manchester, Manchester University Press, 1983, pp. 28–39. And for a critique of the cost of living index, see N. Branson and M. Heinemann, *Britain in the Nineteen Thirties*, St Albans, Panther Books, 1973, pp. 154–56.

7 For a recent analysis of real wages see N. H. Dimsdale, 'Employment And Real Wages In The Inter-War Period', *National Institute Economic Review*, no. 110, November 1984, pp. 94–103.

8 S. Glynn and J. Oxborrow, *Interwar Britain: A Social and Economic History*, London, Allen & Unwin, 1976, pp. 38–40.

9 Quoted in J. Stevenson, *British Society 1914–45*, Harmondsworth, Penguin Books, 1984, p. 127.

10 R. Evans and A. Boyd, *The Use of Leisure in Hull*, Hull, The Hull 'Use of Leisure' Sub-Committee, 1933, p. 5. cf. *Ministry of Labour Gazette*, January 1941, p. 9.

11 R. Stone and D. A. Rowe, *The Measurement of Consumers' Expenditure and Behaviour in the United Kingdom 1920–1938*, vol. 2, Cambridge, Cambridge University Press, 1966, p. 93.

12 This information has been extracted from a number of sources and is meant to show, if only crudely, the average cost of certain leisure products and services.

13 J. D. Owen, *The Price Of Leisure: An Economic Analysis of the Demand for Leisure Time*, Rotterdam, Rotterdam University Press, 1969, p. 18.

14 W. J. Hausman and B. T. Hirsch, 'Wages, Leisure, and Productivity in South Wales Coalmining, 1874–1914: An Economic Approach', *Llafur*, vol. 3, no. 3, 1982?, p. 59.

15 National Union of Foundry Workers, *Journal and Report*, July 1933, p. 4. *The Post*, 2 March 1935, p. 190. *The Typographical Circular*, January 1937, p. 1. National Society of Painters, *Monthly Journal*, February 1937, pp. 36–7.

16 Phelps Brown and Browne, op. cit., p. 208. D. H. Aldcroft, *The Inter-War Economy: Britain, 1919–1939*, London, Batsford, 1970, p. 366. See also J. A. Dowie, '1919–1920 is in Need of Attention', *Economic History Review*, 2nd series, vol. 28, no. 3, 1975, pp. 429–50.

17 Department of Employment and Productivity, op. cit., p. 105. For further information on hours see M. A. Bienefeld, *Working Hours in British Industry*, London, Weidenfeld & Nicolson, 1972. B. McCormick, 'Hours of Work in British Industry', *Industrial and Labour Relations Review*, vol. 12, 1959, pp. 423–33.

18 Public Record Office (hereafter cited as PRO) LAB 2/882/IR 786/ 1933.

19 Scottish TUC *Report*, 1937, p. 152.

20 Department of Employment and Productivity, op. cit., p. 36.

21 *The Listener*, 28 July 1937.

22 Civil War Workers' Committee, *Third Interim Report: Holidays for Munition Workers After the War*, Parliamentary Papers 1918 xiv, cmd 9192, pp. 12–15. S. J. Rodger Charles, *The Development of Industrial Relations in Britain 1911–1939*, London, Hutchinson, 1973, pp. 166, 171, 174, 176. See also University of Warwick Modern

Records Centre (hereafter cited as MRC), Ernest Bevin Papers, Mss 126/EB/HP/2/5ii. For further details of the development of paid holidays, see S. G. Jones, 'Trade Union Policy Between the Wars: The Case of Holidays with Pay', *International Review of Social History*, vol. 31, pt. 1 (1986), from which the following short section is based.

23 *Labour Gazette*, August 1920, p. 421.

24 C. J. Bundock, *The Story of the National Union of Printing, Bookbinding and Paper Workers*, Oxford, Oxford University Press, 1959, p. 418.

25 *Report of the Committee on Holidays with Pay*, Parliamentary Papers 1937–8 xii, cmd 5724, pp. 54, 60. For further details, see PRO LAB 31/1–4.

26 *Hansard* (Commons) 5th series, vol. 338, col. 1533, 14 July 1938.

27 *Minutes of Evidence Taken Before the Committee on Holidays with Pay*, London, HMSO, 1937, p. 2. *Ministry of Labour Gazette*, March 1938, p. 86.

28 Ministry of Labour, *Holidays with Pay*, London, HMSO, 1939, p. 7.

29 MRC, Ernest Bevin Papers, Mss 126/EB/HP/1/27, Holidays with Pay Memorandum dated 23 April 1937.

30 'Holidays With Pay in Great Britain', *International Labour Review*, vol. 51, 1945, p. 741.

31 Aldcroft, op. cit., p. 217.

32 *Minutes Of Evidence Taken Before The Committee on Industry And Trade 1924–1927*, vol. 1, London, HMSO, p. 465.

33 A. Delgado, *The Annual Outing and Other Excursions*, London, Allen & Unwin, 1977, pp. 139–52.

34 C. Delisle Burns, *Leisure In The Modern World*, London, Allen & Unwin, 1932, p. 53.

35 H. Llewellyn Smith (ed.), *The New Survey of London Life and Labour*, vol. 9, *Life And Leisure*, London, P. S. King, 1935, p. 53.

36 R. Sinclair, *Metropolitan Man: The future of the English*, London, Allen & Unwin, 1937, especially pp. 114–20. *The Economist*, 29 October 1938.

37 K. Liepmann, *The Journey To Work*, London, Kegan Paul, Trench, Trubner and Co., 1944, p. 50.

38 PRO CAB 24/74 (GT 6712). Similar demands were also being made in France, the USA and other countries. See G. S. Cross, 'The Quest For Leisure: Reassessing The Eight-Hour Day In France', *Journal of Social History*, vol. 18, no. 2, 1984, pp. 195–216. B. K. Hunnicutt, 'The End Of Shorter Hours', *Labor History*, vol. 25, no. 3, 1984, pp. 373–404.

39 TUC *Report*, 1918, pp. 189–95.

40 *The Post*, 24 January 1920. See also *The Labour Woman*, January 1919, p. 2. *The Typographical Circular*, January 1919, p. 13. *Daily Herald*, 4 April 1919; 25 April 1919.

41 *Daily Herald*, 17 January 1934.

42 *Daily Herald*, 28 June 1934.

43 See S. G. Jones, 'The Trade Union Movement And Work-Sharing Policies In Interwar Britain', *Industrial Relations Journal*, vol. 16, no. 1, 1985, pp. 57–69.

44 *Hansard* (Commons) 5th series, vol. 272, col. 1946, 9 December 1932. See also *The New Leader*, 16 December 1932.

45 *Minutes and Record of the Proceedings of the Biennial Delegate Conference of the Transport and General Workers' Union*, 1933, pp. 45–6.

46 PRO T 172/1708, Notes of a deputation received by the Chancellor of the Exchequer from the TUC, 13 August 1930.

47 *The Democrat*, 28 November 1919. F. Henderson, *The Economic Consequences of Power Production*, London, Allen & Unwin, 1931, p. 210. *Hansard* (Commons) 5th series, vol. 272, col. 2011, 9 December 1932. Scottish TUC *Report*, 1933, p. 108. J. W. Bowen, 'Workers' Leisure', *The Shop Assistant*, 17 June 1933.

48 National Society of Painters, *Monthly Journal*, 10 June 1929. *The Labour Woman*, September 1933, p. 133.

49 *The Post*, 24 August 1929. National Union of Foundry Workers, *Journal and Report*, October 1934, p. 6.

50 *Daily Herald*, 16 February 1934.

51 *The Typographical Circular*, April 1924, p. 6; April 1931, p. 73. *The Printing Federation Bulletin*, July 1934, p. 1.

52 TUC *Report*, 1934, p. 280.

53 A. E. Musson, 'Technological Change and Manpower', *History*, vol. 67, no. 220, 1982, p. 245.

54 Labour Party, *For Socialism and Peace*, London, Labour Party, 1938, p. 28.

55 R. Lowe, 'Hours of Labour: Negotiating Industrial Legislation in Britain, 1919–39', *Economic History Review*, 2nd series, vol. 35, no. 2, 1982, pp. 254–71.

56 T. Savage, 'Is There Any Hope?', United Society of Boilermakers and Iron and Steel Shipbuildiers, *Monthly Report*, December 1921, p. 40.

57 *The Record*, December 1921, p. 1. *The Railway Review*, 23 December 1921. *The Labour Pioneer*, 22 December 1921; 16 February 1922. *British Trades Union Review*, January 1922, pp. 5–9; February 1922, pp. 2–6. *The Workers' Union Record*, March 1922, p. 15. Amalgamated Engineering Union, *Monthly Journal*, February

1923, p. 52. *The Post*, 17 February 1923. *Daily Herald*, 19 February 1923. National Society of Painters, *Monthly Journal*, March 1923, pp. 3–6, 59–61. National Union of Foundry Workers, *Monthly Report and Journal*, April 1923, p. 3. *The Typographical Circular*, April 1923, p. 5. Post Office Engineering Union, *The Journal*, 9 June 1923; 7 July 1923.

58 *The Record*, July 1923, pp. 12–13; August 1923, pp. 8–9; September 1923, p. 8; October 1923, p. 9; December 1923, p. 9.

59 PRO CAB 24/115 (CU 17), Cabinet Committee on Unemployment, Short Time as an Alternative to Unemployment: Memorandum by the Minister of Labour, 14 September 1920.

60 PRO PREM 1/217, W. Citrine to O. S. Cleverly, 3 May 1937.

61 See *Daily Herald*, 27 July 1920. *The Worker*, 12 June 1926. *The Tribune*, 6 August 1937.

62 *Lansbury's Labour Weekly*, 17 April 1926; 11 June 1927; 9 July 1927.

63 *The Economist*, 4 June 1938.

64 E. Brunner, *Holiday Making and the Holiday Trades*, Oxford, Nuffield College, 1945, p. 3.

65 *Oldham Chronicle*, 30 August 1929; 25 August 1939.

66 *Ashton-Under-Lyne-Reporter*, 23 August 1930. A similar picture can be painted for the mining areas. See 'The Working Week', *Our History*, pamphlet no. 12, Winter 1958, p. 21.

67 *Cotton Factory Times*, 12 August 1932.

68 M. Tebbutt, *Making Ends Meet: Pawnbroking and Working Class Credit*, Leicester, Leicester University Press, 1983. S. Humphries, *Hooligans or Rebels? An Oral History of Working-Class Childhood and Youth 1889–1939*, Oxford, Basil Blackwell, 1981, p. 166.

69 J. K. Walton, *The Blackpool Landlady: A social history*, Manchester, Manchester University Press, 1978, p. 184. cf. A. Hern, *The Seaside Holiday*, London, Cresset Press, 1967, p. 172.

70 AEU, *National Committee Report*, May 1929, p. 103. AEU, *The Engineers' Charter*, London, AEU, 1932, p. 7.

71 Aircraft Shop Stewards' National Council, *The Aircraft Workers' Case*, London, Aircraft Shop Stewards' National Council, n.d., p. 15.

72 *The Millgate*, July 1936, pp. 569–70. *Minutes of Evidence Taken Before the Committee on Holidays With Pay*, op. cit., p. 309.

73 Jones, op. cit.

74 See J. Mensch, 'The Urban Workers' Need For Holidays', *The Labour Magazine*, March 1932, pp. 502–3.

75 *Cotton Factory Times*, 27 August 1920.

76 *The Typographical Circular*, April 1919, p. 7. H. S. Temple, 'Trade Unionism in the Print Industry', in G. D. H. Cole *et al.*, *British Trade Unionism Today*, London, Gollancz, 1939, p. 373.

77 TUC *Report*, 1919, pp. 375–6. See also Scottish TUC *Report*, 1919, pp. 104–5. General Federation of Trade Unions, *General Council Report*, 1919, p. 33.

78 S. G. Jones, 'The British Labour Movement and Working Class Leisure 1918–1939', unpublished Ph.D. thesis, Manchester University, 1983, pp. 166–78.

79 *The Times*, 15 July 1933. *Minutes and Record of the Proceedings of the Biennial Delegate Conference of the Transport and General Workers' Union*, 1933, p. 14.

80 E. Bevin, 'The People Will Not Be Denied Their Rights', *The Record*, June 1936, p. 263.

81 TUC Archives, Minutes of the TUC General Council, 24 February 1937. PRO PREM 1/218, Notes of a Deputation from the TUC Received by the Prime Minister, 15 February 1937. MRC, Ernest Bevin Papers, Mss 126/EB/HP/1/3, Memorandum headed deputation, 15 February 1937. PRO LAB 10/53/IR/280, File on Annual Holiday Bill, 1936.

82 Labour Party Archives, Minutes of the Publicity, Research and Local Government Committee of the Labour Party, 22 July 1937 Minutes of the Campaign Committee of the Labour Party, 26 July 1937. *Labour*, August 1937, p. 279. Labour Party, *Annual Conference Report*, 1937, pp. 23, 59.

83 Jones, 'The British Labour Movement and Working Class Leisure 1918–1939', pp. 185–91.

84 A. Robertson, *The Trade Unions*, London, H. Hamilton, 1965, p. 11.

85 See *The Record*, June 1937, p. 282. Post Office Engineering Union, *The Journal*, 13 August 1937. *The Shop Assistant*, 21 August 1937; 23 April 1938; 7 May 1938. National Union of Foundry Workers, *Journal and Report*, April 1938, p. 5.

86 Although private agreements were not included in the figures collected by the *Ministry of Labour Gazette*, it is clear from press reports that many companies gave holidays with pay.

87 *Daily Herald*, 9 September 1937. It must be added that with the spread of scientific management some employers may have been willing to concede shorter hours and holidays in exchange for changes in the work process.

88 Quoted in A. Briggs, *Social Thought and Social Action: A Study of the Work of Seebohm Rowntree 1871–1954*, London, Longman, 1961, p. 299.

89 *Industrial Welfare*, April 1938, p. 134. ILO, *Facilities for the Use of Workers' Leisure During Holidays*, Geneva, ILO, 1939, p. 33.
90 See *Daily Express*, 5 April 1938.
91 General Federation of Trade Unions *Report*, 1937, p. 18. *Manchester Guardian*, 19 January 1938.

Chapter 2   Commercialization and the growth of the leisure industry

1 See W. Vamplew, 'The Sport of Kings and Commoners: The Commercialization of British Horse-Racing in the Nineteenth Century', in R. Cashman and M. McKernan (eds), *Sport in History: The Making of Modern Sporting History*, Queensland, Queensland University Press, 1979, pp. 307–25. S. Tischler, *Footballers and Businessmen: The Origins of Professional Soccer in England*, New York, Holmes & Meier, 1981. P. Bailey, *Leisure and Class in Victorian England: Rational recreation and the contest for control*, London, Routledge & Kegan Paul, 1978, especially pp. 150–2. J. K. Walton, *The English Seaside Resort: A Social History 1750–1914*, Leicester, Leicester University Press, 1983, *passim*.
2 A. Briggs, *Mass Entertainment: The Origins of a Modern Industry*, Adelaide, Griffen Press, 1960, p. 9.
3 R. Stone and D. A. Rowe, *The Measurement of Consumers' Expenditure and Behaviour in the United Kingdom 1920–1938*, vol. 2, Cambridge, Cambridge University Press, 1966, p. 78.
4 S. Rowson, 'A Statistical Survey of the Cinema Industry in Great Britain in 1934', *Journal of the Royal Statistical Society*, vol. 99, 1936, pp. 67–118.
5 A. Briggs, *The History of Broadcasting in the UK*, vol. 2, *The Golden Age of Wireless*, Oxford, Oxford University Press, 1965, p. 450. *Investors' Chronicle*, 12 November 1938.
6 H. Llewellyn Smith (ed.), *The New Survey of London Life and Labour*, vol. 9, *Life and Leisure*, London, P. S. King, 1935, pp. 55–6.
7 'The Football Industry – 1', *Planning*, vol. 17, no. 324, 1951, p. 168.
8 J. Walvin, *The People's Game: A Social History of British Football*, London, Allen Lane, 1975, p. 135. S. G. Jones, 'The Economic Aspects of Association Football in England', *The British Journal of Sports History*, vol. 1, no. 3, 1984, pp. 286–99.
9 J. Walvin, *Leisure and Society 1830–1950*, London, Longman, 1978, p. 140.

10 R. McKibbon, 'Working-Class Gambling in Britain 1880–1939', *Past and Present*, no. 82, 1979, p. 152.

11 Cited in B. Seebohm Rowntree and G. R. Lavers, *English Life and Leisure. A Social Study*, London, Longmans, 1951, p. 125.

12 B. Seebohm Rowntree, *Poverty and Progress: A Second Social Survey of York*, London, Longmans, 1942, p. 403.

13 *The Economist*, 1 January 1938.

14 Ministry of Labour and National Service, *Development of the Catering, Holiday, and Tourist Industry*, London, HMSO, 1946, pp. 52–3.

15 C. H. Feinstein, *National Income, Expenditure and Output of the United Kingdom 1855–1965*, Cambridge, Cambridge University Press, 1972, Table 70.

16 *The Economist*, 7 March 1936.

17 ibid.

18 *Royal Commission On Lotteries and Betting 1932–3: Final Report*, Parliamentary Papers 1932–33 xiv, cmd 4341, p. 58.

19 *The Economist*, 16 April 1932.

20 *The Economist*, 8 April 1939.

21 *Daily Herald*, 28 August 1936.

22 *The Listener*, 1 July 1931, Supplement no. 14.

23 *Investors' Chronicle*, 9 January 1937.

24 G. B. Wilson (ed.), *Alliance Year Book And Temperance Reformers Handbook*, Manchester, United Kingdom Alliance, 1940, pp. 110–12.

25 A. L. Chapman and R. Knight, *Wages and Salaries in the United Kingdom 1920–1938*, Cambridge, Cambridge University Press, 1953, pp. 207, 210–11.

26 British Association, *Britain in Depression*, London, Sir Isaac Pitman, 1935, p. 441.

27 W. H. Beveridge, *Full Employment in a Free Society*, London, Allen & Unwin, 1944, p. 63.

28 E. Brunner, *Holiday Making and the Holiday Trades*, Oxford, Nuffield College, 1945, p. 11. H. Frankel, 'The Industrial Distribution of the Population of Great Britain in July, 1939', *Journal of The Royal Statistical Society*, vol. 108, 1945, pp. 418–19.

29 *The Economist*, 8 April 1939.

30 *Fifth Census of Production*, Part 3, London, HMSO, 1940, pp. 573, 583.

31 *The Listener*, 1 June 1939.

32 *Census of England and Wales 1931. Occupation Tables*, London, HMSO, 1934, p. 679.

33 *Daily Herald*, 21 July 1933.

34 Jones, op. cit., p. 293.

35 D. Smith and G. Williams, *Fields of Praise: The Official History of the Welsh Rugby Union 1881–1981*, Cardiff, University of Wales Press, 1980, p. 225.

36 C. H. Feinstein, *Domestic Capital Formation in the United Kingdom 1920–1938*, Cambridge, Cambridge University Press, 1965, p. 198.

37 R. Low, *The History of the British Film*, vols 4, 7, London, Allen & Unwin, 1971, 1985.

38 ibid., *passim*. Rowson, op. cit., p. 76. The Arts Enquiry, *The Factual Film*, London, Oxford University Press, 1947, p. 198.

39 Llewellyn Smith (ed.), op. cit., p. 45. D. Caradog Jones (ed.), *The Social Survey of Merseyside*, vol. 3, Liverpool, Liverpool University Press and Hodder & Stoughton, 1934, p. 279. J. Richards, 'The Cinema and cinema-going in Birmingham in the 1930s', in J. K. Walton and J. Walvin (eds), *Leisure in Britain 1780–1939*, Manchester, Manchester University Press, 1983, p. 35.

40 N. Branson and M. Heinemann, *Britain in the Nineteen Thirties*, St Albans, Panther Books, 1973, p. 275.

41 M. Balcon, 'The Film Industry', in H. J. Schofield (ed.), *The Book of British Industries*, London, Denis Archer, 1933, p. 154.

42 J. McMillan, *The Way It Was: 1914–1934*, London, William Kimber, 1979, p. 145.

43 F. Rust, *Dance in Society*, London, Routledge & Kegan Paul, 1969, p. 97.

44 P. Wild, 'Recreation in Rochdale 1900–40', in J. Clarke, C. Critcher and R. Johnson (eds), *Working Class Culture: Studies in history and theory*, London, Hutchinson, 1979, p. 149.

45 R. Graves and A. Hodge, *The Long Week-End: A Social History of Great Britain 1918–1939*, London, Faber & Faber, 1940, p. 235.

46 F. Johnston (ed.), *The Football Who's Who*, London, Associated Sporting Press, 1935, p. 11.

47 'The Football Industry – I', op. cit., p. 172.

48 W. Vamplew, *The Turf: A Social and Economic History of Horse Racing*, London, Allen Lane, 1976, p. 72.

49 J. Walvin, *Beside the Seaside: A Social History of the Popular Seaside Holiday*, London, Allen Lane, 1978, p. 117.

50 *Report of the Committee on Land Utilisation in Rural Areas*, Parliamentary Papers 1941–42 iv, cmd 6378, p. 25.

51 D. J. Jeremy, 'Butlin, Sir William Heygate Edmund Colbourne (1899–1980): Pioneer in the mass leisure industry', in D. J. Jeremy

(ed.), *Dictionary of Business Biography*, vol. 1, London, Butterworths, 1984, pp. 535–41.

52 *Financial News*, 4 August 1938.

53 *Investors' Chronicle*, 21 January 1939.

54 H. Clay (ed.), *The Inter-War Years and Other Papers: A Selection from the writings of Hubert Douglas Henderson*, Oxford, Clarendon Press, 1955, p. 64.

55 See *Report of the Committee on the Disinterested Management of Public Houses*, Parliamentary Papers 1927 x, cmd 2862. E. Selley, *The English Public House As It Is*, London, Longmans, Green & Co., 1927, pp. 109–22. B. Oliver, *The Renaissance of the English Public House*, London, Faber & Faber, 1947.

56 A. Crawford and R. Thorne, *Birmingham Pubs 1890–1939*, Birmingham, University of Birmingham, 1975.

57 *Investors' Chronicle*, 12 December 1931.

58 D. H. Aldcroft, *The Inter-War Economy: Britain, 1919–1939*, London, Batsford, 1970, p. 236.

59 *Fifth Census of Production*, op. cit., p. 583. J. B. Jefferys, *Retail Trading in Britain 1850–1950*, Cambridge, Cambridge University Press, 1954, p. 419. The most well-known sports companies included Bukta, Dunlop, Slazenger and Spalding.

60 See B. Dabscheck, 'The Wage Determination Process For Sportsmen', *Economic Record*, vol. 51, no. 133, 1975, pp. 52–65. J. A. Schofield, 'The Development Of First-Class Cricket in England: An Economic Analysis', *The Journal of Industrial Economics*, vol. 30, no. 4, 1982, pp. 337–60. P. J. Sloane, 'The Economics Of Professional Football: The Football Club As A Utility Maximiser', *Scottish Journal of Political Economy*, vol. 18, no. 2, 1971, pp. 121–46. W. Vamplew, 'The Economics of a Sports Industry: Scottish Gate-Money, 1890–1914', *Economic History Review*, 2nd Series, vol. 35, no. 4, 1982, pp. 549–67.

61 'The Football Industry – II', *Planning*, vol. 17, no. 325, p. 191.

62 C. Korr, 'The men at the top: The board of directors of the West Ham United Football Club', in W. Vamplew (ed.), *The Economic History Of Leisure: Papers presented at the Eighth International Economic History Congress*, Budapest, 1982, p. 6. S. Tischler, 'The basis for professionalism in English football clubs', in Vamplew (ed.), op. cit., p. 26. cf. S. Wagg, *The Football World: A Contemporary Social History*, Brighton, Harvester Press, 1984, pp. 31–3.

63 J. Walvin, *The People's Game*, London, Allen Lane, 1975, pp. 128–33. S. Studd, *Herbert Chapman, Football Emperor: A Study in the Origins of Modern Soccer*, London, Peter Owen, 1981.

64 McMillan, op. cit., p. 195.
65 N. Kaldor and R. Silverman, *A Statistical Analysis of Advertising Expenditure and of the Revenue of the Press*, Cambridge, Cambridge Universty Press, 1948, p. 10.
66 *Hansard* (Commons) 5th series, vol. 264, col. 1208, 15 April 1932.
67 *Daily Express*, 21 April 1932.
68 *Investors' Chronicle*, 8 January 1938.
69 See M. Pegg, *Broadcasting and Society 1918–1939*, London, Croom Helm, 1983. J. Redmond, *Broadcasting: The Developing Technology*, London, BBC Publications, 1974, p. 4. S. G. Sturmey, *The Economic Development of Radio*, London, Duckworth, 1958.
70 J. H. E. Williams, 'The Radio Industry', in Schofield (ed.), op. cit., p. 289.
71 D. L. Lemahieu, 'The Gramophone: Recorded Music and the Cultivated Mind in Britain Between the Wars', *Technology and Culture*, vol. 23, no. 3, 1982, p. 379.
72 A. Briggs, *Mass Entertainment: The Origins of a Modern Industry*, Adelaide, Griffen Press, 1960, p. 18.
73 D. E. Channon, *The Strategy and Structure of British Enterprise*, London, Macmillan, 1973, p. 100.
74 *The Economist*, 14 December 1929; 12 December 1932. See also G. Jones, 'The Gramophone Company: An Anglo-American Multinational, 1898–1931', *Business History Review*, vol. 51, no. 1, 1985, pp. 76–100.
75 L. Hannah, *The Rise of the Corporate Economy*, London, Methuen, 1976, p. 97.
76 *Investors' Chronicle*, 18 May 1935. cf. R. E. Catterall, 'Electrical Engineering', in N. K. Buxton and D. H. Aldcroft (eds), *British Industry Between the Wars: Instability and Industrial Development 1919–1939*, London, Scolar Press, 1979, p. 264.
77 *Investors' Chronicle*, 11 December 1937.
78 *The Times*, 7 December 1935.
79 *Financial Times*, 16 January 1929.
80 PEP, *The British Film Industry*, London, PEP, 1952, pp. 45–78. F. D. Klingender and S. Legg, *Money Behind the Screen*, London, Lawrence & Wishart, 1937. For a detailed treatment of cinema history, see J. Curran and V. Porter (eds), *British Cinema History*, London, Weidenfeld & Nicolson, 1983. Low, op. cit.
81 Mass Observation, *The Pub and the People: A Worktown Study*, London, Gollancz, 1943, pp. 33, 45. *Report of the Royal Commission on Licensing (England and Wales) 1929–31*, Parliamentary Papers 1931–32 xi, cmd 3988, p. 156. For the development of liquor advertising, see G. Prys Williams and G.

Thompson Brake, *Drink in Great Britain 1900 to 1979*, London, Edsall, 1980, pp. 193–206.

82 K. H. Hawkins and C. L. Pass, *The Brewing Industry: A Study in Industrial Organisation and Public Policy*, London, Heinemann, 1979, p. 48.

83 J. Vaizey, *The Brewing Industry 1886–1951: An Economic Study*, London, Sir Isaac Pitman & Sons, 1960, pp. 27–9.

84 *Financial News*, 4 February 1936.

85 J. Hilton, *Why I Go In For The Pools*, London, Allen & Unwin, 1936.

86 J. White, 'Campbell Bunk: A Lumpen Community in London Between the Wars', *History Workshop Journal*, no. 8, 1979, pp. 25–6.

87 See *The New Statesman*, 18 June 1921. *The Nation and Athenaeum*, 26 January 1929. *Daily Herald*, 14 July 1932.

88 *Ashton-Under-Lyne Reporter*, 12 July 1930.

89 Quoted in Graves and Hodge, op. cit., p. 114.

90 E. M. Roberts, *Working Class Barrow and Lancaster 1890–1930*, Lancaster, University of Lancaster Occasional Paper no. 2, 1976, p. 54.

91 Quoted in Wild, op. cit., p. 148.

92 J. Stevenson, 'Myth and Reality: Britain in the 1930s', in A. Sked and C. Cook (eds), *Crisis and Controversy: Essays in Honour of A. J. P. Taylor*, London, Macmillan, 1976, p. 91. See also J. Stevenson and C. Cook, *The Slump: Society And Politics During The Depression*, London, Quartet Books, 1979, especially chapters 1–2.

93 A. Howkins and J. Saville, 'The 1930s: A revisionist history', *The Socialist Register 1979*, London, Merlin Press, 1979, pp. 92–4. A. Exell, 'Morris Motors in the 1930s', *History Workshop Journal*, no. 6, 1978, pp. 52–78; no. 7, 1979, pp. 45–65. See also G. Harkell, 'The Migration of Mining Families to the Kent Coalfield Between the Wars', *Oral History*, vol. 6, 1978, pp. 98–113.

94 E. D. Smithies, 'The Contrast Between North and South in England 1918–1939: A Study of Economic, Social and Political Problems With Particular Reference to the Experience of Burnley, Halifax, Ipswich and Luton', unpublished Ph.D. thesis, Leeds University, 1974.

95 C. Cameron, A. J. Lush and G. Meara (eds), *Disinherited Youth*, Edinburgh, Carnegie United Kingdom Trust, 1943, p. 6.

96 See C. Forman, *Industrial Town. Self Portrait of St Helens in the 1920s*, St Albans, Granada Publishing, 1979, pp. 127–36. D. Gittens, *Fair Sex: Family size and structure, 1900–39*, London, Hutchinson, 1982, pp. 131–51. J. Greave, 'A Woman's Life in

Oldham before 1914 . . . 56 hours a week at the looms and housework on top', *Spare Rib*, June 1984, pp. 52–3. R. Hoggart, *The Uses of Literacy*, Harmondsworth, Penguin Books, 1977, pp. 41–53. J. Lewis, 'In search of a Real Equality: Women Between the Wars', in F. Gloversmith (ed,), *Class, Culture and Social Change: A New View of the 1930s*, Brighton, Harvester Press, 1980, pp. 208–39. *Oral History: Women's History Issue*, vol. 5, no. 2, 1977. S. Rowbotham, *Hidden From History: 300 Years of Women's Oppression and the Fight Against It*, London, Pluto Press, 1977, pp. 137–58. P. Taylor, 'Daughters and mothers – maids and mistresses: domestic service between the wars', in Clarke, Critcher and Johnson (eds), op. cit., pp. 121–39. B. Williamson, *Class, Culture and Community: A Biographical Study of Social Change in Mining*, London, Routledge & Kegan Paul, 1982, pp. 118–32.

97 See M. Spring Rice, *Working Class Wives: Their Health and Conditions*, Harmondsworth, Penguin Books, 1939. J. Lewis, *The Politics of Motherhood: Child and Maternal Welfare in England 1900–1939*, London, Croom Helm, 1980, *passim*. C. Webster, 'Healthy or Hungry Thirties?', *History Workshop Journal*, no. 13, 1982, pp. 110–29.

98 Spring Rice, op. cit., p. 108. See also F. Zweig, *Women's Life and Labour*, London, Gollancz, 1952, pp. 141–8.

99 Forman, op. cit., p. 128. Compare with the comments of the middle-class philanthropist, Constance Harris, about the women of Bethnal Green:

> I believe it is true to say that a great number of them do not make the best use of their time. They can be seen at any hour of the day in many of the streets, with untidy hair and torn clothing, gossiping with each other, waiting for the public-house to open, ready with their jugs for the daily drink of beer or stout.

C. Harris, *The Use of Leisure in Bethnal Green: A Survey of Social Conditions in the Borough 1925 to 1926*, London, Lindsey Press, 1927, p. 33.

100 *The Socialist*, 24 August 1922.

101 Harris, op. cit., pp. 35–6.

102 *Manchester Guardian*, 26 August 1931. *Daily Worker*, 26 March 1932; 17 August 1935.

103 *Cotton Factory Times*, 7 July 1933. See also *The Labour Woman*, 1 September 1927; June 1937, pp. 90–1.

104 Spring Rice, op. cit., pp. 109–15.

105 J. Richards, *The Age Of The Dream Palace: Cinema And Society*

In Britain 1930–1939, London, Routledge & Kegan Paul, 1984, pp. 13–16.

Chapter 3   Leisure provision in the voluntary sector

1 A. Howkins and J. Lowerson, *Trends In Leisure, 1919–1939*, London, The Sports Council and Social Science Research Council, 1979, pp. 55, 46.
2 See D. Prynn, 'The Clarion Clubs, Rambling and the Holiday Associations in Britain since the 1890s', *Journal of Contemporary History*, vol. 11, nos 2 and 3, 1976, pp. 65–77.
3 *The YHA Rucksack*, Easter 1938, p. 30.
4 Manchester Central Reference Library Archives Department, Mss 111, Manchester School Camps Association, *Report of the 15th Annual Camp*, 1930, p. 3; *Report of the 17th Annual Camp*, 1932, p. 3.
5 *Camping*, June 1930, p. 90.
6 Benny Rothman, interview with the author, 3 August 1981.
7 Martin Bobker, interview with the author, 18 August 1981.
8 D. Caradog Jones (ed.), *The Social Survey of Merseyside*, vol. 3, Liverpool, Liverpool University Press and Hodder & Stoughton, 1934, p. 295. B. Seebohm Rowntree, *Poverty and Progress: A Second Social Survey of York*, London, Longmans, 1942, p. 396. H. Llewellyn Smith (ed.), *The New Survey of London Life and Labour*, vol. 9, *Life and Leisure*, London, P. S. King, 1935, p. 61.
9 See R. Q. Gray, *The Labour Aristocracy in Victorian Edinburgh*, Oxford, Clarendon Press, 1976. G. Crossick, *An Artisan Elite in Victorian Society: Kentish London*, London, Croom Helm, 1978.
10 T. Middleton, 'An Enquiry into the Use of Leisure Amongst the Working Classes of Liverpool', unpublished M.A. thesis, Liverpool University, 1931, p. 122.
11 R. Evans and A. Boyd, *The Use of Leisure in Hull*, Hull, The Hull 'Use of Leisure' Sub-Committee, 1933, p. 15. Seebohm Rowntree, op. cit., pp. 387–9.
12 Llewellyn Smith, op. cit., p. 61.
13 T. Young, *Becontree and Dagenham: A Report Made For The Pilgrim Trust*, London, Becontree Social Survey Committee, 1934, pp. 222–3.
14 J. Springhall, 'The Boy Scouts, Class and Militarism in relation to British Youth Movements 1908–1930', *International Review of Social History*, vol. 16, 1971, pp. 140–1. J. Springhall, *Youth, Empire and Society: British Youth Movements, 1883–1940*, London, Croom Helm, 1977, p. 78. cf. M. Blanch, 'Imperialism, nationalism and

organised youth', in J. Clarke, C. Critcher and R. Johnson (eds), *Working Class Culture: Studies in history and theory*, London, Hutchinson, 1979, pp. 115–17.

15 W. G. Jackson, 'A Historical Study of the Provision of Facilities for Play and Recreation in Manchester', unpublished M.Ed. thesis, Manchester University, 1940, pp. 142, 148. Llewellyn Smith (ed.), op. cit., pp. 155–6, 197. See generally F. Dawes, *A Cry From The Streets: The Boys' Club Movement from the 1850s to the Present Day*, Hove, Wayland Publishers, 1975.

16 See *How To Sustain A Branch of The Junior Imperial and Constitutional League*, London, Headquarters, n.d. *The Blackshirt*, March 1933, p. 4; 1 April 1933, p. 3; 16–22 February 1934, p. 4; 23–9 March 1934, p. 3; 30 March–5 April 1934, p. 3; 11–17 May 1934, p. 1.

17 *The Amateur Theatre and Playwrights' Journal*, 8 April 1938; 22 April 1938.

18 M. Rooff, *Youth And Leisure: A Survey Of Girls' Organisations In England And Wales*, Edinburgh, Carnegie United Kingdom Trust, 1935.

19 J. H. Richardson, *Industrial Relations in Great Britain*, Geneva, International Labour Organisation, 1933, p. 165.

20 See for example T. C. Barker, *The Glassmakers. Pilkington: the rise of an international company 1826–1976*, London, Weidenfeld & Nicolson, 1977, pp. 403–4. R. A. Church, *Kenricks in Hardware: A Family Business 1791–1966*, Newton Abbot, David & Charles, 1969, p. 302. A. E. Musson, *Enterprise in Soap and Chemicals: Joseph Crosfield & Sons Ltd.*, Manchester, Manchester University Press, 1965, pp. 154–5, 317–18. H. Nockolds, *Lucas: The First 100 Years, vol. 1, The King of the Road*, Newton Abbot, David & Charles, 1976, pp. 191–2. A. Plummer and R. E. Early, *The Blanket Makers 1669–1969: A History of Charles Early and Marriott (Witney) Ltd*, London, Routledge & Kegan Paul, 1969, p. 123.

21 H. A. Mess, *Industrial Tyneside: A Social Survey*, London, Ernest Benn, 1928, p. 148. R. Whiting, 'The Working Class in the "New Industry" Towns Between the Wars: The Case of Oxford', unpublished D.Phil. thesis, Oxford University, 1978, pp. 162–3, 172–3, 288.

22 Leeds Archive Centre, Acc 1951/36, 128, The Montague Burton Archives, Newscutting Books. See also *Unity*, February 1931, pp. 216–17.

23 TUC *Report*, 1932, p. 73.

24 'The New Industrial England: Where the Foundations of Industrial Peace are Laid', *Unity*, January 1928–September 1935, *passim*.

25 *Industrial Welfare*, October 1938, p. 414.
26 *Sunday Referee*, 27 January 1935. Evans and Boyd, op. cit., pp. 7, 14.
27 Caradog Jones, op. cit., pp. 310–12. Middleton, op. cit., p. 123.
28 *The New Dawn*, 28 April 1923; 12 May 1923. *The Yorkshire Factory Times and Workers' Weekly Record*, 12 October 1922. I have examined company recreation in some detail in two papers: 'Recreation and Company Welfare Policy in Britain Between the Wars'; 'Cotton Employers and Industrial Welfare Between the Wars' (to be published in a volume edited by A. McIvor and T. Jowett).
29 See for example *The Labour Year Book*, 1919, pp. 296–8. B. T. Hall, 'Workmen's Clubs: An Organ of Democratic Reform', *The Labour Magazine*, June 1922, pp. 84–5. *Daily Herald*, 21 July 1927.
30 *Minutes of Evidence Taken Before The Royal Commission on Licensing (England and Wales)*, London, HMSO, 1930–2, p. 1218.
31 Note the comments of B. T. Hall:

> I am keenly interested in the Labour Party and I should say that is true of 18 out of 20 of our Executives. There would be the gravest possible reluctance, and indeed it would be almost fratricidal to do any thing to bring us in conflict with the Labour Party.

Labour Party Archives LIQ/22/330/1, Evidence of B. T. Hall to the Special Sub-Committee on the Liquor Trade Problem, 28 March 1923.
32 See *The Labour Pioneer*, 4 March 1920; 11 March 1920. *Daily Herald*, 27 July 1927. *The Co-operative News*, 8 December 1934.
33 Section 20(1), Mining Industry Act, 1920.
34 *Report of the Departmental Committee of Inquiry into the Miners' Welfare Fund*, Parliamentary Papers 1932–33 xv, cmd 4236, pp. 26–35.
35 P. Brook Long, 'The Economic and Social History of the Scottish Coal Industry 1925–1939, With Particular Reference to Industrial Relations', unpublished Ph.D. thesis, Strathclyde University, 1978, p. 320.
36 S. Macintyre, *Little Moscows: Communism and Working-Class Militancy in Inter-War Britain*, London, Croom Helm, 1980, p. 72.
37 ibid., p. 26. H. Francis and D. Smith, *The Fed: A History of the South Wales Miners in the Twentieth Century*, London, Lawrence & Wishart, 1980, p. 160. cf. R. J. Waller, *The Dukeries Transformed: The Social and Political Development of a Twentieth Century Coalfield*, Oxford, Clarendon Press, 1983, pp. 189–207.

38 J. Mott, 'Miners, weavers and pigeon racing', in M. A. Smith, S. Parker and C. S. Smith (eds), *Leisure and Society in Britain*, London, Allen Lane, 1973, pp. 86–96. E. Bird, 'Jazz Bands of North East England: The Evolution of a Working Class Cultural Activity', *Oral History*, vol. 4, 1976, pp. 79–88. J. B. Priestley, *English Journey*, Harmondsworth, Penguin Books, 1979, pp. 314–15. C. Forman, *Industrial Town. Self Portrait of St Helens in the 1920s*, St Albans, Granada Publishing, 1979, pp. 185–7, 197. Llewellyn Smith (ed.), op. cit., p. 70. W. Feaver, 'How a Colliery Art Class Took Peking By Storm', *Observer Magazine*, 27 October 1980.

39 R. Hoggart, *The Uses of Literacy*, Harmondsworth, Penguin Books, 1977, p. 24. See also Howkins and Lowerson, op. cit., 'Preface'. J. Power. 'Aspects Of Working Class Leisure During the Depression Years: Bolton In the 1930s', unpublished M.A. thesis, Warwick University, 1980, pp. iii–iv, 18.

40 Hoggart, op. cit., p. 35. See also D. Gittens, *Fair Sex: Family size and structure, 1900–39*, London, Hutchinson, 1982, especially p. 183. B. Williamson, *Class, Culture and Community: A Biographical Study of Social Change in Mining*, London, Routledge & Kegan Paul, 1982, pp. 105–6.

41 For instance, in one very poor Sheffield family, under the initiative of mother, games such as cards or ludo were played, 'as that is cheaper than the pictures – I have no money for pictures'. M. Spring Rice, *Working Class Wives: Their Health and Conditions*, Harmondsworth, Penguin Books, 1939, p. 112. For the growth of gardening, see S. Constantine, 'Amateur Gardening and Popular Recreation in the 19th and 20th Centuries', *Journal of Social History*, vol. 14, no. 3, 1981, especially pp. 394–9.

42 G. Orwell, *The Lion and the Unicorn: Socialism And The English Genius*, Harmondsworth, Penguin Books, 1982, p. 39.

43 See Howkins and Lowerson, op. cit., pp. 13–19. cf. C. Delisle Burns, *Leisure In The Modern World*, London, Allen & Unwin, 1932, pp. 36–48.

44 Caradog Jones (ed.), op. cit., pp. 274, 276. Gittens, op. cit., pp. 56–7. Hoggart, op. cit., pp. 120–31. Seebohm Rowntree, op. cit., pp. 376–85. See also C. L. White, *Women's Magazines 1693–1968*, London, Michael Joseph, 1970. K. Drotner, 'Schoolgirls, Madcaps, and Air Aces: English Girls and their Magazine Reading between the Wars', *Feminist Studies*, vol. 9, no. 1, 1983, pp. 33–52.

45 R. Roberts, *The Classic Slum: Salford Life in the First Quarter of the Century*, Harmondsworth, Penguin Books, 1980, p. 49.

46 C. Harris, *The Use of Leisure in Bethnal Green: A Survey of Social*

Conditions in the Borough 1925 to 1926, London, Lindsey Press, 1927, p. 14. Rooff, op. cit., p. 85.

47 Manchester Central Reference Library Archives Department, Mss 8/5/13, Minutes of the Manchester Chamber of Commerce, 1 June 1932. See also Manchester Chamber of Commerce, *Monthly Record*, 30 June 1932.

48 Mass Observation, *The Pub and the People: A Worktown Study*, London, Gollancz, 1943, p. 17.

49 J. Stevenson, *British Society 1919–45*, Harmondsworth, Penguin Books, 1984, p. 166.

50 *South London Press*, 9 April 1926.

51 Women's Group on Public Welfare, *Our Towns: A Close-Up*, London, Oxford University Press, 1943, p. 15.

52 See M. McLaren, 'The London Public House', *London Mercury*, May 1928, pp. 30–8.

53 For further information about working class gambling, see R. McKibbon, 'Working Class Gambling in Britain 1880–1939', *Past and Present*, no. 82, 1979, pp. 147–78. W. Vamplew, *The Turf: A Social and Economic History of Horse Racing*, London, Allen Lane, 1976, pp. 199–212. R. Samuel, *East End Underworld: Chapters in the life of Arthur Harding*, London, Routledge & Kegan Paul, 1981, pp. 175–86.

54 Harris, op. cit., pp. 49–50.

55 A. Hutt, *The Condition Of The Working Class In Britain*, London, Martin Lawrence, 1933, p. 176.

56 T. Willis, *Whatever Happened to Tom Mix? The Story of One of My Lives*, London, Cassell, 1970, pp. 34–9. cf. Roberts, op. cit., pp. 153–5. Llewellyn Smith (ed.), op. cit., pp. 71–2.

57 S. Humphries, *Hooligans or Rebels: An Oral History of Working-Class Childhood and Youth 1889–1939*, Oxford, Basil Blackwell, 1981, pp. 121–49.

58 Willis op. cit., pp. 47–8.

59 G. Stedman Jones, 'Working-Class Culture and Working-Class Politics In London, 1870–1900; Notes on the Remaking of a Working Class', *Journal of Social History*, vol. 7, no. 4, 1974, pp. 460–508.

60 E. and S. Yeo, 'Perceived Patterns: Competition and Licence versus Class and Struggle' in E. and S. Yeo (eds), *Popular Culture and Class Conflict 1590–1914: Explorations in the History of Labour and Leisure*, Brighton, Harvester Press, 1981, pp. 292–7. It must be added, however, that the Yeos acknowledge that there has been resistance to this process, and that 'demands for real, mutual nexuses of *social* life' live on (p. 273).

61 F. R. Leavis, 'Mass Civilisation and Minority Culture', in *For Continuity*, Cambridge, Minority Press, 1933, pp. 13–46. R. Sinclair, *Metropolitan Man: The Future of the English*, London, Allen & Unwin, 1937, p. 114. J. L. Hammond, *The Growth of Common Enjoyment*, London, Oxford University Press, 1933, p. 20. Given the view that modern forms of leisure had emerged by the late Victorian period, it has been suggested that historians of leisure have chartered the rise of mass culture to this very same period. See C. Waters, ' "All Sorts and Any Quantity of Outlandish Recreations": History, Sociology, and the Study of Leisure in England, 1820 to 1870', *Historical Papers/Communications historiques*, A selection from the papers presented at the annual meeting of the Canadian Historial Association, 1981, pp. 8–33.

62 *The Plebs*, March 1929, p. 5. *The Socialist Review*, June 1930, pp. 92–3. *Red Stage*, January 1932, p. 6.

63 *Westminster Gazette*, 11 May 1927. Harris, op. cit., pp. 64–70.

64 N. Branson and M. Heinemann, *Britain in the Nineteen Thirties*, St Albans, Panther Books, 1973, p. 270. For contemporary comments, see Evans and Boyd, op. cit., p. 22. F. Young, 'The Art of Listening', *BBC Handbook 1928*, p. 349.

65 For further discussion, see T. Lovell, 'The Social Relations of Cultural Production: Absent Centre of a New Discourse', in S. Clarke *et al.*, *One-Dimensional Marxism: Althusser and the Politics of Culture*, London, Allison Busby, 1980, pp. 232–56. By stressing the importance of consumer demand one is not trying to conceal history for capital as the Yeos seem to suggest, but rather to admit that people are quite able to make decisions for themselves and to be aware of the significance of those decisions. E. and S. Yeo, op. cit., pp. 279–81.

66 A. Howkins, 'Leisure in the Inter-war Years: an auto-critique', in A. Tomlinson (ed.), *Leisure and Social Control*, Brighton, Brighton Polytechnic, 1981, pp. 79–81.

67 D. Hebdige, 'Towards a Cartography of Taste 1935–1962', in B. Waites, T. Bennett and G. Martin (eds), *Popular Culture: Past and Present*, London, Croom Helm, 1982, p. 216.

68 Mass Observation, op. cit., *passim*.

69 For examples of crowd disturbance, see *The Daily Mail*, 5 January 1923. *The Sporting Chronicle*, 14 January 1925; 28 January 1925. *The Sporting Chronicle and Athletic News*, 2 December 1935.

70 R. Miliband, *Marxism and Politics*, Oxford, Oxford University Press, 1977, pp. 51–2.

71 See P. Stead, 'The people and the pictures: The British working class and film in the 1930s', in N. Pronay and D. W. Spring (eds),

Propaganda, Politics And Film, 1918–1945, London, Macmillan, 1982, especially, p. 93.

72 See introduction.

73 J. Foster, 'British Imperialism and the Labour Aristocracy', in J. Skelley (ed.), *The General Strike 1926*, London, Lawrence & Wishart, 1976, p. 32.

74 J. Hargreaves, 'The Political Economy of Mass Sport', in S. Parker, N. Ventris, J. Haworth and M. Smith (eds), *Sport And Leisure In Contemporary Society*, London, Polytechnic of Central London, 1975, p. 60. T. Aldgate, 'Ideological Consensus in British Feature Films, 1935–1947', in K. R. M. Short (ed.), *Feature Film as History*, London, Croom Helm, 1981, pp. 103, 111. R. L. Taylor, *Art, An Enemy Of The People*, Hassocks, Harvester Press, 1978, p. 47.

Chapter 4   State provision: the role of central and municipal authorities

1 For further details of the State, see R. Miliband, *The State in Capitalist Society*, London, Quartet Books, 1980.

2 E. Higgs, 'Leisure and the State: The History of Popular Culture as Reflected in the Public Records', *History Workshop Journal*, no. 15, 1983, pp. 141–50. D. A. Robinson, 'Sport In Surrey', *British Society Of Sports History Bulletin*, no. 3, 1985, p. 32.

3 R. Storch, 'Introduction: Persistence And Change In Nineteenth-Century Popular Culture', in R. Storch (ed.), *Popular Culture and Custom in Nineteenth Century England*, London, Croom Helm, 1982, p. 16.

4 H. E. Meller, *Leisure and the Changing City, 1870–1914*, London, Routledge & Kegan Paul, 1976. D. A. Reid, 'Municipalities and Leisure: Birmingham 1838–1875', paper given at the Urban History Society Conference, 1981.

5 Richard Roberts, 'The Corporation as impresario: the municipal provision of entertainment in Victorian and Edwardian Bournemouth', in J. K. Walton and J. Walvin (eds), *Leisure in Britain 1780–1939*, Manchester, Manchester University Press, 1983, pp. 136–57. J. K. Walton, 'Municipal government and the holiday industry in Blackpool, 1876–1914', in Walton and Walvin (eds), op. cit., pp. 158–85.

6 A. Marwick, 'British Life and Leisure and the First World War', *History Today*, vol. 15, no. 6, 1965, pp. 409–19. J. Walvin, *Leisure and Society 1830–1950*, London, Longman, 1978, pp. 128–32.

7 *Final Report of the Health of Munition Workers Committee on*

Industrial Health and Efficiency, Parliamentary Papers 1918 xii, cmd 9065, p. 117.

8 R. Middleton, *Towards the Managed Economy: Keynes, the Treasury and the Fiscal Policy Debate of the 1930s*, London, Methuen, 1985. A. Booth and M. Pack, *Employment, Capital and Economic Policy: Great Britain 1918–1939*, Oxford, Basil Blackwell, 1985. J. Tomlinson, *British Macroeconomic Policy since 1940*, London, Croom Helm, 1985, p. 40. D. H. Aldcroft, *Full Employment*, Brighton, Wheatsheaf, 1984, p. 30.

9 A. Howkins and J. Lowerson, *Trends in Leisure, 1919–1939*, London, The Sports Council and Social Science Research Council, 1979, pp. 6, 55. Though compare with their more recent contribution, 'Leisure in the Thirties', in A. Tomlinson (ed.), *Leisure and Social Control*, Brighton, Brighton Polytechnic, 1981, pp. 70–92.

10 G. Mequet, 'Possibilities of International Action in regard to Workers' Spare Time', *International Labour Review*, vol. 30, 1934, p. 593.

11 A. Marwick, *The Explosion of British Society 1914–1970*, London, Macmillan, 1971, p. 51. See also M. Dickinson and S. Street, *Cinema and State: The Film Industry and the British Government 1927–84*, London, British Film Institute, 1985.

12 A. L. Stevenson, 'The Development of Physical Education in the State Schools of Scotland 1900–1960', unpublished M.Litt. thesis, Aberdeen University, 1978, p. 167.

13 *Physical Training and Recreation: Memorandum explaining the Government proposals for the development and extension of the facilities available*, Parliamentary Papers 1937 xxi, cmd 5364, p. 6.

14 TUC Archives, Minutes of the TUC General Council, 22 June 1938.

15 National Fitness Council, *The National Fitness Campaign*, London, issued by the National Fitness Council, 1939, p. 23.

16 *Royal Commission On National Museums and Galleries. Final Report, Part 1*, Parliamentary Papers 1929–30 xvi, cmd 3401, p. 81. *Royal Commission On National Museums and Galleries. Interim Report*, Parliamentary Papers 1928–29 viii, cmd 3192, p. 59. *Report of the Committee On Local Expenditure (England and Wales)*, Parliamentary Papers 1932–33 xiv, cmd 4200, pp. 86–7. *Report of the Committee On Local Expenditure (Scotland)*, Parliamentary Papers 1932–33 xiv, cmd 4201, pp. 128–9. See generally J. Minihan, *The Nationalization of Culture: The Development of State Subsidies of the Arts in Great Britain*, London, Hamish Hamilton, 1977.

17 D. Caradog Jones (ed.), *The Social Survey of Merseyside*, vol. 3,

Liverpool, Liverpool University Press and Hodder & Stoughton, 1934, pp. 287–8.

18 W. G. Jackson, 'An Historical Study of the Provision of Facilities for Play and Recreation in Manchester', unpublished M.Ed. thesis, Manchester University, 1940, p. 139. Manchester Corporation Parks and Cemetries Department, *Short Historical Survey*, Manchester, the Corporation, 1938. Despite this, F. T. Moore suggested 'that many of the adolescents of Hulme spend their leisure time mainly in walking about, standing on the street corner and visiting the cinema.' F. T. Moore, 'The Hulme Youth Problem'. *Social Welfare*, vol. 4, no. 7, 1941, p. 124. H. E. O. James and F. T. Moore, *Adolescent Leisure in a Working-Class District*, London, Occupational Psychology, 1940.

19 H. Llewellyn Smith (ed.), *The New Survey of London Life and Labour*, vol. 9, *Life and Leisure*, London, P. S. King, 1935, p. 57.

20 *News Chronicle*, 23 January 1935; 6 April 1939.

21 *Hansard* (Commons) 5th series, vol. 127, col. 1851, 15 April 1920; vol. 175, cols 1973–4, 8 July 1924; vol. 182, cols 1316–19, 1 April 1925.

22 *Manchester Guardian*, 23 May 1933.

23 *Cotton Factory Times*, 21 October 1927. *Manchester Guardian*, 25 January 1928.

24 *Manchester Guardian*, 7 September 1936.

25 *The Times*, 20 May 1936; 23 May 1936.

26 *Daily Herald*, 30 May 1934.

27 R. Roberts, *The Classic Slum: Salford Life in the First Quarter of the Century*, Harmondsworth, Penguin Books, 1980, pp. 237–8.

28 J. Stevenson, *British Society 1914–45*, Harmondsworth, Penguin Books, 1984, p. 398.

29 B. Seebohm Rowntree, *Poverty and Progress: A Second Social Survey of York*, London, Longmans, 1942, p. 377.

30 W. Dougill, 'The British Coast and its Holiday Resorts', *The Town Planning Review*, vol. 16, no. 4, 1935, p. 278. C. Musgrave, *Life in Brighton: from the earliest times to the present*, London, Faber, 1970, p. 391.

31 J. K. Walton, *The Blackpool Landlady: A social history*, Manchester, Manchester University Press, 1978, pp. 176–7.

32 *Hansard* (Commons) 5th series, vol. 191, cols 1694–5, 16 February 1926; vol. 202, cols 772–3, 15 February 1927; vol. 217, col. 170, 8 May 1928; vol. 260, col. 28, 23 November 1931.

33 E. Wilkinson, *The Town That Was Murdered*, London, Gollancz, 1939, p. 231.

34 M. Rooff, *Youth And Leisure: A Survey Of Girls' Organisations In*

England And Wales, Edinburgh, Carnegie United Kingdom Trust, 1935, pp. 41–58.

35 Howkins and Lowerson, op. cit., p. 31.

36 Labour Party Archives, National Conference of Labour Women, *Report*, 1934. See also, for example, TUC *Report*, 1921, pp. 341–2; 1929, pp. 454–5. Scottish TUC *Report*, 1921, p. 75; 1922, pp. 98–9; 1929, p. 170; 1939, p. 237.

37 Manchester Central Reference Library Archives Department, Mss 351/5, Manchester and District Dramatic Federation, *Journal*, November–December 1931, p. 2.

38 Reg Cordwell interview, 21 July 1977, Tape number 455, Manchester Studies Unit, Manchester Polytechnic.

39 *Report of the National Conference: 'The Leisure of The People'*, Manchester, 17–20 November 1919, p. 31.

40 *Daily Herald*, 26 May 1919.

41 *Manchester Guardian*, 29 September 1928.

42 See D. H. Aldcroft, 'Control of the liquor trade in Great Britain 1914–21', in W. H. Chaloner and B. M. Ratcliffe (eds), *Trade And Transport: Essays in economic history in honour of T. S. Willan*, Manchester, Manchester University Press, 1977, pp. 242–57. M. E. Rose, 'The Success of Social Reform? The Central Control Board (Liquor Traffic) 1915–21', in M. R. D. Foot (ed.), *War and Society: Historical Essays in honour and memory of J. R. Western 1928–1971*, London, Elek, 1973, pp. 71–84. J. Turner, 'State Purchase Of The Liquor Trade In The First World War', *The Historical Journal*, vol. 23, no. 3, 1980, pp. 589–615.

43 *The Spectator*, 13 September 1919; 27 September 1919.

44 Labour Party Archives, Minutes of the Labour Party Executive Committee, 4 June 1919; 5 June 1919; 12 November 1919.

45 *The Spectator*, 20 December 1919. See also A. Greenwood, *Public Ownership of the Liquor Trade*, London, Leonard Parsons, 1920, pp. 29–30.

46 Labour Party Archives, LIQ/22/74, Profiteering in the Liquor Trade And Abolition of Private Ownership: Evidence Submitted by the Tailors and Garment Workers' Union to the Labour Party Special Sub-Committee on the Liquor Traffic, 1923, p. 1.

47 Labour Party Archives, LIQ/22/79, J. Turner to J. S. Middleton, 12 March 1923.

48 See the following publications by the Labour Campaign for the Public Ownership and Control of the Liquor Trade: A. Greenwood, *Publicans and Politics*, London, n.d. A. Greenwood, *The Brewers Repentant*, London, n.d. 'Investigator', *The Liquor Trade In Politics*, London, 1926. Not all Labour men and women were arch

enemies of the Trade. Ben Tillett, for instance, spoke at meetings of the Glasgow Licensed Trade Local Veto Defence Association and The True Temperance Association, and acquired a reputation as a heavy drinker. See *Forward*, 23 October 1920. *Glasgow Herald*, 26 October 1920. *The Morning Advertiser*, 27 March 1925. J. Schneer, *Ben Tillett: Portrait of a Labour Leader*, London, Croom Helm, 1982, p. 219.

49 *Minutes of Evidence Taken Before The Royal Commission on Licensing (England and Wales)*, London, HMSO, 1930–2, p. 2038.

50 E. Selley, *The English Public House As It Is*, London, Longmans, Green & Co., 1927, p. 125. cf. A. Susan Lawrence, *Women and the Drink Trade*, London, Labour Campaign for the Public Ownership and Control of the Liquor Trade, n.d. *The Spectator*, 13 September 1919.

51 *Daily Herald*, 25 September 1919. See also J. H. Thomas, *When Labour Rules*, London, W. Collins, 1920, p. 112. *The Railway Review*, 8 July 1921. *Daily Herald*, 2 April 1923. *Record*, September–October 1926, pp. 33–6; March–April 1927, pp. 9–11.

52 *The Spectator*, 27 September 1919.

53 Rose, op. cit., p. 80.

54 See *The Locomotive Journal*, July 1925, pp. 300–1; August 1925, pp. 351–2. *Record*, July–August 1925, pp. 1–5; April 1928, pp. 1–4. *Leeds Weekly Citizen*, 12 February 1926. *Minutes of Evidence Taken Before The Royal Commission on Licensing (England and Wales)*, op. cit., pp. 2039–40.

55 *The Spectator*, 20 October 1933; 12 November 1937. *Manchester Guardian*, 17 November 1935.

56 *Report of the Broadcasting Committee*, Parliamentary Papers 1923 x cmd 1951, p. 32.

57 P. Scannell and D. Cardiff, 'Serving The Nation: Public Service Broadcasting Before The War', in B. Waites, T. Bennett and G. Martin (eds), *Popular Culture: Past and Present*, London, Croom Helm, 1982, p. 162.

58 ibid. P. Scannell, ' "A conspiracy of silence". The state, the BBC and public opinion in the formative years of British broadcasting, 1922–39', in G. McLennan, D. Held and S. Hall (eds), *State and Society in Contemporary Britain*, Cambridge, Polity Press, 1984.

59 S. G. Jones, 'The British Labour Movement and Working Class Leisure 1918–1939', unpublished Ph.D. thesis, Manchester University, 1983, p. 267.

60 *The BBC Year Book*, 1930, p. 36.

61 *Report of the Broadcasting Committee, 1935*, Parliamentary Papers 1935 vii, cmd 5091, p. 28.

62 M. Pegg, *Broadcasting and Society 1918–1939*, London, Croom Helm, 1983, pp. 195–217.
63 R. Lucas, *The Voice of a Nation?: A concise account of the BBC in Wales 1923–1973*, Llandysul, Gomer Press, 1981, pp. 27–31.
64 *BBC Handbook 1928*, pp. 50–5 reveals the complex structure.

Chapter 5 Work, leisure and unemployment

1 J. Stevenson and C. Cook, *The Slump: Society And Politics During The Depression*, London, Quartet Books, 1979, p. 57.
2 D. W. Harding, 'Varieties of Work and Leisure', *Occupational Psychology*, vol. 12, no. 2, 1938, p. 104.
3 S. Parker, *Leisure and Work*, London, Allen & Unwin, 1983. For further details of the issues taken up in this section, see S. G. Jones, 'Work, Leisure and Unemployment in Western Europe Between the Wars', in *The British Journal of Sports History*, vol. 3, no. 1, 1986.
4 G. Stedman Jones, 'Class expression versus social control? A critique of recent trends in the social history of leisure', *History Workshop Journal*, no. 4, 1977, p. 169.
5 U. Harva, 'Marxist conception of leisure', *Adult Education In Finland*, vol. 14, no. 2, 1977, pp. 4–6.
6 A. Barratt Brown, *The Machine and the Worker*, London, Ivor Nicholson & Watson, 1934, pp. 182–4.
7 H. Mannion, 'I Was in a Gas Works', in J. Common (ed.), *Seven Shifts*, London, Secker & Warburg, 1938, pp. 164, 167.
8 A. Howkins and J. Lowerson, *Trends In Leisure, 1919–1939*, London, The Sports Council and Social Science Research Council, 1979, pp. 41–5.
9 W. Boyd, 'Leisure Time Education', in A. E. Campbell (ed.), *Modern Trends in Education*, Wellington, New Education Fellowship, 1938, p. 44.
10 D. H. Aldcroft, *The Inter-War Economy: Britain, 1919–1939*, London, B. T. Batsford, 1970, pp. 147, 209.
11 R. McKibbon, 'Work and hobbies in Britain, 1880–1950', in J. Winter (ed.), *The Working Class in Modern Britain, 1880–1950: Essays in Honour of Henry Pelling*, Cambridge, Cambridge University Press, 1983, p. 142.
12 G. Mackenzie, 'World Images And The World of Work', in G. Esland, G. Salaman and M. A. Speakman (eds), *People And Work*, Edinburgh, Holmes McDougall, 1975, p. 173.

13 L. Jones, *We Live: The Story Of A Welsh Mining Valley*, London, Lawrence & Wishart, 1980, pp. 93, 96.

14 See R. Hoggart, *The Uses of Literacy*, Harmondsworth, Penguin Books, 1977. cf. S. Macintyre, *Little Moscows: Communism and Working-class Militancy in Inter-war Britain*, London, Croom Helm, 1980, pp. 137–49.

15 W. W. Daniel, *Strategies for Displaced Employees*, London, PEP, 1970, p. 8.

16 G. Orwell, *The Road to Wigan Pier*, Harmondsworth, Penguin Books, 1979, p. 77.

17 S. Constantine, *Unemployment in Britain between the Wars*, Harlow, Longman, 1980, p. 40.

18 K. Mourby, 'The Wives And Children Of The Teeside Unemployed 1919–1939', *Oral History and Labour History*, vol. 11, no. 2, 1983, p. 56.

19 Cited in J. Stevenson, *Social Conditions In Britain Between The Wars*, Harmondsworth, Penguin Books, 1977, p. 263.

20 Harding, op. cit.

21 Parker, op. cit., p. 65. See also, M. A. Smith, S. Parker and C. S. Smith (eds), *Leisure and Society in Britain*, London, Allen Lane, 1973, p. 7.

22 A. Shimmin, 'Leisure', in *Report of the Annual Convention of the Joint Industrial Council of the Printing and Allied Trades of Great Britain and Ireland*, 1936, p. 20.

23 *Morning Post*, 15 August 1935.

24 *Industrial Welfare*, May 1934, p. 26.

25 The Pilgrim Trust, *Men Without Work*, Cambridge, Cambridge University Press, 1938, pp. 94–7.

26 Mourby, op. cit., pp. 59–60.

27 Orwell, op. cit., pp. 80–1.

28 C. L. Mowat, *Britain Between The Wars 1918–1940*, London, Methuen, p. 485.

29 N. Pronay, 'British Newsreels in the 1930s. 1. Audience and Producers', *History*, vol. 56, 1971, p. 413.

30 J. Power, 'Aspects Of Working Class Leisure During The Depression Years: Bolton In The 1930s', unpublished M.A. thesis, Warwick University, 1980, p. 24.

31 Mowat, op. cit., p. 485.

32 Cited in Constantine, op. cit., p. 95. The unemployed were therefore quite aware that the cinema offered an opportunity for escapism.

33 The Pilgrim Trust, op. cit., pp. 98–100.

34 J. B. Priestley, *English Journey*, Harmondsworth, Penguin Books, 1979, p. 312.

35 Stevenson and Cook, op. cit., p. 92.

36 *Licensing Statistics*, Parliamentary Papers 1937–38 xxviii, cmd 5869, p. 5.

37 J. Corrie, *Rebel Poems*, London, ILP Publications, 1932, p. 12.

38 For the voluntary service schemes, see A. C. Richmond, 'The Action of Voluntary Organisations To Provide Occupation for Unemployed Workers in Great Britain', *International Labour Review*, vol. 37, 1938, pp. 644–51. R. Hayburn, 'The Voluntary Occupational Centre Movement, 1932–39', *Journal of Contemporary History*, vol. 6, no. 3, 1977, pp. 156–71. L. Opie, 'Voluntary Effort to Help The Unemployed in the 1930s', unpublished M.A. thesis, Manchester University, 1975.

39 *The Times*, 28 January 1932.

40 *The Times*, 24 November 1932.

41 *The Times*, 17 December 1932.

42 *Manchester Guardian*, 4 August 1936.

43 *Manchester Guardian*, 4 May 1934.

44 *Manchester Guardian*, 8 April 1935.

45 S. Meyers and E. Ramsay, *London Men and Women: An Account of the L.C.C. Men's and Women's Institutes*, London, British Institute of Adult Education, 1936, p. 38.

46 B. Seebohm Rowntree, *Poverty and Progress: A Second Social Survey of York*, London, Longmans, 1942, p. 345. See also, Priestley's description of the Hebburn Council of Social Service. Priestley, op. cit., pp. 296–7.

47 BBC, *8th Annual Report*, 1934, p. 12.

48 *The Times*, 10 November 1933.

49 *Morning Post*, 28 February 1936. See also National Council of Social Service, *Unemployment and Community Service*, London, NCSS, 1936, pp. 18–21, 35, 44.

50 *Third Report of The Commissioner For the Special Areas (England and Wales)*, Parliamentary Papers 1936–37 xii, cmd 5303, p. 137.

51 *The Times*, 9 February 1939.

52 *Manchester Guardian*, 23 October 1931; 18 June 1934.

53 See, for example, *Observer*, 9 February 1936. *News Chronicle*, 20 November 1936.

54 For the Lincoln People's Service Club, see A. M. Cameron, *Civilisation And The Unemployed*, London, Student Christian Movement Press, 1935, pp. 61–91. And for Lindsay and the problem of unemployment, D. Scott, *A. D. Lindsay: A Biography*, Oxford, Basil Blackwell, 1971, pp. 149–72.

55 See Scott, op. cit., pp. 160–4. *Daily Herald*, 16 June 1933. *The Co-operative News*, 23 September 1933. *Manchester Guardian*, 28

February 1936. A. D. Lindsay, 'Unemployment and Education', in W. Boyd and V. Ogilvie (eds), *The Challenge of Leisure*, London, New Education Fellowship, 1936, especially pp. 20–3.

56 *Daily Herald*, 4 July 1933.

57 E. Wilkinson, *The Town That Was Murdered*, London, Gollancz, 1939, p. 232.

58 *The Times*, 24 November 1932; 22 December 1932.

59 *The Railway Review*, 31 March 1933.

60 For details of the Associations, see A. Clinton, *The Trade Union Rank and File: Trades Councils in Britain 1900–40*, Manchester, Manchester University Press, 1977, pp. 156–66.

61 *Daily Herald*, 27 October 1932. *Labour*, December 1938, p. 59.

62 *Daily Herald*, 27 July 1932. TUC *Report*, 1932, p. 100.

63 TUC *Report*, 1937, p. 116.

64 Letter from Joe Norman to the author, 15 October 1981. Mick Jenkins also claims that the Openshaw branch used the Whitworth Hall for its social functions. M. Jenkins, interview with the author, 7 September 1981. cf. Stevenson and Cook, op. cit., p. 161.

65 *Daily Worker*, 18 April 1933. See also Marx Memorial Library, 'Developing Social Life of the Branches', Report of the National Administrative Council Meeting of the NUWM, 27 and 28 May 1933, p. 7.

66 Marx Memorial Library, 'Memorandum on the Development of Social Life in the NUWM', Report of the National Administrative Council Meeting of the NUWM, 26 and 27 August 1933, pp. 10–12.

67 Marx Memorial Library, 'Social Activities', Report of the National Administrative Council Meeting of the NUWM, 14 and 15 July 1934, p. 5. NUWM, *The Fight Against Unemployment and Poverty: Our Plan For Action*, London, NUWM, n.d., pp. 6–7.

68 *The Unemployed Leader*, May 1934, p. 6. *Daily Worker*, 2 May 1934. Marx Memorial Library, 'NUWM Holiday Camps', Report of the National Administrative Council of the NUWM, 25 and 26 May 1935, p. 5. For further details of the slave camps, see D. Colledge and J. Field, ' "To Recondition Human Material . . .": an Account of a British Labour Camp in the 1930s. An Interview with William Heard', *History Workshop Journal*, no. 15, 1983, pp. 152–66.

69 *Daily Worker*, 10 August 1934; 17 August 1934.

70 E. Bird, 'Jazz Bands of North East England: The Evolution Of A Working Class Cultural Activity', *Oral History*, vol. 4, no. 2, 1976, pp. 79–88.

71 C. Delisle Burns, *Leisure in the Modern World*, London, Allen & Unwin, 1932, p. 17. C. Delisle Burns, 'The Leisure of the Workless', *The Spectator*, 5 May 1933.

72 *The New Leader*, 21 August 1925.
73 *Daily Herald*, 10 September 1935. See also *Daily Herald*, 16 August 1927; 14 September 1935. *Rochdale Labour News*, March 1932, p. 2. *The Railway Review*, 24 February 1933. *Leeds Weekly Citizen*, 13 April 1934.
74 R. Price, 'Rethinking Labour History: The Importance Of Work', in J. Cronin and J. Schneer (eds), *Social Protest and the Political Order in Modern Britain*, London, Croom Helm, 1982, pp. 179–214. R. Price, 'The labour process and labour history', *Social History*, vol. 8, no. 1, pp. 57–75. See also J. Cronin, *Labour and Society in Britain 1918–1979*, London, Batsford, 1984, pp. 51–69.
75 *The Post*, 24 January 1920; 8 October 1932; 13 May 1933; 1 June 1935.
76 J. Dale, 'Railwaymen and Leisure', *The Railway Review*, 6 June 1919. See also chapter 1.
77 *Resolutions to be submitted to the 34th Annual Conference of the I.L.P., 1926*, p. 72. See also *The Railway Review*, 14 April 1933.
78 B. Russell, 'In Praise of Idleness', *The Review of Reviews*, 10 October 1932.
79 *The (Merthyr) Pioneer*, 2 October 1920.
80 Contribution of Margaret Cohen to the 1982 Spring Conference of the North West Labour History Society.
81 *The Workers' Union Record*, September 1928, p. 2.
82 TUC *Report*, 1931, p. 335. *The Workers' Union Record*, September 1926, p. 9. See also J. Beard, 'Share the work and Share the Leisure: The Unemployment Problem *Can* Be Solved', *The Labour Magazine*, April 1930, pp. 556–7.
83 *The Times*, 21 February 1934.
84 H. Durant, *The Problem of Leisure*, London, G. Routledge & Sons, 1938, p. 18.
85 *The Post*, 1 June 1935.
86 For the actions of the Parisian working class, see M. Seidman, 'The Birth of the Weekend and the Revolts Against Work: The Workers of the Paris Region during the Popular Front (1936–38)', *French Historical Studies*, vol. 12, no. 2, 1981, pp. 249–76.
87 Quoted in I. Britain, *Fabianism And Culture: A Study in British Socialism and the Arts c. 1884–1918*, Cambridge, Cambridge University Press, 1982, p. 247.

Chapter 6   The Labour Movement and working-class leisure

1 S. Macintyre, *A Proletarian Science: Marxism in Britain 1917–1933*, Cambridge, Cambridge University Press, 1980, pp. 47–65.

2 Labour Party Archives, Minutes of the Labour Party Executive Committee, 10 February 1920.
3 *12 Years of Labour Rule on the Bermondsey Borough Council 1922–34: Labour's Magnificent Record*, London, Labour Party, 1934, pp. 33–8. Minutes of the Pontypridd Trades and Labour Council, 27 August 1923; 3 September 1923; 22 October 1923. B. S. Keene, 'Our Parks', *The East Ham North Citizen*, August 1930, p. 2. *Labour Party Manifesto (Sheffield) Municipal Elections*, 1932, p. 5. Minutes of the South Shields Labour Party and Trades Council, 17 May 1931; 14 June 1931. *The (Bolton) Citizen*, October 1934, p. 1. *Rochdale Labour News*, October 1926, p. 3; 13 October 1928, p. 7; October 1936, p. 2.
4 *Report of the National Conference of Labour Women*, 1927, p. 14. *Women and the General Election: Report to be presented by the Standing Joint Committee of Industrial Women's Organisations to the National Conference of Labour Women*, Buxton, 23–5 April 1929, p. 33. Labour Party Archives, Report and Minutes of the Standing Joint Committee of Industrial Women's Organisations, 19 September 1929.
5 *The Labour Woman*, November 1932, p. 171.
6 *Labour's Immediate Programme*, London, Labour Party, 1937, p. 6. *Leisure and Culture*, London, Labour Party Leaflet, no. 53, 1937. *Let Us Face the Future: A Declaration of Labour Policy for the Consideration of the Nation*, London, Labour Party, 1945, p. 9. Another important development was the interest shown in leisure by the International Labour Organisation (ILO) – an international committee on workers' leisure had been formed in the mid-1930s. See ILO, *Recreation and Education: Reports presented to the International Conference on Workers' Spare Time* (Brussels, 15–17 June 1935), Geneva, ILO, 1935. ILO, *Facilities for the Use of Workers' Leisure During Holidays*, Geneva, ILO, 1939.
7 See, for example, G. Lansbury, 'Playing Fields Make For Prosperity', *The Labour Magazine*, August 1931, pp. 146–9.
8 M. Cole, 'The Society for Socialist Inquiry and Propaganda', in A. Briggs and J. Saville (eds), *Essays in Labour History 1918–1939*, London, Croom Helm, 1977, p. 192.
9 C. Waters, 'Social Reformers, Socialists, and the Opposition to the Commercialisation of Leisure in Late Victorian England', in W. Vamplew (ed.), *The Economic History Of Leisure: Papers presented at the Eighth International Economic History Congress*, Budapest, 1982, pp. 106–24.
10 TUC *Report*, 1921, pp. 341–2; 1929, pp. 454–5; 1930, pp. 328–30;

1933, pp. 393–4; 1934, pp. 179–80, 308. Scottish TUC *Report*, 1921, p. 75; 1922, pp. 98–9; 1929, p. 170; 1930, pp. 144, 147–8; 1939, p. 237.

11 *The New Leader*, 18 July 1930.

12 *Daily Herald*, 19 February 1923.

13 Harvester Press Microfilm series, card 208, May Day Leaflet, 1936, issued by the National Council of Labour.

14 A. E. Ford, 'Wise Use of Leisure', AEU, *Monthly Journal*, December 1938, p. 497.

15 TUC *Report*, 1938, p. 75. See also H. H. Elvin, 'Workers' Leisure', *Industrial Welfare*, October 1938, p. 413. This was not exactly a new idea; in 1936, G. S. Crossley, a director of Rowntrees, had made a similar suggestion. *Manchester Guardian*, 9 April 1936.

16 Prof. Rausehendusch, 'The Dignity of Leisure', quoted in *All Power* (organ of the Red International of Labour Unions), July 1922, p. 5. T. Morris, 'Have You Ever Worked This Out?', *The Bus Wheel* (a communist newsheet), July 1931.

17 See, for example, *Class Against Class: The General Election Programme of the Communist Party of Great Britain*, 1929. *The Worker*, 4 April 1931.

18 *We Ask For Life Based on the Report of John Gollan to the Eighth National Conference of the Communist Youth Movement*, London, Young Communist League, 1936, p. 15. *Challenge*, December 1936, p. 4. *Communist Plan For Life in Southall*, London, Southall CP, n.d., pp. 7–8. *Communist Plan For Life in Finsbury*, London, Finsbury CP, n.d., p. 12. *Communist Plan For Life in Westminster*, London, Westminster CP, n.d., pp. 8, 16.

19 *Where's That Fact?*, London, London District Committee of the CP, n.d., pp. 18–19. *Leisure*, London, CP Leaflet no. 7, n.d.

20 E. Rickwood, *War and Culture: The Decline of Culture Under Capitalism*, London, CP, n.d., p. 1.

21 For the views of Lenin, see V. I. Lenin, *On Culture and Cultural Revolution*, Moscow, Progress Publishers, 1978. C. Claudin-Urondo, *Lenin and the Cultural Revolution*, Hassocks, Harvester Press, 1977.

22 E. Upward, 'The Island', *The Left Review*, January 1935, p. 108.

23 *Daily Worker*, 31 March 1934.

24 ibid. For the general relations between British Labour and the Soviet Union, see B. Jones, *The Russia Complex: The British Labour Party and the Soviet Union*, Manchester, Manchester University Press, 1977. This suggests that in the thirty years or so after 1917 the Labour Party was 'enchanted' with the Soviet Union, and to a lesser extent with their policy objectives and achievements.

25 See *Russia Today*, September 1931, p. 2; February 1932, pp. 6–7; April 1935, p. 6; August 1931, pp. 6–7; August 1933, p. 2; October 1933, p. 9; November 1935, pp. 8–9. cf. *The New Russia* (Supplement to *The New Leader*), 9 December 1932.

26 *For Soviet Britain: Resolutions adapted by the xiiith Congress of the Communist Party*, London, CP, 1935, especially p. 39.

27 E. Yeo, 'Robert Owen and Radical Culture', in S. Pollard and J. Salt (eds), *Robert Owen, Prophet of the Poor*, London, Macmillan, 1971, pp. 84–114. E. Yeo, 'Culture and Constraint in Working-Class Movements, 1830–1850', in E. and S. Yeo (eds), *Popular Culture and Class Conflict 1590–1914: Explorations in the History of Labour and Leisure*, Brighton, Harvester Press, 1981, pp. 155–86. J. Epstein, 'Some Organisational and Cultural Aspects of the Chartist Movement in Nottingham', in J. Epstein and D. Thompson (eds), *The Chartist Experience: Studies in Working Class Radicalism and Culture, 1830–1860*, London, Macmillan, 1982, pp. 221–68.

28 S. Yeo, 'A New Life: The Religion of Socialism in Britain 1883–1896', *History Workshop Journal*, no. 3, 1977, especially p. 31.

29 D. Clark, *Colne Valley: Radicalism to Socialism*, London, Longman, 1981, p. 52.

30 S. G. Jones, 'The British Labour Movement And Working Class Leisure 1918–1939', unpublished Ph.D. thesis, Manchester University, 1983.

31 See, for example, the column under the heading 'Social Complimentary and Propaganda' in the AEU, *Monthly Journal*, 1922–40.

32 National Amalgamated Union of Shop Assistants, Warehousemen and Clerks, *Annual Report*, 1931, p. 17.

33 W. Milne Bailey, *Trade Unions and the State*, London, Allen & Unwin, 1934, pp. 93–4. H. Durant, *The Problem of Leisure*, London, G. Routledge & Sons, 1938, pp. 255–6. A. Clinton, *The Trade Union Rank and File: Trades Councils in Britain 1900–40*, Manchester, Manchester University Press, 1977, p. 181.

34 *Labour*, March 1939, p. 48.

35 *The People's Year Book 1928*, pp. 61–4. See also F. Whittle, 'The Leisure Hours of Co-operation', *The Co-operative News*, 22 July 1933.

36 See, for example, D. Caradog Jones (ed.), *The Social Survey of Merseyside*, vol. 3, Liverpool, Liverpool University Press and Hodder & Stoughton, 1934, pp. 308–9. T. Young, *Becontree and*

Dagenham: A Report Made For The Pilgrim Trust, London, Becontree Social Survey Committee, 1934, p. 223.

37 Harvester Press Microfilm series, card 138, Programme of the Festival of Labour, The Crystal Palace, 21 July 1928.

38 For the pre-1914 labour clubs, see Clark, op. cit., pp. 32–5, 47–50, 117–25, 162–5.

39 Colne Valley Divisional Labour Party, *Annual Report*, 1933.

40 *Daily Herald*, 13 May 1929. *Oldham Chronicle*, 27 July 1929. *Salford City Reporter*, 5 August 1932. *Leeds Weekly Citizen*, 30 July 1937.

41 Minutes of the Cambridge Trades Council and Labour Party, 5 May 1920; 1 September 1920. Minutes of the Annual General Meeting of the Cambridgeshire Trades Council and Divisional Labour Party, 14 April 1928. Minutes of the Executive Committee of the Sheffield Trades and Labour Council, 23 April 1929; 17 March 1931. Minutes of the South Shields Labour Party and Trades Council, 6 January 1925; 11 January 1925; 8 March 1925; 17 March 1925.

42 *The London Citizen* (Tottenham edition), October 1923, p. 4.

43 *Cambridge Daily News*, n.d. (Newspaper cutting in the archives of the Cambridgeshire Trades Council and Divisional Labour Party.) The executive committee also reported in 1928 that, 'During the winter months our chief activity has been with concerts and socials. Again the smaller villages have been attacked with great success. The Foxton Follies have continued to give their service and we cannot easily estimate their worth to our cause. They have visited 22 villages for us this season.' *Cambridgeshire Trades Council and Divisional Labour Party Report of the Executive Committee for the Year Ending March 1928*, p. 5.

44 See *Rochdale Labour News*, *The Bolton Citizen*, and *Oldham Labour Gazette*.

45 Minutes of the Pontypridd Trades and Labour Council, 7 May 1919; 4 June 1919; 20 February 1920; 19 March 1920; 1 April 1920; 21 May 1920; 11 December 1922; 25 February 1924. See also Minutes of the South Shields Labour Party and Trades Council, 30 January 1919; 3 February 1919; 10 February 1919.

46 *Cambridge Daily News*, 19 April 1926. Anon, 'The Building of the Romsey Town Labour Club', in D. Hardman (ed.), *1912–1937: The First Twenty-Five Years in the History of the Cambridge Borough Trades Council and Labour Party*, Cambridge, Cambridge Trades Council and Labour Party, 1937, pp. 17–18. T. H. Amey, 'Romsey Labour Club', *The Cambridge Labour Review*, no. 2, 1947, pp. 5–6.

47 Eric Jones (a secretary of the Union in the 1980s), interview with the author, 27 May 1982.

48 National Union of Labour and Socialist Clubs, *Annual Bulletin*, 1936, pp. 14–15.

49 London School of Economics, Beatrice Webb Manuscript Diaries, vol. 37, 15 January 1924. For further details, see Webb Diaries, vol. 36, 24 April 1921; 27 June 1921; 16 July 1921; Xmas 1921; vol. 37, 12 December 1923; 15 January 1924; 18 January 1924.

50 See *The Labour Magazine*, May 1924, pp. 12–14; August 1929, pp. 164–7; February 1933, pp. 449–53.

51 *Leeds Weekly Citizen*, 22 April 1932.

52 G. Hicks, *Give New Life and Purpose to the Labour Clubs!*, London, Federation of Trade Union, Labour, Socialist, and Co-operative Clubs, 1928, p. 4. See also *Daily Herald*, 8 October 1928; 11 May 1929; 13 June 1929.

53 Quoted in R. Whiting, 'The Working Class in the "New Industry" Towns between the Wars: the case of Oxford', unpublished D.Phil. thesis, Oxford University, 1978, p. 162.

54 *The Amalgamated Engineers' Monthly Journal and Report*, July 1920, p. 76.

55 *The Locomotive Journal*, July 1924, pp. 263–4.

56 For a more sympathetic view of welfarism, see *British Trades Union Review*, October 1921, p. 10. *Yorkshire Factory Times and Workers' Weekly Record*, 3 August 1922. *The Locomotive Journal*, August 1923, pp. 320–1.

57 *Minutes and Record of the Proceedings of the Third Biennial Delegate Conference of the Transport and General Workers' Union*, 1929, p. 15.

58 TUC *Report*, 1932, pp. 72–5.

59 See *The Record*, November 1936, p. 88; June 1938, p. 295. *Industrial Welfare*, October 1938, pp. 415–16.

60 Minutes of the Annual General Meeting of the Colne Valley Divisional Labour Party, 16 February 1929.

61 AEU, *Monthly Journal*, January 1934, p. 21. See also *Trade Union Recruitment: Memorandum for discussion at the Annual Conference of Trades Councils*, 1936, pp. 3–5.

62 See *Oldham Labour Gazette*, December 1924, p. 1; December 1934, p. 4. *Leeds Weekly Citizen*, 12 March 1926. Colne Valley Divisional Labour Party, *Annual Report*, 1929. *The East Ham North Citizen*, August 1930, p. 3; September 1930, p. 4. *Gloucester Labour News*, October 1937, p. 4.

63 Quoted in C. Howard, 'Expectations born to death: Local Labour Party expansion in the 1920s', in J. Winter (ed.), *The Working Class*

in Modern Britain, 1880–1950: Essays in Honour of Henry Pelling, Cambridge, Cambridge University Press, 1983, p. 75.

64 For an excellent study of socialist youth and cultural formation, see D. L. Prynn, 'The Socialist Sunday Schools, The Woodcraft Folk and Allied Movements: Their Moral Influence on the British Labour Movement Since the 1890s', unpublished M.A. thesis, Sheffield University, 1971.

65 J. Ferris, 'The Labour Party League of Youth 1924–1940', unpublished M.A. thesis, Warwick University, 1977, especially pp. 138–92.

66 Leeds Archive Department, Acc 2102/L.P./98, Minutes of the Youth Advisory Committee of the Leeds Labour Party League of Youth, 1935–1938, *passim*.

67 Contribution of Jill Norris to the 1982 Spring Conference of the North West Labour History Society. See also K. Hunt, 'Women and the Social Democratic Federation: Some notes on Lancashire', *North West Labour History Society Bulletin*, no. 7, 1980–1, pp. 58–63.

68 Lancashire Record Office, DDX 1274/2/18, Minutes of the Committee of the Burnley Power Loom Weavers' Association, 12 November 1930; 3 March 1931; 8 April 1931; 5 May 1931; 30 December 1931. Minutes of a Meeting of the Meltham ILP branch, 11 December 1927; 25 November 1928.

69 Photograph in J. Gorman, *To Build Jerusalem: A Photographic Remembrance of British Working Class Life 1875–1950*, London, Scorpion Publications, 1980, p. 117.

70 *Workers' Life*, 5 August 1927.

71 Mick Jenkins, interview with the author, 7 September 1981. Thus one Young Communist League factory and trade union social was said to offer 'A Real Workers' Programme', including football, pictures and dancing. *The Spark*, February 1925, p. 4.

72 University of Warwick Modern Records Centre, George Renshaw Papers, Mss 104, Programme of the event.

73 *Daily Worker*, 13 June 1933.

74 *Daily Worker*, 8 August 1934.

75 John Rylands University Library, CP Pamphlet collection, Programme of a meeting at St Pancras Town Hall, 21 January 1939.

76 S. Macintyre, *Little Moscows: Communism and Working-class Militancy in Inter-war Britain*, London, Croom Helm, 1980, *passim*. H. Francis and D. Smith, *The Fed: A History of the South Wales Miners in the Twentieth Century*, London, Lawrence & Wishart, 1980, p. 160. See also I. Macdougall (ed.), *Militant Miners: Recollections of John McArthur, Buckhaven; and letters,*

1924–26, of David Proudfoot, Methil to G. Allen Hutt, Edinburgh, Polygon Books, 1981, *passim*.

77 For a theoretical underpinning of this view, see Q. Hoare and G. Nowell (eds), *Antonio Gramsci: Selections from the Prison Notebooks*, London, Lawrence & Wishart, 1971.

78 The Economic League, *The Innocents Clubs*, London, The Economic League, series no. 7, 1934.

79 *Programme of the Young Communist International*, London, Young Communist League, 1929, p. 60.

80 Communist Party Archives, George Sinfield Papers, Membership Card of the British Workers' Sports Federation. For further details, see S. G. Jones, 'Sport, Politics and the Labour Movement: The British Workers' Sports Federation, 1923–1935', *The British Journal of Sports History*, vol. 2, no. 2, 1985, pp. 154–78.

81 *Daily Worker*, 15 May 1935.

82 H. Pollitt, *Harry Pollitt Speaks . . . A Call to all Workers*, London, CP, n.d., pp. 40–1.

83 In fact, quite a lot has been written about both the workers' film and theatre movements. See especially J. Clark, M. Heinemann, D. Margolies and C. Snee (eds), *Culture and Crisis in Britain in the Thirties*, London, Lawrence & Wishart, 1979. R. Samuel, E. MacColl and S. Cosgrove, *Theatres Of The Left: Workers' Theatre Movements in Britain and America 1880–1935*, London, Routledge & Kegan Paul, 1984.

84 The first issue of the *Sunday Worker* contained a set of weekly notes stressing 'the great importance of the theatre to the Labour movement'. *Sunday Worker*, 15 March 1925.

85 National Minority Movement, *Annual Conference Report*, 1925, p. 30. R. Samuel, 'Editorial Introduction', *History Workshop Journal*, no. 4, 1977, pp. 104–5.

86 T. Thomas, 'A Propertyless Theatre for the Propertyless Class', *History Workshop Journal*, no. 4, 1977, p. 126.

87 *Sunday Worker*, 30 October 1926.

88 Thomas, op. cit., pp. 115–19.

89 L. Jones, 'The Workers' Theatre Movement in the Twenties', *Zeitschrift Für Anglistik und Amerikanistik*, vol. 14, no. 3, 1966, p. 268.

90 *Sunday Worker*, 19 April 1925; 6 June 1926; 22 August 1926.

91 *Sunday Worker*, 18 March 1928.

92 *Lansbury's Labour Weekly*, 14 May 1927.

93 *Daily Worker*, 11 January 1930.

94 *Daily Worker*, 10 May 1932.

95 *The Red Stage*, November 1931, p. 1.

96 *Red Stage*, March 1932, p. 2.
97 Samuel, op. cit., p. 107.
98 Thomas, op. cit., p. 121. *Red Stage*, February 1932, pp. 1, 6.
Before the German tour, however, the first conference of the
WTM had stressed the need for street performances 'by which
propaganda may be carried over in a simple and direct manner
with dramatic symbolism'. *Daily Worker*, 29 December 1930.
99 R. and E. Frow, 'Working Class Theatre in Manchester
1928–1934', unpublished paper, p. 2.
100 J. Loveman, 'Workers' Theatre: Personal Recollections of political
theatre in Greenwich during the 1920s and 1930s', *Red Letters*, no.
13, Spring 1982, p. 44.
101 *Red Stage*, April–May 1932, p. 3. *Daily Worker*, 4 January 1932.
There was also a Jewish group in the East End of London called
Proltet, which by 1933 threatened to absorb the WTM. R.
Waterman, 'Proltet: The Yiddish Speaking Group of the Workers'
Theatre Movement', *History Workshop Journal*, no. 5, 1978,
pp. 174–8.
102 *Red Stage*, January 1932, p. 7.
103 *Daily Worker*, 15 September 1931; 7 January 1932; 31 August 1932.
104 *Red Stage*, February 1932, p. 4.
105 Samuel, op. cit., p. 106.
106 *Red Stage*, December 1931, pp. 2–3. Thomas, op. cit., p. 123.
107 'The Workers' Theatre Movement: an interview with Philip Poole
by Jon Clark and David Margolies', *Red Letters*, no. 10, n.d., p. 6.
108 *The New Leader*, 11 August 1933.
109 Cf. 'The Workers' Theatre Movement: an interview with Philip
Poole . . .' op. cit., p. 10.
110 A. Van Gyseghem, 'British Theatre in the Thirties: An
Autobiographical Record', in J. Clark *et al*. (eds), op. cit., p. 212.
111 For details, see E. MacColl, 'Grass Roots of Theatre Workshop',
Theatre Quarterly, vol. 3, 1973, pp. 60–4.
112 For further discussion of Unity theatre, see M. Page, 'The Early
Years at Unity', *Theatre Quarterly*, vol. 1, 1971, pp. 60–6. J. Clark,
'Agitprop and Unity Theatre: Socialist Theatre in the Thirties', in
J. Clark *et al*. (eds), op. cit., pp. 224–39. R. Travis, 'The Unity
Theatre of Great Britain 1936–1946: A Decade of Production',
unpublished M.A. thesis, Southern Illinois University, 1968.
113 *Daily Worker*, 16 November 1932.
114 *New Red Stage*, June–July 1932, pp. 1–2.
115 *The Communist Review*, April 1930, p. 151. As was also stated:
'We cannot fulfil the bold tasks we have set ourselves unless we
are organising all kinds of cultural, recreational and sporting and

social activities within our ranks.' *Youth of Britain Advance. Report and Resolutions of the 9th Congress of the Y.C.L.*, 1937, p. 25.

116 See *Report of the Central Committee to the 14th National Congress of the C.P.G.B.*, 1937, p. 18.

117 D. Proudfoot to G. A. Hutt, 31 October 1926, in Macdougall (ed.), op. cit., pp. 305–6.

118 *Report on Organisation presented by the Party Commission to the Annual Conference of the C.P.G.B.*, 1922, p. 61.

119 *Lansbury's Labour Weekly*, 1 January 1927. George Lansbury similarly suggested that the arts should be 'a means of bringing us all together, not of perpetuating our little sectarian squabbles'. *Lansbury's Labour Weekly*, 5 September 1925.

120 Working Class Movement Library, F4 Box 3, Stockport Labour Fellowship (SLP), *Syllabus and Year Book*, 1931–2, pp. 1, 3. Snow White was even produced as an operetta. Stockport Library Archive Centre (hereafter cited as SLAC), B/MM/3/22, Minutes of the Propaganda Committee of the SLF, 15 September 1931.

121 Working Class Movement Library, F4 Box 3, SLF, *Coming-of-Age-Syllabus*, n.d., pp. 2–3. SLAC, B/MM/3/22, Minutes of the Annual General Meeting of the SLF, 19 April 1931.

122 SLAC, B/MM/3/22, SLF Account Book.

123 SLAC, B/X/7/12, SLF, Handbooks of Lectures, 1924–1928; B/MM/3/22–3, Minutes of the Propaganda Committee of the SLF, 26 January 1932; Minutes of the Executive Committee of the SLF, 12 January 1934.

124 SLAC, B/X/7/12, SLF, *Syllabus of Lectures* 1927–8, p. 1.

125 SLAC, B/MM/3/23, Minutes of the Annual General Meeting of the SLF, 30 April 1933.

126 For further discussion of 'the social democratic, fabian, reformist' cultural tradition, and the 'marxist revolutionary' cultural tradition, see D. Allen, ' "Culture" and the Scottish Labour Movement', *Scottish Labour History Society Journal*, no. 14, 1980, pp. 30–9.

Chapter 7　The politics of leisure

1 B. Jones, 'The Politics Of Popular Culture', Centre for Contemporary Cultural Studies, University of Birmingham, Stencilled Occasional Papers, n.d., pp. 3–4. See also C. W. E. Bigsby, 'The Politics of Popular Culture', *Cultures*, vol. 1, no. 2, 1973, pp. 15–35. C. Critcher, 'The Politics of Leisure – Social Control and Social Development', in *Work And Leisure: The*

Implications Of Technological Change, Leisure Studies Seminar 1980, Tourism and Recreation Unit, University of Edinburgh, 1982, pp. 43–53. H. Cunningham, *Leisure in the Industrial Revolution, 1780–1880*, London, Croom Helm, 1980, p. 11. G. Eley and K. Nield, 'Why does social history ignore politics?', *Social History*, vol. 5, no. 2, 1980, p. 268. E. and S. Yeo, 'Ways of Seeing: Control and Leisure versus Class and Struggle', in E. and S. Yeo (eds), *Popular Culture and Class Conflict 1590–1914: Explorations in the History of Labour and Leisure*, Brighton, Harvester Press, 1981, pp. 128–54. G. Whannel, *Blowing the Whistle: The Politics of Sport*, London, Pluto Press, 1983.

2 For the social sciences, see I. Craven, 'Leisure', in *Encyclopaedia of the Social Sciences*, vol. 9, London, Macmillan & Co., 1933, pp. 402–6. D. W. Harding, 'The Place of Entertainment in Social Life', *The Sociological Review*, vol. 26, no. 4, 1934, pp. 393–406. For architecture and town planning, see Leeds and Bradford Region Joint Town Planning Committee, *Preliminary Report*, 1926, pp. 63–6. P. Abercrombie and B. F. Brueton, *Bristol and Bath Regional Planning Scheme*, Liverpool, Liverpool University Press, 1930, pp. 112–15. D. Pilcher, 'Leisure as an Architectural Problem', *The Architectural Review*, vol. 84, no. 505, December 1938, pp. 231–310. For hygiene, see C. W. Salleby, 'A Civic Sense in England? The Hygiene of Recreation', *The Spectator*, 5 April 1924. S. Alstead, 'Leisure and Health', in L. R. Missen, *The Employment of Leisure*, Exeter, A. Wheaton & Co., 1935, pp. 56–74. For history, see J. L. Hammond, *The Growth of Common Enjoyment*, London, Oxford University Press, 1933. J. L. Hammond, 'The Background of the Problem of Leisure', *Industrial Welfare*, September 1939, pp. 333–6.

3 *The Shop Assistant*, 22 August 1931. See also *The New Age*, 10 September 1931; 11 February 1932; 18 February 1932; 25 February 1932. M. Butchart (ed.), *A. R. Orage: Political And Economic Writings*, London, Stanley Nott, 1936, especially pp. 137–8. Before this at least one commentator had advocated the formation of a Leisure Party 'devoted to the improvement of Leisure'. L. P. Jacks, 'Preface' to C. Harris, *The Use Of Leisure In Bethnal Green: A Survey of Social Conditions in the Borough 1925 to 1926*, London, The Lindsay Press, 1927, p. vi.

4 E. Barker, *The Uses of Leisure*, London, British Institute of Adult Education, n.d., p. 6.

5 'Leisure and Education', *The Democrat*, 13 February 1920.

6 *Industrial Welfare*, October 1934, pp. 42–3. *The Post*, 17 October 1936.

7 *The Co-operative News*, 11 April 1936. See also *The Amalgamated Engineers' Monthly Journal and Report*, January 1919, pp. 52–4. National Amalgamated Furnishing Trades Association, *Monthly Report*, February 1929, p. 25. Post Office Engineering Union, *The Journal*, 14 October 1932. *The Locomotive Journal*, February 1933, pp. 72–3. *The New Leader*, 13 January 1933.
8 Missen, op. cit.
9 *The Times*, 18 July 1935. W. Boyd and W. Rawson, *The Story of the New Education*, London, Heinemann, 1965, p. 99.
10 *News Chronicle*, 19 November 1937.
11 J. J. Findlay, 'Spare Time', *The Labour Magazine*, August 1922, p. 163.
12 R. H. Tawney, 'Introduction', in W. Boyd and V. Ogilvie (eds), *The Challenge of Leisure*, London, New Education Fellowship, 1936, pp. xiii–xiv.
13 J. Lowerson, 'Studying Inter-War Leisure: the context and some problems', in A. Tomlinson (ed.), *Leisure and Social Control*, Brighton, Brighton Polytechnic, 1981, p. 71.
14 A. Salter, *The Prospect before the Temperance Movement of this Country*, London, International Order of Good Templars, 1939, p. 8.
15 *Southwark Recorder*, 22 June 1928.
16 *The English Review*, February 1924, p. 224.
17 S. G. Jones, 'The British Labour Movement and Working Class Leisure 1918–1939', unpublished Ph.D. thesis, Manchester University, 1983, pp. 228–59.
18 *The Methodist Leader*, 29 November 1928.
19 *Forward*, 20 November 1920.
20 See *Report From The Select Committee on Betting Duty Together with The Proceedings of the Committee, Minutes of Evidence, Appendices and Index*, Parliamentary Papers 1923 v, pp. 392–417. *The New Statesman*, 28 July 1923. *The Spectator*, 21 November 1931.
21 *Hansard* (Commons) 5th series, vol. 310, col. 2317, 3 April 1936.
22 ibid., vol. 220, cols 519–22, 18 July 1928; cols 682–7, 714–6, 769–70, 19 July 1928.
23 ibid., vol. 217, col. 622, 11 May 1928.
24 ibid., vol. 308, cols 2347–56, 7 February 1936.
25 H. Llewellyn Smith (ed.), *The New Survey of London Life and Labour*, vol. 9, *Life and Leisure*, London, P. S. King, 1935, pp. 75–7.
26 *The Times*, 7 July 1923.
27 *Tottenham and Edmonton Weekly Herald*, 4 July 1930.
28 J. Richards, 'The cinema and cinema-going in Birmingham in the

1930s', in J. K. Walton and J. Walvin (eds), *Leisure in Britain 1780–1939*, Manchester, Manchester University Press, 1983, p. 40.

29 *Manchester Guardian*, 18 December 1930.

30 *Hansard* (Commons) 5th series, vol. 251, cols 655–62, 20 April 1931. *Oldham Chronicle*, 25 April 1931. When a poll was held in Oldham on the question of opening cinemas on a Sunday, a majority of 8,865 were against. *The Times*, 22 December 1932.

31 See *Hansard* (Commons) 5th series, vol. 266, cols 715–800, 27 May 1932; vol. 267, cols 1821–1984, 29 June 1932.

32 Public Record Office (hereafter cited as PRO) HO 45/17521. *Daily Herald*, 21 May 1935.

33 Quoted in J. Walvin, *Leisure and Society 1830–1950*, London, Longman, 1978, p. 136.

34 COPEC, *Leisure*, London, Longman, Green & Co., 1924.

35 Quoted in J. Richards, *The Age Of The Dream Palace: Cinema and Society in Britain 1930–1939*, London, Routledge & Kegan Paul, 1984, p. 51.

36 J. Donald and C. Mercer, *The State and Popular Culture (2)*, Milton Keynes, The Open University, 1982.

37 *The C.T.C. Gazette*, December 1918, p. 123; September 1934, p. 302. During 1935 many of the district associations of the Cyclists' Touring Club held protest meetings: Liverpool and Birmingham in February; Bolton, Bristol and Cardiff in March; East Kent, East Surrey, Essex, Glasgow, Leicestershire and Rutland, Manchester, London, Norfolk, Northamptonshire, North Lincolnshire, Oxford and Sheffield also in March; Derby, Hull and East Riding, Northumberland and Durham, North West Lancs, Notts, Devon, Mid-Yorkshire, Birmingham and Midland, North Staffordshire and Wessex in April; and so on. *The C.T.C. Gazette*, 1935, *passim*.

38 *The C.T.C. Gazette*, April 1935, p. 122.

39 Labour Party Archives, Minutes of the Executive Committee of the Labour Party, 29 September 1935; 26 February 1936. Manchester Central Reference Library Archives Department,016/I Box 1/2, Minutes of the National Committee of the Clarion Cycling Club, 12 and 13 June 1936; 12 and 13 September 1936. *Daily Worker*, 19 June 1936.

40 *The Northern Cyclist and Athlete*, December 1929, p. 3.

41 *Drama*, March 1929, pp. 82–3; July 1929, p. 148.

42 Stockport Library, Microfilm Box no. 220, Thomas Middleton's Scrapbook, vol. 1, p. 218. Quoted in S. G. Jones, 'Recreational and Cultural Provision In Hyde Between The Wars', in A. Lock (ed.), *Looking Back At Hyde*, Forthcoming, Tameside Libraries and Arts Committee, 1986.

43 Stalybridge Local History Library, CA/HYD/119/4, Borough of Hyde, Minutes of the Cemetery and Park Committee, 31 January 1927; 21 August 1933.

44 *Ashton-Under-Lyne Reporter*, 27 August 1932. See also Critcher, op. cit., p. 45.

45 Quoted in J. E. Williams, *The Derbyshire Miners. A Study in Industrial and Social History*, London, Allen & Unwin, 1962, p. 790.

46 *Daily Herald*, 28 May 1923.

47 D. Smith and G. Williams, *Fields of Praise: The Official History of The Welsh Rugby Union 1881–1981*, Cardiff, University of Wales Press, 1980, p. 230.

48 *The Communist*, 21 January 1922. *The Locomotive Journal*, September 1923, p. 394.

49 PRO CAB 24/96 (CP 462).

50 PRO CAB 24/74 (GT 6713).

51 Richards, op. cit.

52 N. Pronay, 'The First Reality: Film Censorship In Liberal England', in K. R. M. Short (ed.), *Feature Films as History*, London, Croom Helm, 1981, p. 125. See also N. Pronay, 'The Political Censorship of Films in Britain between the wars', in N. Pronay and D. W. Spring (eds), *Propaganda, Politics and Film 1918–1945*, London, Macmillan, 1982, pp. 98–125. Richards, op. cit., pp. 89–152. cf. T. Aldgate, 'Comedy, Class and Containment: The British Domestic Cinema of the 1930s', in J. Curran and V. Porter (eds), *British Cinema History*, London, Weidenfeld & Nicolson, 1983, pp. 257–71. J. C. Robertson, *The British Board of Film Censors: Film Censorship in Britain, 1896–1950*, London, Croom Helm, 1985.

53 *Report of the Colonial Films Committee*, Parliamentary Papers 1930 viii, cmd 3630, p. 18.

54 See, for example, *Hansard* (Commons) 5th series, vol. 204, cols 2240–1, 7 April 1927; vol. 240, col. 972, 24 June 1930; vol. 240, cols 1587–8, 30 June 1930; vol. 240, col. 1934, 2 July 1930. *The Times*, 16 June 1930. T. J. Hollins, 'The Conservative Party and Film Propaganda Between the Wars', *English Historical Review*, vol. 96, no. 379, pp. 359–69.

55 *Manchester Guardian*, 5 May 1931; 29 June 1931. Reg Cordwell interview, 21 July 1977, Tape number 455, Manchester Studies Unit, Manchester Polytechnic. Indeed, censorship caused plenty of difficulties for the society. See *Manchester Guardian*, 10 April 1933.

56 *The Times*, 12 March 1930. *Manchester Guardian*, 31 July 1930. *Daily Worker*, 5 October 1931; 20 February 1934. See also D.

Macpherson (ed.), *Traditions Of Independence: British Cinema in the Thirties*, London, British Film Institute, 1980, pp. 96–115.

57 Alf Williams interview, 19 January 1978, Tape number 566, Manchester Studies Unit, Manchester Polytechnic.

58 *Daily Worker*, 9 October 1933; 10 October 1933; 17 October 1933.

59 P. McIntosh, *Fair Play: Ethics in Sport and Education*, London, Heinemann, 1979, p. 143.

60 For a general discussion of British cultural policy overseas see P. Taylor, *The Projection of Britain: British Overseas Publicity and Propaganda*, Cambridge, Cambridge University Press, 1981.

61 *Hansard* (Commons) 5th series, vol. 238, cols 349–50, 1 May 1930.

62 PRO FO 371/14883.

63 P. J. Beck, 'England v Germany, 1938', *History Today*, vol. 32, June 1982, p. 34. See also Foreign Office News Dept. file PRO FO 395/568.

64 PRO HO 45/16425.

65 PRO FO 371/18884/5184/354, Newspaper cutting, *The Star*, 15 October 1935.

66 *The New Leader*, 22 November 1935.

67 PRO HO 45/16425, Notes of Deputation from the Trades Union Congress to the Home Secretary, 2 December 1935. See also TUC Archives, Minutes of the TUC General Council, 20 November 1935; 18 December 1935.

68 PRO FO 371/18884/5184/375, Sir W. Citrine to Sir J. Simon, 18 November 1935.

69 *Daily Worker*, 5 December 1935.

70 PRO FO 371/18884/5184/352.

71 PRO FO 371/18884/5184/357, 359.

72 PRO FO 371/18884/5184/371–3.

73 PRO FO 371/18884/5184/379.

74 PRO HO 45/11880, file relating to boxing contests between coloured men and white men.

75 *Hansard* (Commons) 5th series, vol. 262, col. 1416, 4 March 1932.

76 *The Listener*, 26 August 1936.

77 *Westminster Gazette*, 18 July 1927. *Manchester Guardian*, 17 November 1930.

78 *Daily Telegraph*, 20 December 1930. *The Journal of the Commons, Open Spaces and Footpaths Preservation Society*, January 1931, p. 17.

79 *Out-O'-Doors*, May 1932, p. 87.

80 For the history of the BWSF, see S. G. Jones, 'Sport, Politics and the Labour Movement: The British Workers' Sports Federation',

1923–1935', *The British Journal of Sports History*, vol. 2, no. 2, 1985, pp. 154–78.

81 C. Owen, 'The Scarlet Ramblers: Communists After the Hikers', *Daily Mail*, 3 July 1931.

82 See M. Jenkins, 'Salute to "riotous" ramblers', *Morning Star*, 5 July 1969. P. W. Rickwood, 'Public Enjoyment of the Open Countryside In England and Wales 1919–1939', unpublished Ph.D. thesis, Leicester University, 1973, pp. 227–34. D. Cook, 'The Battle For Kinder Scout', *Marxism Today*, vol. 21, no. 8, 1977, pp. 241–3. H. Hill, *Freedom To Roam: The Struggle For Access To Britain's Moors and Mountains*, Ashbourne, Moorland Publishing, 1980, pp. 62–9. J. Lowerson, 'Battles For The Countryside', in F. Gloversmith (ed.), *Class, Culture and Social Change*, Brighton, Harvester Press, 1980, pp. 272–3. B. Rothman, *The 1932 Kinder Trespass: A personal view of the Kinder Scout Trespass*, Timperley, Willow Publishing, 1982.

83 For this view, see Hill, op. cit. Rothman, op. cit. C. Brasher, 'Back to the Battlefield', *The Observer*, 25 April 1982. J. Batsleer, 'The Right To Roam', *WEA News*, no. 22, 1982, p. 3.

84 T. M. Condon, *The Fight for the Workers' Playing Fields*, London, British Workers' Football Council, n.d., p. 6.

85 *Daily Worker*, 12 September 1930; 16 September 1930. The decision to ban Sunday games was passed by a majority of two at a Council meeting on 15 July 1930. Bruce Castle Museum, Minutes of the Tottenham Urban District Council (hereafter cited as TUDC Minutes), 15 July 1930. *Tottenham and Edmonton Weekly Herald*, 18 July 1930. *North Tottenham Citizen*, August 1930, p. 1.

86 *Daily Worker*, 2 October 1930; 25 October 1930; 14 November 1930; 27 January 1931. TUDC Minutes, 20 January 1931. *Tottenham and Edmonton Weekly Herald*, 24 October 1930; 26 December 1930; 23 January 1931.

87 TUDC Minutes, 20 June 1930; 15 July 1930; 16 June 1931. See also the conflict between the workers' sports movement and the religious community in the correspondence columns of the *Tottenham and Edmonton Weekly Herald*, February 1931 to May 1931, *passim*.

88 *Tottenham and Edmonton Weekly Herald*, 10 April 1931.

89 TUDC Minutes, 19 May 1931. It should be noted that it was the Labour group who finally cast their vote in favour of Sunday sport.

90 *The Worker Sportsman*, June 1932, p. 11; July 1932, p. 11. *Daily Worker*, 16 August 1932. *Young Worker*, 27 August 1932.

91 Greater London Record Office, Minutes of the Parks and Open Spaces Committee of the LCC (hereafter cited as LCC Parks

Committee Minutes), 22 April 1932. *Daily Worker*, 6 June 1932.
Organized Sunday football in the LCC area had been banned since
1922. However, there were no regulations which prevented the
playing of 'friendly' matches. *The Times*, 24 July 1922.
92 LCC Parks Committee Papers, 17 June 1932, no. 34; 21 October
1932, no. 26; 15 July 1932, no. 4. T. M. Condon to the Parks
Committee, 4 June 1932; 1 September 1932. A. C. Brown (secretary
of the Tooting Workers' Sports Club) to the Parks Committee, 18
June 1932.
93 T. M. Condon, *The Case for Organised Sunday Football: A
Statement of the case put forward by an All-London deputation
before the London County Council on February 10th, 1933*, London,
London Workers' Football Council, 1933, p. 2.
94 LCC Parks Committee Papers, 10 March 1933, no. 31. Report by
P. Maud to the Parks Committee, 10 March 1933.
95 LCC Parks Committee Minutes, 24 March 1933.
96 LCC Parks Committee Papers, 8 December 1933, no. 22. Report
by P. Maud to the Parks Committee, 8 December 1933.
97 LCC Parks Committee Minutes, 10 July 1934. *Daily Worker*, 12 July
1934.
98 Martin Bobker, interview with the author, 18 August 1981.
99 *Daily Worker*, 18 May 1933; 25 May 1933; 22 June 1933.

Conclusion

1 C. L. Mowat, *Britain Between The Wars 1918–1940*, London,
Methuen, 1955, pp. 231, 454.
2 R. Carr, *English Fox Hunting: A History*, London, Weidenfeld &
Nicolson, 1976, pp. 237–9.
3 See R. W. Cox, *Theses and Dissertations on the History of Sport,
Physical Education and Recreation Accepted for Higher Degrees
and Advanced Diplomas in British Universities 1900–1981*,
Liverpool, Bibliographical Centre for the History of Sport, 1982.
4 *Royal Commission On Licensing (England and Wales): Extracts
From Written Statements Submitted To The Commission*, London,
HMSO, 1932, p. 34.
5 See A. Marwick, *British Society Since 1945*, Harmondsworth,
Penguin Books, 1982, *passim*. J. Walvin, *Leisure and Society
1830–1950*, London, Longman, 1978, pp. 148–60.
6 S. Pollard, *The Development of the British Economy 1914–1980*,
London, Edward Arnold, 1983, p. 322.

7 See Incomes Data Services, *Hours and Holidays 1984*, study 323, October 1984.
8 *Sunday Times*, 8 July 1984.
9 *Sunday Times*, 25 November 1984; 3 February 1985.
10 Committee of Enquiry Into Sports Sponsorship, *The Howell Report*, London, The Central Council of Physical Recreation, 1983, p. 11.
11 Central Statistical Office, *Social Trends*, no. 6, 1975, p. 100.
12 Central Statistical Office, *Social Trends*, no. 15, 1985, p. 150.
13 Central Statistical Office, *Monthly Digest of Statistics*, no. 475, February 1985, p. 123.
14 *Market Research Europe*, vol. 17, February 1985, p. 7.
15 Central Statistical Office, *Monthly Digest of Statistics*, no. 475, February 1985, p. 123.
16 Central Statistical Office, *Social Trends*, no. 15, 1985, p. 150.
17 C. Critcher, 'Football since the war', in J. Clarke, C. Critcher and R. Johnson (eds), *Working Class Culture: Studies in history and theory*, London, Hutchinson, 1979, pp. 168–9. See also P. J. W. N. Bird, 'The demand for league football', *Applied Economics*, vol. 14, 1982, pp. 637–49.
18 The Sports Council, *Sport in the Community: The Next Ten Years*, London, Sports Council, 1982, p. 15.
19 ibid., p. 42.
20 ibid., p. 15.
21 See L. Allison, *The Condition of England: Essays and Impressions*, London, Junction Books, 1981, pp. 39–51.
22 *The Director*, September 1983, p. 24.
23 *The Guardian*, 10 October 1983.
24 *The Guardian*, 26 August 1983. See also S. G. Jones, 'The Worksharing Debate in Western Europe', *National Westminster Bank Quarterly Review*, February 1985, pp. 30–41.
25 A. Gorz, *Farewell to the Working Class*, London, Pluto Press, 1982, p. 137.
26 See 'Shorter hours through national agreements', *Employment Gazette*, October 1983, pp. 432–6. F. Walz, 'Shorter Working Hours And Their Impact On Overall Employment', *Swiss Bank Corporation Economic And Financial Prospects*, no. 1, 1984, pp. 3–5. R. A. Hart, 'Worksharing and factor prices', *European Economic Review*, vol. 24, no. 2, 1984, pp. 165–88. B. Williams, 'Shorter Hours – Increased Employment?', *Three Banks Review*, no. 143, 1984, pp. 3–16.

Select bibliography

This bibliography is composed mainly of material directly relevant to this study.

Collections of primary sources

Bruce Castle Museum, Borough of Haringey, London
A selection of local newspapers.
Tottenham Urban District Council: Minutes of Proceedings.
Communist Party Archives, London
George Sinfield Papers: Records of the British Workers' Sports Federation.
Greater London Record Office
London County Council: Minutes and papers of the Parks and Open Spaces Committee. Proceedings of the full Council.
John Rylands University Library, Manchester
Newspaper cuttings collection.
Labour Party Archives, London
Labour Party Special Sub-Committee on the Liquor Traffic, 1923: Three boxes of correspondence and papers (Subject files vol. 3 LP/LIQ/22).
Minutes of the Labour Party Executive Committee, Sub-Committees and other papers.
Lancashire Record Office, Preston
Burnley Power Loom Weavers' Association: Minute books and journal (DDX 1274).
Leeds Archives Department
Montague Burton Collection: Newscuttings books (Acc 1951/36, 128).
Manchester Central Reference Library Archives Department

Clarion Cycling Club: Minute books, annual reports, programmes, handbooks, pamphlets and other records (016).

Manchester Chamber of Commerce: Minute books, together with *Monthly Record* (Mss 8).

Manchester and District Dramatic Federation: Journal and other records (Mss 351/5).

Manchester School Camps Association: Reports (Mss 111).

Marx Memorial Library

National Unemployed Workers' Movement: Records of the National Administrative Council.

Other relevant items are found in the library's pamphlet and periodicals collection.

Microfilm Collection

EP Microform: Origins and Development of the Labour Party at local level. Collections of minute books, annual reports and other records of local Labour Parties at Cambridge, Colne Valley, Gloucester, Penistone, Pontypridd, Sheffield and South Shields.

Public Record Office, Kew

CAB 24/96 (CP 462), Directorate of Intelligence (Home Office), 'A Survey of Revolutionary Feeling during the year 1919'.

CAB 24/74 (GT 6713), 'Fortnightly Report on Revolutionary Organisations in the United Kingdom and Morale Abroad', Report no. 31, n.d.

CAB 24/79 (GT 6712), 'Memorandum on Movements for Reduction in Hours of Labour', n.d.

CAB 24/115 (CU 17), Cabinet Committee on Unemployment, Short Time as an Alternative to Unemployment: Memorandum by the Minister of Labour.

CAB 24/117 (CP 2363–4), Draft letters suggesting introduction of short time to alleviate unemployment.

HO 45/11880, File on boxing.

HO 45/16425, Notes of a Deputation from the Trades Union Congress to the Home Secretary, 2 December 1935.

HO 45/17521, File on Sunday cinemas.

LAB 2/867/ED 196, Copies of letters regarding short time as a remedy for unemployment.

LAB 2/882/IR/786, Pronouncements on the desirability of avoiding overtime.

LAB 2/2047/176/2, Resolutions from trade unions and others regarding the forty-hour week.

LAB 10/53/IR/280, File on the Annual Holiday Bill, 1936.

LAB 31/1–4, Papers relating to the Departmental Committee on Holidays with Pay, 1937–8.

PREM 1/218, Correspondence and papers relating to the TUC deputation urging legislation for holidays with pay.

PREM 1/217, Correspondence and papers relating to the TUC claim for the forty-hour week.

PRO FO 371/14883, Foreign Office General Correspondence.

PRO FO 371/18884/5184, File on the England versus Germany football match, 1935.

PRO FO 395/568, Foreign Office News Department file.

T 172/1708, Notes of a deputation received by the Chancellor of the Exchequer from the TUC, 13 August 1930.

Stalybridge Local History Library

Hyde Cemetery and Park Committee: Minute book (CA/HYD/119/4).

Stockport Library

Microfilm Box no. 220, Thomas Middleton's Scrapbook, vol. 1.

Stockport Labour Fellowship: Minute books, account book, handbooks, programmes and related material (B/MM/3/20–2; B/X/7/12).

University of Warwick Modern Records Centre

Ernest Bevin Papers: File on holidays with pay (Mss 126/EB/HP).

Joseph Hallsworth Papers: File on holidays with pay (Mss 70/3/15).

National Amalgamated Union of Life Assurance Workers: File on holidays with pay (Mss 141/10).

National Union of Railwaymen: Reports, proceedings, journals and other related material (Mss 127).

George Renshaw Papers: Short runs of rank and file papers and other related material (Mss 104).

Transport and General Workers' Union: Biennial Delegate Conference Reports, General Executive Council minutes and other related material. Also, records of the Workers' Union (Mss 126).

Working Class Movement Library, Manchester

Records of many labour and working-class organizations.

Official Publications and Parliamentary Papers (PP)

Census of England and Wales 1931. Occupation Tables, London, HMSO, 1934.

Cinematograph Films Act 1927: Report of a Committee Appointed by the Board of Trade, PP 1936 ix, cmd 5320.

Civil War Workers' Committee, *Third Interim Report: Holidays for Munition Workers After the War*, PP 1918 xiv, cmd 9192.

Fifth Census of Production, Part 3, London, HMSO, 1940.

Final Report of the Commissioners for the Special Areas (England and Wales), PP 1934–5 x, cmd 4957.

Final Report of the Health of Munition Workers' Committee on Industrial Health and Efficiency, PP 1918 xii, cmd 9065.

Hansard

Licensing Statistics, PP 1937–8 xxviii, cmd 5869.

Ministry of Labour, *Holiday With Pay*, London, HMSO, 1939.

Ministry of Labour and National Service, *Development of the Catering, Holiday, and Tourist Industry*, London, HMSO, 1946.

Minutes of Evidences Taken Before the Committee on Holidays with Pay, London, HMSO, 1937–8.

Minutes of Evidence Taken Before the Committee on Industry and Trade, vol. 1, London, HMSO, 1924–7.

Minutes of Evidence Taken Before the Royal Commission on Licensing (England and Wales), London, HMSO, 1930–2.

Physical Training and Recreation: Memorandum explaining the Government's proposals for the development and extension of the facilities available, PP 1937 xxi, cmd 5364.

Report From the Select Committee on Betting Duty Together with the Proceedings of the Committee, Minutes of Evidence, Appendices and Index, PP 1923 v.

Report of the Broadcasting Committee, PP 1923 x, cmd 1951.

Report of the Broadcasting Committee, PP 1936 vii, cmd 5091.

Report of the Colonial Films Committee, PP 1930 viii, cmd 3630.

Report of the Committee on the Disinterested Management of Public Houses, PP 1927 x, cmd 2862.

Report of the Committee on Holidays with Pay, PP 1937–8 xii, cmd 5724.

Report of the Committee on Land Utilisation in Rural Areas, PP 1941–2 iv, cmd 6378.

Report of the Committee on Local Expenditure (England and Wales), PP 1932–3 xiv, cmd 4200.

Report of the Committee on Local Expenditure (Scotland), PP 1932–3 xiv, cmd 4201.

Report of the Departmental Committee on Crowds, PP 1924 viii, cmd 2088.

Report of the Departmental Committee of Inquiry into the Miners' Welfare Fund, PP 1932–3 xv, cmd 4236.

Report of the Royal Commission on Licensing (England and Wales) 1929–1931, PP 1931–2, xi, cmd 3988.

Royal Commission on Licensing (England and Wales): Extracts From Written Statements Submitted to the Commission, London, HMSO, 1932.

Royal Commission on Lotteries and Betting 1932–3: Final Report, PP 1932–3 xiv, cmd 4341.

Royal Commission on National Museums and Galleries. Interim Report,
  PP 1928–9 viii, cmd 3192.
*Royal Commission on National Museums and Galleries. Final Report
  Part 1*, PP 1929–30 xvi, cmd 3401.
*Third Report of the Commissioner For The Special Areas (England and
  Wales)*, PP 1936–7 xii, cmd 5303.

Newspapers and journal publications

AEU, *Monthly Journal*
Ashton-Under-Lyne Reporter
British Trades Union Review
Camping
Cotton Factory Times
Daily Express
Daily Herald
Daily Mirror
Daily Telegraph
Daily Worker
Drama
Financial News
Forward
Industrial Welfare
International Labour Review
Investors' Chronicle
Labour
Lansbury's Labour Weekly
Leeds Weekly Citizen
Manchester Guardian
Ministry of Labour Gazette
National Society of Painters, *Monthly Journal*
National Union of Foundry Workers, *Journal and Report*
New Red Stage
Oldham Labour Gazette
Oldham Chronicle
Out-O'-Doors
Record (Organ of the Labour Campaign for the Public Ownership and
  Control of the Liquor Trade)
Red Stage
Rochdale Labour News
Russia Today

Sport and Games
Sunday Worker
The Amateur Theatre and Playwrights' Journal
The Blackshirt
The (Bolton) Citizen
The Co-operative News
The C.T.C. Gazette
The East Ham North Citizen
The Economist
The English Review
The Journal of the Commons, Open Spaces and Footpaths Preservation Society
The Labour Magazine
The Labour Woman
The Left Review
The Listener
The Locomotive Journal
The London Citizen
The Millgate
The Nation and Athenaeum
The New Age
The New Dawn
The New Leader
The New Statesman
The Northern Cyclist and Athlete
The Plebs
The Post
The Printing Federation Bulletin
The Railway Review
The Record
The Shop Assistant
The Socialist
The Socialist Review
The Spectator
The Sporting Chronicle
The Times
The Tribune
The Typographical Circular
The Worker Sportsman
The Workers' Union Record
The Y.H.A. Rucksack
Tottenham and Edmonton Weekly Herald
Unity

Westminster Gazette
Workers' Life

Contemporary books and pamphlets

AEU, *The Engineers' Charter*, London, AEU, 1932.

E. Barker, *The Uses of Leisure*, London, British Institute of Adult Education, n.d.

A. Barratt Brown, *The Machine And The Worker*, London, Ivor Nicholson & Watson, 1934.

W. Boyd and V. Ogilvie (eds), *The Challenge Of Leisure*, London, New Education Fellowship, 1936.

British Association, *Britain In Depression*, London, Sir Isaac Pitman, 1938.

M. Butchart (ed.), *A. R. Orage: Political And Economic Writings*, London, Stanley Nott, 1936.

A. M. Cameron, *Civilisation And The Unemployed*, London, Student Christian Movement Press, 1935.

C. Cameron, A. J. Lush and G. Meara (eds), *Disinherited Youth*, Edinburgh, Carnegie United Kingdom Trust, 1943.

A. E. Campbell (ed.), *Modern Trends in Education*, Wellington, New Education Fellowship, 1938.

D. Caradog Jones (ed.), *The Social Survey of Merseyside*, 3 vols, Liverpool, Liverpool University Press and Hodder & Stoughton, 1934.

E. B. Castle, A. K. C. Ottaway and W. T. R. Rawson, *The Coming of Leisure*, London, New Education Fellowship, 1935.

G. D. H. Cole *et al.*, *British Trade Unionism Today*, London, Gollancz, 1939.

J. Common (ed.), *Seven Shifts*, London, Secker & Warburg, 1938.

T. M. Condon, *The Fight for the Workers' Playing Fields*, London, British Workers' Football Council, n.d.

T. M. Condon, *The Case for Organised Sunday Football*, London, London Workers' Football Council, 1933.

Conference on Christian Politics, Economics and Citizenship, *Leisure*, London, Longman, Green & Co., 1924.

J. Corrie, *Rebel Poems*, London, ILP Publications, 1932.

C. Delisle Burns, *Leisure In The Modern World*, London, Allen & Unwin, 1932.

H. Durant, *The Problem of Leisure*, London, G. Routledge & Sons, 1938.

R. Evans and A. Boyd, *The Use of Leisure in Hull*, Hull, The Hull 'Use of Leisure' Sub-Committee, 1935.

A. Greenwood, *Publicans and Politics*, London, Labour Campaign for the Public Ownership and Control of the Liquor Trade, n.d.

A. Greenwood, *The Brewers Repentant*, London, Labour Campaign for the Public Ownership and Control of the Liquor Trade, n.d.

A. Greenwood, *Public Ownership of the Liquor Trade*, London, Leonard Parsons, 1920.

J. L. Hammond, *The Growth of Common Enjoyment*, London, Oxford University Press, 1933.

C. Harris, *The Use of Leisure in Bethnal Green: A Survey of Social Conditions in the Borough 1925 to 1926*, London, Lindsey Press, 1927.

F. Henderson, *The Economic Consequences of Power Production*, London, Allen & Unwin, 1931.

G. Hicks, *Give New Life and Purpose To The Labour Clubs!*, London, Federation of Trade Union, Labour, Socialist and Co-operative Clubs, 1928.

J. Hilton, *Why I Go In For The Pools*, London, Allen & Unwin, 1936.

A. Hutt, *The Condition of the Working Class in Britain*, London, Martin Lawrence, 1933.

International Labour Office, *Holidays with Pay Report*, Geneva, International Labour Organisation, 1935.

International Labour Office, *Recreation and Education: Reports presented to the International Conference on Workers' Spare Time*, Geneva, International Labour Organisation, 1935.

International Labour Office, *Facilities for the Use of Workers' Leisure During Holidays*, Geneva, International Labour Organisation, 1939.

'Investigator', *The Liquor Trade In Politics*, London, Labour Campaign for the Public Ownership and Control of the Liquor Trade, 1926.

H. E. O. James and F. T. Moore, *Adolescent Leisure in a Working-Class District*, London, reprinted from *Occupational Psychology*, 1940.

F. Johnston (ed.), *The Football Who's Who*, London, Associated Sporting Press, 1935.

L. Jones, *We Live: The Story of a Welsh Mining Valley*, London, Lawrence & Wishart, 1939.

Labour Party, *Labour's Immediate Programme*, London, Labour Party, 1937.

Labour Party, *For Socialism and Peace*, London, Labour Party, 1938.

A. S. Lawrence, *Women and the Drink Trade*, London, Labour Campaign for the Public Ownership and Control of the Liquor Trade, n.d.

F. R. Leavis, *For Continuity*, Cambridge, Minority Press, 1933.

K. Liepmann, *The Journey To Work*, London, Kegan Paul, Trench, Trubner & Co., 1944.

H. Llewellyn Smith (ed.), *The New Survey of London Life and Labour*, vol. 9, *Life and Leisure*, London, P. S. King, 1935..

Mass Observation, *The Pub and The People: A Worktown Study*, London, Gollancz, 1943.

H. A. Mess, *Industrial Tyneside: A Social Survey*, London, Ernest Benn, 1928.

S. Meyers and E. Ramsay, *London Men and Women: An Account of the L.C.C. Men's and Women's Institutes*, London, British Institute of Adult Education, 1936.

L. R. Missen, *The Employment of Leisure*, Exeter, A. Wheaton & Co., 1935.

National Council of Social Service, *Unemployment and Community Service*, London, National Council of Social Service, 1936.

National Fitness Council, *The National Fitness Campaign*, London, National Fitness Council, 1939.

G. Orwell, *The Road to Wigan Pier*, Harmondsworth, Penguin Books, 1979. First published 1937.

G. Orwell, *The Lion and the Unicorn: Socialism and the English Genius*, Harmondsworth, Penguin Books, 1982. First published 1941.

The Pilgrim Trust, *Men Without Work*, Cambridge, Cambridge University Press, 1938.

J. B. Priestley, *English Journey*, Harmondsworth, Penguin Books, 1979. First published 1934.

Report of the National Conference: 'The Leisure of The People', Manchester, 17–20 November 1919.

Report on Organisation presented by the Party Commission to the Annual Conference of the C.P.G.B., 1922.

J. H. Richardson, *Industrial Relations in Great Britain*, Geneva, International Labour Organisation, 1933.

E. Rickwood, *War and Culture: The Decline of Culture Under Capitalism*, London, Communist Party, n.d.

M. Rooff, *Youth and Leisure: A Survey of Girls' Organisations In England and Wales*, Edinburgh, Carnegie United Kingdom Trust, 1935.

B. Seebohm Rowntree, *Poverty and Progress: A Second Social Survey of York*, London, Longmans, 1942.

A. Salter, *The Prospect before the Temperance Movement of this Country*, London, International Order of Good Templars, 1939.

H. J. Schofield (ed.), *The Book of British Industries*, London, Denis Archer, 1933.

E. Selley, *The English Public House As It Is*, London, Longmans, Green & Co., 1927.

R. Sinclair, *Metropolitan Man: The future of the English*, London, Allen & Unwin, 1937.

M. Spring Rice, *Working-Class Wives. Their Health and Conditions*, Harmondsworth, Penguin Books, 1939.

J. H. Thomas, *When Labour Rules*, London, W. Collins, 1920.

H. Tout, *The Standard of Living in Bristol*, Bristol, Bristol University Press, 1938.

E. Wilkinson, *The Town That Was Murdered*, London, Gollancz, 1939.

G. B. Wilson (ed.), *Alliance Year Book And Temperance Reformers Handbook*, Manchester, United Kingdom Alliance, 1940.

Women's Group on Public Welfare, *Our Towns: A Close-Up*, London, Oxford University Press, 1943.

T. Young, *Becontree and Dagenham: A Report Made For The Pilgrim Trust*, London, Becontree Social Survey Committee, 1934.

Secondary publications

1 Articles

D. H. Aldcroft, 'Control of the liquor trade in Great Britain 1914–1921', in W. H. Chaloner and B. M. Ratcliffe (eds), *Trade and Transport: Essays in honour of T. S. Willan*, Manchester, Manchester University Press, 1977, pp. 242–57.

T. Aldgate, 'Ideological Consensus in British Feature Films, 1935–1947', in K. R. M. Short (ed.), *Feature Film as History*, London, Croom Helm, 1981, pp. 94–112.

D. Allen, ' "Culture" and the Scottish Labour Movement', *Scottish Labour History Society Journal*, no. 14, 1980, pp. 30–9.

L. Althusser, 'Ideology and Ideological State Apparatuses (Notes towards an Investigation)', in *Lenin and Philosophy and other essays*, London, New Left Books, 1971, pp. 121–73.

W. J. Baker, 'The State of British Sport History', *Journal of Sport History*, vol. 10, no. 1, 1983, pp. 53–66.

P. J. Beck, 'England v Germany, 1938', *History Today*, vol. 32, June 1982, pp. 29–34.

C. W. E. Bigsby, 'The Politics of Popular Culture', *Cultures*, vol. 1, no. 2, 1973, pp. 15–35.

E. Bird, 'Jazz Bands of North East England: The Evolution of a Working Class Cultural Activity', *Oral History*, vol. 4, no. 2, 1976, pp. 79–88.

M. Blanch, 'Imperialism, nationalism and organised youth', in J.

Clarke, C. Critcher and R. Johnson (eds), *Working-Class Culture: Studies in history and theory*, London, Hutchinson, 1979, pp. 103–20.

A. Bush, 'Musicians and the Working Class in Britain', in P. M. Kemp-Ashraf and J. Mitchell (eds), *Essays in honour of William Gallacher*, Berlin, Humboldt University, 1966, pp. 177–80.

G. C. Cameron, 'The Growth of Holidays with Pay in Britain', in G. L. Reid and D. J. Robertson (eds), *Fringe Benefits, Labour Costs and Social Security*, London, Allen & Unwin, 1965, pp. 273–99.

D. Colledge and J. Field, ' "To Recondition Human Material . . .": an Account of a British Labour Camp in the 1930s. An Interview with William Heard', *History Workshop Journal*, no. 15, 1983, pp. 152–66.

S. Constantine, 'Amateur Gardening and Popular Recreation in the 19th and 20th Centuries', *Journal of Social History*, vol. 14, no. 3, 1981, pp. 387–406.

D. Cook, 'The Battle for Kinder Scout', *Marxism Today*, vol. 21, no. 8, 1977, pp. 241–3.

C. Critcher, 'The Politics of Leisure – Social Control and Social Development', in *Work and Leisure: The Implications of Technological Change*, Leisure Studies Seminar 1980, Tourism and Recreation Unit, University of Edinburgh, 1982, pp. 43–53.

H. Cunningham, 'Leisure', in J. Benson (ed.), *The Working Class In England 1875–1914*, London, Croom Helm, 1985, pp. 133–64.

B. Dabaschek, 'The Wage Determination Process for Sportsmen', *Economic Record*, vol. 51, no. 133, 1975, pp. 52–65.

B. Dabaschek, ' "Defensive Manchester": a History of the Professional Footballers' Association', in R. Cashman and M. McKernan (eds), *Sport in History: The Making of Modern Sporting History*, Queensland, Queensland University Press, 1979, pp. 227–57.

T. Dennett, 'England: The (Workers') Film and Photo League', in *Photography/Politics: One*, London, Photography Workshop, 1979, pp. 100–17.

N. H. Dimsdale, 'Employment and Real Wages in the Inter-war Period', *National Institute Economic Review*, no. 110, 1984, pp. 94–103.

D. Dixon, 'Gambling and the Law: The Street Betting Act, 1906, as an Attack on Working Class Culture' in A. Tomlinson (ed.), *Leisure and Social Control*, Brighton, Brighton Polytechnic, 1981, pp. 1–32.

W. Dougill, 'The British Coast and its Holiday Resorts', *The Town Planning Review*, vol. 16, no. 4, 1935, pp. 265–78.

K. Drotner, 'Schoolgirls, Madcaps, and Air Aces: English Girls and their Magazine Reading between the Wars', *Feminist Studies*, vol. 9, no. 1, 1983, pp. 33–52.

A. Exell, 'Morris Motors in the 1930s', *History Workshop Journal*, no. 6, 1978, pp. 52–78; no. 7, 1979, pp. 45–65.

'The Football Industry – 1', *Planning*, vol. 17, no. 324, 1951, pp. 157–84.

'The Football Industry – 2', *Planning*, vol. 17, no. 325, 1951, pp. 185–208.

J. Foster, 'British Imperialism and the Labour Aristocracy', in J. Skelley (ed.), *The General Strike 1926*, London, Lawrence & Wishart, 1976, pp. 3–57.

H. Frankel, 'The Industrial Distribution of the Population of Great Britain in July 1939', *Journal of the Royal Statistical Society*, vol. 108, 1945.

D. W. Harding, 'The Place of Entertainment in Social Life', *The Sociological Review*, vol. 26, no. 4, 1934, pp. 393–406.

D. W. Harding, 'Varieties of Work and Leisure', *Occupational Psychology*, vol. 12, no. 2, 1938, pp. 104–15.

J. Hargreaves, 'The Political Economy of Mass Sport', in S. Parker, N. Ventris, J. Haworth and M. Smith (eds), *Sport and Leisure in Contemporary Society*, London, Polytechnic of Central London, pp. 53–64.

J. Hargreaves, 'Sport, culture and ideology', in J. Hargreaves (ed.), *Sport, Culture and Ideology*, London, Routledge & Kegan Paul, 1982, pp. 30–61.

G. Harkell, 'The Migration of Mining Families to the Kent Coalfield Between the Wars', *Oral History*, vol. 6, 1978, pp. 98–113.

U. Harva, 'Marxist Conception of Leisure', *Adult Education in Finland*, vol. 14, no. 2, 1977, pp. 3–12.

W. J. Hausman and B. T. Hirsch, 'Wages, Leisure, and Productivity in South Wales Coalmining, 1874–1914', *Llafur*, vol. 3, no. 3, 1982?, pp. 58–66.

R. Hayburn, 'The Voluntary Occupational Centre Movement, 1932–39', *Journal of Contemporary History*, vol. 6, no. 3, 1971, pp. 156–71.

D. Hebdige, 'Towards A Cartography of Taste 1935–1962', in B. Waites, T. Bennett and G. Martin (eds), *Popular Culture: Past and Present*, London, Croom Helm, 1982, pp. 194–218.

E. Higgs, 'Leisure and the State: The History of Popular Culture as Reflected in the Public Records', *History Workshop Journal*, no. 15, 1983, pp. 141–50.

B. Hogenkamp, 'Film and the Workers' Movement in Britain, 1929–39', *Sight and Sound*, vol. 45, no. 2, 1976, pp. 68–76.

T. J. Hollins, 'The Conservative Party and Film Propaganda between the Wars', *English Historical Review*, vol. 96, no. 379, 1981, pp. 359–69.

A. Howkins, 'Class Against Class: The Political Culture of the

Communist Party of Great Britain, 1930–1935', in F. Gloversmith (ed.), *Class, Culture and Social Change: A New View of the 1930s*, Brighton, Harvester Press, 1980, pp. 240–57.

A. Howkins and J. Lowerson, 'Leisure in the Thirties', in A. Tomlinson (ed.), *Leisure and Social Control*, Brighton, Brighton Polytechnic, 1981, pp. 70–92.

A. Howkins and J. Saville, 'The 1930s: A revisionist history', *Socialist Register 1979*, London, Merlin Press, 1979, pp. 274–84.

D. Jeremy, 'Butlin, Sir William Heygate Edmund Colbourne (1899–1980): Pioneer in the mass leisure industry', in D. J. Jeremy (ed.), *Dictionary of Business Biography*, vol. 1, London, Butterworths, 1984, pp. 535–41.

L. Jones, 'The General Strike and the Workers' Theatre', in P. M. Kemp-Ashraf and J. Mitchell (eds), *Essays in honour of William Gallacher*, Berlin, Humboldt University, 1966, pp. 153–8.

L. Jones, 'The Workers' Theatre Movement in the Twenties', *Zeitschrift Für Anglistik und Amerikanistik*, vol. 14, no. 3, 1966, pp. 259–81.

L. Jones, 'The Workers' Theatre in the Thirties', *Marxism Today*, vol. 18, no. 9, 1974, pp. 271–80.

S. G. Jones, 'The Economics of Association Football in England, 1918–39', *British Journal of Sports History*, vol. 1, no. 3, 1984, pp. 286–99.

S. G. Jones, 'Die Britische Arbeitersport Föderation, 1923–1935', in A. Krüger and J. Riordan (eds), *Der internationale Arbeitersport. Der Schlüssel zum Arbeitersport in 10 Ländern*, Germany, Pahl-Rugenstein, 1985, pp. 110–23.

S. G. Jones, 'The Leisure Industry In Britain 1918–39', *The Service Industries Journal*, vol. 5, no. 1, 1985, pp. 90–106.

S. G. Jones, 'The Trade Union Movement and Work-Sharing Policies in Interwar Britain', *Industrial Relations Journal*, vol. 16, no. 1, 1985, pp. 57–69.

S. G. Jones, 'Sport, Politics and the Labour Movement: The British Workers' Sports Federation, 1923–1935', *The British Journal of Sports History*, vol. 2, no. 2, 1985, pp. 154–78.

S. G. Jones, 'Trade Union Policy Between the Wars: The Case of Holidays with Pay', *International Review of Social History*, vol. 31, pt. 1 (1986).

D. L. Lemahieu, 'The Gramophone: Recorded Music and the Cultivated Mind in Britain Between the Wars', *Technology and Culture*, vol. 23, no. 3, 1982, pp. 372–91.

J. Lewis, 'In Search of a Real Equality: Women Between the Wars', in F. Gloversmith (ed.), *Class, Culture and Social Change: A New View of the 1930s*, Brighton, Harvester Press, 1980, pp. 208–39.

T. Lovell, 'The Social Relations of Cultural Production: Absent Centre of a New Discourse', in S. Clarke *et al.*, *One-Dimensional Marxism: Althusser and the Politics of Culture*, London, Allison Busby, 1980, pp. 232–56.

J. Loveman, 'Workers' Theatre: Personal Recollections of Political Theatre in Greenwich during the 1920s and 1930s', *Red Letters*, no. 13, Spring 1982, pp. 40–6.

R. Lowe, 'Hours of Labour: Negotiating Industrial Legislation in Britain, 1919–1939', *Economic History Review*, 2nd series, vol. 35, no. 2, 1982, pp. 254–71.

J. Lowerson, 'Battles For the Countryside', in F. Gloversmith (ed.), *Class, Culture and Social Change: A New View of the 1930s*, Brighton, Harvester Press, 1980, pp. 258–80.

E. MacColl, 'Grass Roots of Theatre Workshop', *Theatre Quarterly*, vol. 3, 1973, pp. 58–68.

B. McCormick, 'Hours of Work in British Industry', *Industrial and Labour Relations Review*, vol. 12, 1959, pp. 423–33.

S. Macintyre, 'British Labour, Marxism and Working Class Apathy in the Nineteen Twenties', *The Historical Journal*, vol. 20, no. 2, 1977, pp. 479–96.

R. McKibbon, 'Working-Class Gambling in Britain 1880–1939', *Past and Present*, no. 82, 1979, pp. 147–78.

R. McKibbon, 'Work and hobbies in Britain 1880–1950', in J. Winter (ed.), *The Working Class in Modern British History: Essays in Honour of Henry Pelling*, Cambridge, Cambridge University Press, 1983, pp. 127–46.

A. Marwick, 'British Life and Leisure and the First World War', *History Today*, vol. 15, no. 6, 1965, pp. 409–19.

J. Mott, 'Miners, weavers and pigeon racing', in M. A. Smith, S. Parker and C. S. Smith (eds), *Leisure and Society in Britain*, London, Allen Lane, 1973, pp. 86–96.

K. Mourby, 'The Wives and Children of the Teeside Unemployed 1919–1939', *Oral History and Labour History*, vol. 11, no. 2, 1983, pp. 56–60.

A. E. Musson, 'Technological Change and Manpower', *History*, vol. 67, no. 220, 1982, pp. 237–51.

M. Page, 'The Early Years at Unity', *Theatre Quarterly*, vol. 1, 1971, pp. 60–6.

R. Penn, 'The Course of Wage Differentials between the Skilled and Non-skilled Manual Workers in Britain between 1856 and 1964', *British Journal of Industrial Relations*, vol. 21, no. 1, 1983, pp. 69–90.

D. Pilcher, 'Leisure as an Architectural Problem', *The Architectural Review*, vol. 84, no. 505, 1938, pp. 231–310.

R. Price, 'Rethinking Labour History: The Importance of Work', in J. Cronin and J. Schneer (eds), *Social Protest and the Political Order in Modern Britain*, London, Croom Helm, 1982, pp. 179–214.

R. Price, 'The labour process and labour history', *Social History*, vol. 8, no. 1, 1983, pp. 57–75.

N. Pronay, 'British Newsreels in the 1930s. 1. Audience and Producers', *History*, vol. 56, 1971, pp. 411–18.

N. Pronay, 'British Newsreels in the 1930s. 2. Their Policies and Impact', *History*, vol. 57, 1972, pp. 63–72.

N. Pronay, 'The First Reality: Film Censorship In Liberal England', in K. R. M. Short (ed.), *Feature Films as History*, London, Croom Helm, 1981, pp. 113–37.

D. Prynn, 'The Clarion Clubs, Rambling and the Holiday Associations in Britain since the 1890s', *Journal Of Contemporary History*, vol. 11, no. 2/3, 1976, pp. 65–77.

J. Richards, 'The cinema and cinema-going in Birmingham in the 1930s', in J. K. Walton and J. Walvin (eds), *Leisure in Britain 1780–1939*, Manchester, Manchester University Press, 1983, pp. 31–52.

M. E. Rose, 'The Success of Social Reform? The Central Control Board (Liquor Traffic) 1915–1921', in M. R. D. Foot (ed.), *War and Society: Historical Essays in honour and memory of J. R. Western 1928–1971*, London, Elek, 1973, pp. 71–84.

S. Rowson, 'A Statistical Survey of the Cinema Industry in Great Britain in 1934', *Journal of the Royal Statistical Society*, vol. 99, 1936, pp. 67–118.

D. Rubinstein, 'An Interview with Tom Stephenson', *Bulletin of the Society for the Study of Labour History*, no. 22, 1971, pp. 27–32.

D. Rubinstein, 'Sport and the Sociologist 1890–1914', *British Journal of Sports History*, vol. 1, no. 1, 1984, pp. 14–23.

R. Samuel, 'Editorial Introduction', *History Workshop Journal*, no. 4, 1977, pp. 103–12.

P. Scannell and D. Cardiff, 'Serving The Nation: Public Service Broadcasting Before the War', in B. Waites, T. Bennett and G. Martin (eds), *Popular Culture: Past and Present*, London, Croom Helm, 1982, pp. 161–88.

J. A. Schofield, 'The Development of First-Class Cricket in England. An Economic Analysis', *The Journal of Industrial Economics*, vol. 30, no. 4, 1982, pp. 337–60.

M. Seidman, 'The Birth of the Weekend and the Revolts Against Work: The Workers of the Paris Region during the Popular Front (1936–38)', *French Historical Studies*, vol. 12, no. 2, 1981, pp. 249–76.

P. J. Sloane, 'The Economics of Professional Football: The Football

Club as a Utility Maximiser', *Scottish Journal of Political Economy*, vol. 18, no. 2, 1971, pp. 121–46.

J. Springhall, 'The Boy Scouts, Class and Militarism in Relation to British Youth Movements 1908–1930', *International Review of Social History*, vol. 16, 1971, pp. 125–58.

P. Stead, 'The People and the Pictures: The British working class and film in the 1930s', in N. Pronay and D. W. Spring (eds), *Propaganda, Politics and Film, 1918–1945*, London, Macmillan, 1982, pp. 77–97.

G. Stedman Jones, 'Working-Class Culture and Working-Class Politics in London, 1870–1900; Notes on the Remaking of a Working Class', *Journal of Social History*, vol. 7, no. 4, 1974, pp. 460–508.

G. Stedman Jones, 'Class expression versus social control? A critique of recent trends in the social history of leisure', *History Workshop Journal*, no. 4, 1977, pp. 162–70.

D. A. Steinberg, 'The Workers' Sport Internationals 1920–1928', *Journal of Contemporary History*, vol. 13, no. 2, 1978, pp. 233–51.

J. Stevenson, 'Myth and Reality: Britain in the 1930s', in A. Sked and C. Cook (eds), *Crisis and Controversy: Essays in Honour of A. J. P. Taylor*, London, Macmillan, 1976, pp. 90–109.

B. Stoddart, 'Cricket's Imperial Crisis: the 1932–3 M.C.C. Tour of Australia', in R. Cashman and M. McKernan (eds), *Sport in History: The Making of Modern Sporting History*, Queensland, Queensland University Press, 1979, pp. 124–47.

'The Workers' Theatre Movement: an interview with Philip Poole by Jon Clark and David Margolies', *Red Letters*, no. 10, n.d., pp. 2–10.

T. Thomas, 'A Propertyless Theatre for the Propertyless Class', *History Workshop Journal*, no. 4, 1977, pp. 113–27.

J. Turner, 'State Purchase of the Liquor Trade in the First World War', *The Historical Journal*, vol. 23, no. 3, 1980, pp. 589–615.

W. Vamplew, 'The Economics of a Sports Industry: Scottish Gate-Money 1890–1914', *Economic History Review*, 2nd series, vol. 35, no. 4, 1982, pp. 549–67.

R. Ward, 'British Documentaries of the 1930s', *History*, vol. 62, 1977, pp. 426–31.

R. Waterman, 'Proltet: The Yiddish-Speaking Group of the Workers' Theatre Movement', *History Workshop Journal*, no. 5, 1978, pp. 174–8.

C. Webster, 'Healthy or Hungry Thirties?', *History Workshop Journal*, no. 13, 1982, pp. 110–29.

R. F. Wheeler, 'Organised Sport and Organised Labour: The Workers' Sports Movement', *Journal of Contemporary History*, vol. 13, no. 2, 1978, pp. 191–210.

J. White, 'Campbell Bunk: A Lumpen Community in London Between the Wars', *History Workshop Journal*, no. 8, 1979, pp. 1–49.

P. Wild, 'Recreation in Rochdale 1900–40', in J. Clarke, C. Critcher and R. Johnson (eds), *Working Class Culture: Studies in history and theory*, London, Hutchinson, 1979, pp. 140–60.

G. Williams, 'From Grand Slam to Great Slump: Economy, Society and Rugby Football in Wales During the Depression', *The Welsh History Review*, vol. 11, no. 3, 1983, pp. 338–57.

R. Williams, 'Base and Superstructure in Marxist Cultural Theory', *New Left Review*, no. 82, 1973, pp. 3–16.

E. and S. Yeo, 'Perceived Patterns: Competition and Licence versus Class and Struggle', in E. and S. Yeo (eds), *Popular Culture and Class Conflict 1590–1914: Explorations in the History of Labour and Leisure*, Brighton, Harvester Press, 1981, pp. 271–305.

E. and S. Yeo, 'Ways of Seeing: Control and Leisure versus Class and Struggle', in E. and S. Yeo (eds), *Popular Culture and Class Conflict 1590–1914: Explorations in the History of Labour and Leisure*, Brighton, Harvester Press, 1981, pp. 128–54.

S. Yeo, 'A New Life: The Religion of Socialism in Britain 1883–1896', *History Workshop Journal*, no. 3, 1977, pp. 5–56.

2 Books and pamphlets

D. H. Aldcroft, *The Inter-War Economy: Britain 1919–1939*, London, Batsford, 1970.

D. H. Aldcroft, *The British Economy Between The Wars*, Oxford, Philip Allan, 1983.

B. W. E. Alford, *Depression and Recovery? British Economic Growth 1918–1939*, London, Macmillan, 1972.

The Arts Enquiry, *The Factual Film*, London, Oxford University Press, 1947.

P. Bailey, *Leisure and Class in Victorian England: Rational recreation and the contest for control*, London, Routledge & Kegan Paul, 1978.

M. A. Bienefeld, *Working Hours in British Industry*, London, Weidenfeld & Nicolson, 1972.

N. Branson and M. Heinemann, *Britain in the Nineteen Thirties*, St Albans, Panther Books, 1973.

A. Briggs, *Mass Entertainment: The Origins of a Modern Industry*, Adelaide, Griffen Press, 1960.

A. Briggs, *The History of Broadcasting in the U.K.*, vol. 2, *The Golden Age of Wireless*, Oxford, Oxford University Press, 1965.

A. Briggs, *Communications and Culture 1823–1973: A Tale of Two Centuries*, London, Birkbeck College, 1973.

I. Britain, *Fabianism And Culture: A Study in British socialism and the arts c. 1884–1918*, Cambridge, Cambridge University Press, 1982.

E. Brunner, *Holiday Making and the Holiday Trades*, Oxford, Nuffield College, 1945.

J. Burnett, *A History Of the Cost of Living*, Harmondsworth, Penguin Books, 1969.

F. Capie and M. Collins, *The Inter-war British Economy: A Statistical Abstract*, Manchester, Manchester University Press, 1983.

R. Cashman and M. McKernan (eds), *Sport: Money, Morality and the Media*, Kensington, New South Wales University Press, 1981.

D. E. Channon, *The Strategy and Structure of British Enterprise*, London, Macmillan, 1973.

A. L. Chapman and R. Knight, *Wages and Salaries in The United Kingdom 1920–1938*, Cambridge, Cambridge University Press, 1953.

D. Clark, *Colne Valley: Radicalism to Socialism*, London, Longman, 1981.

J. Clark, M. Heinemann, D. Margolies and C. Snee (eds), *Culture and Crisis in Britain in the Thirties*, London, Lawrence & Wishart, 1979.

C. Claudin-Urondo, *Lenin and the Cultural Revolution*, Hassocks, Harvester Press, 1977.

A. Clinton, *The Trade Union Rank and File: Trades Councils in Britain 1900–40*, Manchester, Manchester University Press, 1977.

M. Cohen, *I Was One of the Unemployed*, London, Gollancz, 1945.

S. Constantine, *Unemployment in Britain Between the Wars*, Harlow, Longman, 1980.

A. Crawford and R. Thorne, *Birmingham Pubs 1890–1939*, Birmingham, Birmingham University, 1975.

J. E. Cronin, *Labour and Society in Britain 1918–1979*, London, Batsford, 1984.

H. Cunningham, *Leisure in the Industrial Revolution, 1780–1880*, London, Croom Helm, 1980.

F. Dawes, *A Cry from the Streets: The Boys' Club Movement in Britain from the 1850s to the Present Day*, Hove, Wayland Publishers, 1975.

A. Delgado, *The Annual Outing and Other Excursions*, London, Allen & Unwin, 1977.

Department of Employment and Productivity, *British Labour Statistics: Historical Abstract 1886–1968*, London, HMSO, 1971.

J. Donald and C. Mercer, *The State and Popular Culture (2)*, Milton Keynes, Open University, 1982.

C. H. Feinstein, *Domestic Capital Formation in the United Kingdom 1920–1938*, Cambridge, Cambridge University Press, 1965.

C. H. Feinstein, *National Income, Expenditure and Output of the United*

Kingdom 1855–1965, Cambridge, Cambridge University Press, 1972.

C. Forman, *Industrial Town. Self Portrait of St Helens in the 1920s*, St Albans, Granada Publishing, 1979.

H. Francis and D. Smith, *The Fed: A History of the South Wales Miners in the Twentieth Century*, London, Lawrence & Wishart, 1980.

D. Gittens, *Fair Sex: Family Size and Structure, 1900–39*, London, Hutchinson, 1982.

S. Glynn and J. Oxborrow, *Interwar Britain: A Social and Economic History*, London, Allen & Unwin, 1976.

J. Gorman, *To Build Jerusalem: A Photographic Remembrance of British Working Class Life 1875–1950*, London, Scorpion Publications, 1980.

R. Graves and A. Hodge, *The Long Week-End; A Social History of Great Britain 1918–1939*, London, Faber & Faber, 1940.

L. Hannah, *The Rise of the Corporate Economy*, London, Methuen, 1976.

G. Harrison and F. C. Mitchell, *The Home Market*, London, Allen & Unwin, 1936.

K. H. Hawkins and C. L. Pass, *The Brewing Industry: A Study in Industrial Organisation and Public Policy*, London, Heinemann, 1979.

A. Hern, *The Seaside Holiday*, London, Cresset Press, 1967.

H. Hill, *Freedom to Roam: The Struggle For Access To Britain's Moors and Mountains*, Ashbourne, Moorland Publishing, 1980.

Q. Hoare and G. Nowell (eds), *Antonio Gramsci: Selections from the Prison Notebooks*, London, Lawrence & Wishart, 1971.

B. Hogenkamp, 'Workers' Newsreels in the 1920s and 1930s', *Our History*, pamphlet no. 68, London, n.d.

R. Hoggart, *The Uses of Literacy*, Harmondsworth, Penguin Books, 1977.

A. Howkins and J. Lowerson, *Trends in Leisure, 1919–1939*, London, The Sports Council and Social Science Research Council, 1979.

S. Humphries, *Hooligans or Rebels? An Oral History of Working-Class Childhood and Youth 1889–1939*, Oxford, Basil Blackwell, 1981.

J. B. Jefferys, *Retail Trading in Britain 1850–1950*, Cambridge, Cambridge University Press, 1954.

B. Jones, 'The Politics of Popular Culture', Centre for Contemporary Cultural Studies, University of Birmingham, Stencilled Occasional Papers, n.d.

N. Kaldor and R. Silverman, *A Statistical Analysis of Advertising Expenditure and of the Revenue of the Press*, Cambridge, Cambridge University Press, 1948.

V. I. Lenin, *On Culture and Cultural Revolution*, Moscow, Progress Books, 1978.

J. Lewis, *The Politics of Motherhood: Child and Maternal Welfare in England 1900–1939*, London, Croom Helm, 1980.

London and Cambridge Economic Service, *The British Economy: Key Statistics 1900–1970*, London, *The Times*, 1971.

R. Low, *The History of the British Film*, vols 4–7, London, Allen & Unwin, 1971–1985.

J. Lowerson and J. Myerscough, *Time to Spare in Victorian England*, Hassocks, Harvester Press, 1977.

R. Lucas, *The Voice of a Nation?: A concise account of the BBC in Wales 1923–1973*, Llandysul, Gomer Press, 1981.

I. Macdougall (ed.), *Militant Miners: Recollections of John McArthur, Buckhaven; and letters, 1924–26, of David Proudfoot, Methil to G. Allen Hutt*, Edinburgh, Polygon Books, 1981.

P. McIntosh, *Fair Play: Ethics in Sport and Education*, London, Heinemann, 1979.

S. Macintyre, *A Proletarian Science: Marxism in Britain 1917–1933*, Cambridge, Cambridge University Press, 1980.

S. Macintyre, *Little Moscows: Communism and Working-class Militancy in Inter-War Britain*, London, Croom Helm, 1980.

J. McMillan, *The Way It Was: 1914–1934*, London, William Kimber, 1979.

D. Macpherson (ed.), *Traditions of Independence: British Cinema in the Thirties*, London, British Film Institute, 1980.

A. Marwick, *The Explosion of British Society 1914–1970*, London, Macmillan, 1971.

A. Marwick, *British Society Since 1945*, Harmondsworth, Penguin Books, 1982.

T. Mason, *Association Football and English Society 1863–1915*, Brighton, Harvester Press, 1980.

H. E. Meller, *Leisure and the Changing City, 1870–1914*, London, Routledge & Kegan Paul, 1976.

R. Miliband, *Marxism and Politics*, Oxford, Oxford University Press, 1977.

R, Miliband, *The State in Capitalist Society*, London, Quartet Books, 1980.

C. L. Mowat, *Britain Between the Wars 1918–1940*, London, Methuen, 1955.

C. Musgrave, *Life in Brighton: from the earliest times to the present*, London, Faber & Faber, 1970.

B. Oliver, *The Renaissance of the English Public House*, London, Faber & Faber, 1947.

J. D. Owen, *The Price of Leisure: An Economic Analysis of the Demand for Leisure Time*, Rotterdam, Rotterdam University Press, 1969.

S. Parker, *Leisure and Work*, London, Allen & Unwin, 1983.

M. Pegg, *Broadcasting and Society 1918–1939*, London, Croom Helm, 1983.

PEP, *The British Film Industry*, London, PEP, 1952.

E. H. Phelps Brown and M. H. Browne, *A Century of Pay*, London, Macmillan, 1968.

J. A. R. Pimlott, *The Englishman's Holiday: A Social History*, London, Faber & Faber, 1947.

S. Pollard, *The Development of the British Economy 1914–1980*, London, Edward Arnold, 1983.

N. Pronay and D. W. Spring (eds), *Propaganda, Politics and Film 1918–1945*, London, Macmillan, 1982.

G. Prys Williams and G. Thompson Brake, *Drink in Great Britain 1900 to 1979*, London, Edsall, 1980.

J. Redmond, *Broadcasting: The Developing Technology*, London, BBC Publications, 1974.

J. Richards, *The Age of the Dream Palace: Cinema and Society in Britain 1930–1939*, London, Routledge & Kegan Paul, 1984.

E. A. M. Roberts, *Working Class Barrow and Lancaster 1890 to 1930*, Lancaster, University of Lancaster Occasional Paper no. 2, 1976.

E. A. M. Roberts, *A Woman's Place: An Oral History of Working-Class Women 1890–1940*, Oxford, Basil Blackwell, 1984.

K. Roberts, *Leisure*, London, Longman, 1971.

R. Roberts, *The Classic Slum: Salford Life in the First Quarter of the Century*, Harmondsworth, Penguin Books, 1980.

S. J. Rodger Charles, *The Development of Industrial Relations in Britain 1911–1939*, London, Hutchinson, 1973.

B. Rothman, *The 1932 Kinder Trespass: A personal view of the Kinder Scout Mass Trespass*, Timperley, Willow Publishing, 1982.

G. Routh, *Occupation and Pay in Great Britain, 1906–60*, Cambridge, Cambridge University Press, 1965.

S. Rowbotham, *Hidden From History: 300 Years of Women's Oppression and the Fight Against It*, London, Pluto Press, 1977.

B. Seebohm Rowntree and G. R. Lavers, *English Life and Leisure. A Social Study*, London, Longmans, 1951.

F. Rust, *Dance In Society*, London, Routledge & Kegan Paul, 1969.

R. Samuel, *East End Underworld: Chapters in the life of Arthur Harding*, London, Routledge & Kegan Paul, 1981.

R. Samuel, E. MacColl and S. Cosgrove, *Theatres of the Left: Workers' Theatre Movements in Britain and America 1880–1935*, London, Routledge & Kegan Paul, 1984.

D. Scott, *A. D. Lindsay: A Biography*, Oxford, Basil Blackwell, 1971.

D. Smith and G. Williams, *Fields of Praise: The Official History of the Welsh Rugby Union 1881–1981*, Cardiff, Wales University Press, 1980.

M. A. Smith, S. Parker and C. S. Smith (eds), *Leisure and Society in Britain*, London, Allen Lane, 1973.

J. Springhall, *Youth, Empire and Society: British Youth Movements, 1883–1940*, London, Croom Helm, 1977.

J. Stevenson, *Social Conditions in Britain Between the Wars*, Harmondsworth, Penguin Books, 1977.

J. Stevenson, *British Society 1914–45*, Harmondsworth, Penguin Books, 1984.

J. Stevenson and C. Cook, *The Slump: Society and Politics During the Depression*, London, Quartet Books, 1979.

R. Stone and D. A. Rowe, *The Measurement of Consumers' Expenditure and Behaviour in the United Kingdom 1920–1938*, vol. 2, Cambridge, Cambridge University Press, 1966.

S. Studd, *Herbert Chapman, Football Emperor: A Study in the Origins of Modern Soccer*, London, Peter Owen, 1981.

S. G. Sturmey, *The Economic Development of Radio*, London, Duckworth, 1958.

M. Swenarton, *Homes Fit For Heroes: The Politics and Architecture of Early State Housing in Britain*, London, Heinemann, 1981.

A. J. P. Taylor, *English History 1914–1945*, Oxford, Oxford University Press, 1965.

P. Taylor, *The Projection of Britain: British Overseas Publicity and Propaganda*, Cambridge, Cambridge University Press, 1981.

R. L. Taylor, *Art, An Enemy of the People*, Hassocks, Harvester Press, 1978.

M. Tebbutt, *Making Ends Meet: Pawnbroking and Working Class Credit*, Leicester, Leicester University Press, 1983.

S. Tischler, *Footballers and Businessmen: The Origins of Professional Soccer In England*, New York, Holmes & Meier, 1981.

A. Tuckett, 'The People's Theatre in Bristol, 1930–1945', *Our History*, pamphlet no. 72, London, n.d.

J. Vaizey, *The Brewing Industry 1886–1951: An Economic Study*, London, Sir Isaac Pitman & Sons, 1960.

W. Vamplew, *The Turf: A Social and Economic History of Horse Racing*, London, Allen Lane, 1976.

W. Vamplew (ed.), 'The Economic History of Leisure', Papers presented at the Eighth International Economic History Congress, Budapest, 1982.

S. Wagg, *The Football World: A Contemporary Social History*, Brighton, Harvester Press, 1984.

J. K. Walton, *The Blackpool Landlady: A social history*, Manchester, Manchester University Press, 1978.

J. K. Walton, *The English Seaside Resort: A Social History 1750–1914*, Leicester, Leicester University Press, 1983.

J. K. Walton and J. Walvin (eds), *Leisure in Britain 1780–1939*, Manchester, Manchester University Press, 1983.

J. Walvin, *The People's Game: A Social History of British Football*, London, Allen Lane, 1975.

J. Walvin, *Beside the Seaside: A Social History of the Popular Seaside Holiday*, London, Allen Lane, 1978.

J. Walvin, *Leisure and Society 1830–1950*, London, Longman, 1978.

G. Whannel, *Blowing the Whistle: The Politics of Sport*, London, Pluto Press, 1983.

C. L. White, *Women's Magazines 1693–1968*, London, Michael Joseph, 1970.

F. Williams, *Journey Into Adventure: The Story of the Workers' Travel Association*, London, Odhams Press, 1960.

B. Williamson, *Class, Culture and Community: A Biographical Study of Social Change in Mining*, London, Routledge & Kegan Paul, 1982.

T. Willis, *Whatever Happened to Tom Mix? The Story of One of My Lives*, London, Cassell, 1970.

E. and S. Yeo (eds), *Popular Culture and Class Conflict 1590–1914: Explorations in the History of Labour and Leisure*, Brighton, Harvester Press, 1981.

S. Yeo, *Religion and Voluntary Organisation in Crisis*, London, Croom Helm, 1976.

F. Zweig, *Women's Life and Labour*, London, Gollancz, 1952.

3 Unpublished theses

P. Brook Long, 'The Economic and Social History of the Scottish Coal Industry 1925–1939, With Particular Reference to Industrial Relations', Ph.D., University of Strathclyde, 1978.

J. Ferris, 'The Labour Party League of Youth 1924–1940', M.A., University of Warwick, 1977.

R. Hayburn, 'The Responses to Unemployment in the 1930s, with particular reference to South-East Lancashire', Ph.D., University of Hull, 1970.

W. G. Jackson, 'A Historical Study of the Provision of Facilities for

Play and Recreation in Manchester', M.Ed., University of Manchester, 1940.

S. G. Jones, 'The British Labour Movement and Working Class Leisure 1918–1939', Ph.D., University of Manchester, 1983.

G. C. Martin, 'Some Aspects of the Provision of Annual Holidays for the English Working Classes down to 1947', M.A., University of Leicester, 1968.

T. Middleton, 'An Enquiry into the Use of Leisure Amongst the Working Classes of Liverpool', M.A., University of Liverpool, 1931.

L. Opie, 'Voluntary Effort to Help the Unemployed in the 1930s', M.A., University of Manchester, 1975.

J. Power, 'Aspects of Working Class Leisure During the Depression Years: Bolton in the 1930s', M.A., University of Warwick, 1980.

D. L. Prynn, 'The Socialist Sunday Schools, The Woodcraft Folk and Allied Movements: Their Moral Influence on the British Labour Movement Since the 1890s', M.A., University of Sheffield, 1971.

P. W. Rickwood, 'Public Enjoyment of the Open Countryside in England and Wales 1919–1939', Ph.D., University of Leicester, 1973.

E. D. Smithies, 'The Contrast Between North and South in England 1918–1939: A Study of Economic, Social and Political Problems With Particular Reference to the Experience of Burnley, Halifax, Ipswich and Luton', Ph.D., University of Leeds, 1974.

A, L. Stevenson, 'The Development of Physical Education in the State Schools of Scotland 1900–1960', M.Litt., University of Aberdeen, 1978.

R. Travis, 'The Unity Theatre of Great Britain 1936–1946: A Decade of Production', M.A., University of Southern Illinois, 1968.

R. Whiting, 'The Working Class in the "New Industry" Towns Between the Wars: The Case of Oxford', D.Phil., University of Oxford, 1978.

Index